An Age Without Samples

An Age
Without
Samples

Ikutaro Kakehashi

Hal Leonard Books

An Imprint of Hal Leonard LLC

Published in 2017 by Hal Leonard Books
An Imprint of Hal Leonard LLC
7777 West Bluemound Road
Milwaukee, WI 53213

Trade Book Division Editorial Offices
33 Plymouth St., Montclair, NJ 07042

Printed in the United States of America
Book design by Snow Creative

Library of Congress Cataloging-in-Publication Data
Names: Kakehashi, Ikutaro, 1930– author.
Title: An age without samples : originality and creativity in the digital world / Ikutaro Kakehashi.
Other titles: Sanpuru no nai jidai. English
Description: Milwaukee, WI : Hal Leonard Books, 2016. | Includes bibliographical references.
Identifiers: LCCN 2016023571 | ISBN 9781495069277 (hardcover)
Subjects: LCSH: Kakehashi, Ikutaro, 1930- | Roland Corporation. | Musical instrument makers—Japan—Biography. | Electronic musical instruments—History.
Classification: LCC ML424.K24 A3 2016 | DDC 784.19092 [B] --dc23
LC record available at https://lccn.loc.gov/2016023571

www.halleonardbooks.com

Contents

Introduction

IN THE FIFTEEN YEARS SINCE I PUBLISHED MY 2001 MEMOIR, *I BELIEVE in Music*, many people have asked me if I had plans to publish a sequel. And having been awarded the Technical Grammy in February 2013, thirty years after MIDI was born, I felt this was a good time to add to what I have previously written on MIDI and its history.

In Japan, many of us are asking ourselves, how do we need to be moving forward in business? Of course, this is equally true in the United States, Europe, and even China, nations that have lost their sense of direction. In a way, we are all groping in the dark in an age without samples. First, I need clarify the phrase "age without samples." In the world of digital music making, sampling refers to the act of digitally recording a portion or sample of one sound recording and reusing it in a different recording. In other words, it isn't original, wasn't created from scratch; rather it is borrowed, reinvented, or built upon in a new musical work. This has been the Japanese model for many years now. We take something that already exists and improve and innovate. Today, we do not have samples we can borrow from, to build upon and create new innovations. Then how do we move forward in this "age without samples"? I believe that what we need to do now is to resurrect the "venture spirit," the one that we saw from the late sixties and early seventies through the eighties. I also believe that, with the enormous change brought about by information technology, social networking, and other developments, we are seeing a very rare opportunity for new ventures in businesses that need the vision of creative and original thinking.

Such are the times we live in, and this is what drove me to write about the age without samples. Based on a solid footing in my area of specialty, electronic musical instruments, I wished to consider how we might navigate such an age, based on my personal experience and other real-world examples.

While the laptop PC played an important role in making the Internet an integral part of the lives of many, there is something I have been feeling strongly since the explosive proliferation of the latest mobile devices, including iPads and smartphones. The very environment in which we currently find ourselves is in the process of birthing an uncharted era, and we, in the midst of these changes, are struggling to stay grounded and see ourselves objectively. Recently, I've come to realize that the age we live in makes it very difficult to ask ourselves exactly what it means to live in an "age without samples."

From my point of view, I live in a truly wonderful world in which I am able to communicate with people three or even four generations apart from me, not only in Japanese but also in English. But it is also true that personal relationships are becoming increasingly complex. It's misleading to think that you can share a mutual understanding with another just because you both speak the same language.

The following suggestion may sound idealistic, but my feeling is that each of us needs to take up a specific focus as we ponder how best to move forward in what we all likely see as challenging times. So for me personally, I felt the need to take a fresh look at *I Believe in Music*, and rewrite the book after determining which parts of it had endured the test of time, as well as what values we can expect to change and how such change might come about. I think this is what gives meaning to the publication of this new book. While electronic-only publishing has become popular, I opted for a hard-copy book format because I did not feel the electronic publishing platform had fully matured, particularly in Japan. This book also features QR codes that have been widely used for some time now; by presenting a hybrid product consisting of the book (hardware) and video (software), I hope to create a new book-reading experience, one that "has no samples," for my readers.

Now that I have retired from active work, I have often been referred to as a "visionary." Having said that, simply expounding on my visions does not make me a "sample" that can be built upon. I believe that I have lived my life so far through a combination of vision and action. I have put into action visions I truly believed in and was convinced I could achieve.

Yet looking back now, I think this was only the first step toward the future. This is because there are no clear-cut positions or roles for electronic musical instruments in the world of music. They are still in their nascent stages and I don't think anyone has a clear picture of what might lie around the corner. While the first electronic instruments were developed nearly a century ago, compared to all other instruments, which have long histories, they are analogous to a newborn baby who has just been given a name and had his or her birth papers filed.

When we find ourselves in a worse state than when we originally made a commitment and decided to move forward, I believe the best philosophy for reaching our goals is to persevere, refusing to throw in the towel.

There would be no greater joy for me than to be able to present my ideas in the context of electronic instruments, part of our greater scope of industries, and to have my discussions act as an impetus to readers to ponder the "age without samples."

1

An Age Without Samples

Forecasts and Reality

NOTHING CAN BE MORE DIFFICULT THAN FORECASTING THE FUTURE. While a variety of forecasts were made during the 1990s—a decidedly chaotic period in our world—in the area of the economy as well as in communication, which was undergoing the so-called IT revolution, a large percentage of these forecasts never came to pass. In the eighties, we saw the emergence of individuals who called themselves futurists, but these people largely lost their relevance after the collapse of the bubble economy. Nevertheless, I have great respect for these people who approached their areas of expertise with diligence and had the courage to announce their visions of the future. No forecast can ever be 100 percent correct. What is more important in my view is whether or not the directionality of a forecast is correct. Futurists are much more courageous than economists and commentators who make vague inferences based on past data. Even if their forecasts do not come to pass, there is value in the willingness to state one's view clearly.

In the Victorian era, when steam locomotives first came into commercial use, records show that the first passenger train traveled at a speed of about eight miles per hour. Scientists of this era theorized that trains could cause huge tornados if their speeds exceeded fifty miles per hour, or that they would never be able to travel faster than that owing to air resistance. Some scientists even predicted that if a train were to travel faster than one hundred miles per hour, all the air inside the train cars would be sucked out, causing certain death to all passengers by asphyxiation. We now know that passengers traveling

---

* These QR codes give you access to videos related to each chapter, which are informative and also fun to watch.

on the Shinkansen (the Japanese bullet train) or the TGV in France leisurely enjoy their drinks, conversations, and meals. While these earlier forecasts completely missed the mark, no one is laughing at these scientists.

A decade ago, we saw a range of self-proclaimed futurists expounding on their theories. These individuals have now changed their title and are making new predictions. They are putting forth commentaries that differ from their earlier views with an air of dignified seriousness. That there are very few people whose views are consistent with what they were saying a decade ago shows us how difficult it is to maintain an unchanging view over the years.

1. Kenzuishi and Kentoshi (circa seventh century AD)
    - Imported culture from China into Japan and formed a nation based on the Ritsuryo code.

2. Meiji Restoration (late nineteenth century)
    - Imported Western civilization into Japan. The beginning of the modern age.

3. Postwar (mid-twentieth century/1945)
    - Americanization.

4. Present
    - An age without samples.
    - Originality/venture.

Three Foreign Cultures That We Learned From

It is said that you must study large amounts of information and have the capability to analyze that information to make a forecast. Each country has its own unique culture, and when we look back, we see that Japan has imported a large amount of wisdom from other countries to be where it is today. In other words, it has "sampled" from each of these countries, including their cultures and business models—absorbing, transforming, and innovating based on these samples.

About 1,400 years ago, the emperor of Japan sent *kenzuishi* and *kentoshi*, diplomatic delegations to the Sui and Tang dynasties of China, respectively, with the goal of incorporating the advanced political institutions and culture encountered there. This resulted in an influx of information on the state of affairs beyond Japanese borders, and the superior political institutions and advanced technologies of Tang, as well as Buddhist and Confucianist scripture. As kanji (Chinese characters) made their way into the Japanese language, scholars imported works such as the nine Chinese classics and studied from books written in vertical text. The Ritsuryo code system that China had developed over millennia to govern the various tribes was brought to Japan, so that Japan soon became a nation based on the Ritsuryo code as well.

Chinese (Sui and Tang) culture and the culture of other parts of the world transmitted via Tang became the "samples" for Japan fourteen centuries ago. This was the first major transformation in Japanese history.

The second major change was the Meiji Restoration. While there had been many major historic developments leading up to that point—including the Genji-Heike Wars, the Warring States period, and the warless, peaceful Edo period—in the context of how the country was impacted by culture that was imported from abroad, the changes that the country went through during the Meiji era (1868–1912) are more noteworthy.

The Meiji government actively and systematically sent young, talented individuals overseas in an effort to catch up with other countries. The government officials who developed these plans were in their thirties and forties—quite young from our current perspective—and those they sent abroad were in their twenties. These young people concentrated on absorbing as much culture as they could and bringing it back to Japan. Thus, Japan learned about navies from England, armies from France, and physics and medicine from Germany. Literary author Ogai Mori traveled to Germany to study medicine. Other groups who went to America, by this time long independent from Europe, learned about schools and education, and this had a major impact on Japan's current education system. Umeko Tsuda, one of the female students who studied abroad, later went on to found the Joshi Eigaku Juku, the present-day Tsuda College.

The Japanese learned music from Italy and Germany, thanks in part to the influence of pianos. The composer Rentaro Taki was another of the students who went abroad. While he is most famous for writing the song "Kojo no Tsuki," he is known for writing many other songs as well. The songs sung in Japan in those days included many Scottish and Irish folk songs. Novels from the early part of the Meiji era were written in a formal literary style, and songs such as "Ware wa Umi no Ko" were as well. And then in the mid-Meiji era, writers of novels and song lyrics began using a colloquial style instead. On a formative level, people began writing both vertical and horizontal text. Books written in vertical text would start from the right, and those written in horizontal text would start from the left, but in either case, the pages were bound in the opposite direction of foreign books. In those days, kanji were often accompanied by phonetic *furigana*, a reading aid, so that all readers would be able to decipher the kanji. People also began writing Arabic numerals and the English alphabet. With these imports, the way people wrote books and the writing itself underwent many changes.

As you can see, the Meiji Restoration was a time of great change, and it was the European and American cultures that the Japanese of the time took as their "samples." The music Japanese people listen to daily also bears the influence of the Meiji Restoration. Indeed, I think the decision made by the Meiji government to include music as a mandatory part of the school curriculum was a very significant development. Japan is the only industrialized country that includes music as a mandatory part of its school curriculum.

Because I am involved in the music business, I have always been very interested in music education in Japan. While the West has developed a method of notation common to most instruments, traditional Japanese music uses different notations for different instruments. Even then, what might remotely be referred to as notation is often simply made up of auxiliary symbols that provide little more than hints to the player. Another characteristic of traditional Japanese music training is the one-on-one relationship between teacher and student. More to the point, in the Japanese style, music is learned more with the body than with the rational mind.

This way of doing things is shared not only among traditional musicians but among traditional craftspersons as well. The traditional way of transmitting skills in Japan is by observing and then "stealing" what you've observed from your master, as opposed to learning through verbal exchange.

I had the great honor of being given the Technical Grammy Award in 2013 for my contribution to the development of MIDI (Musical Instrument Digital Interface). Whereas notation is the mode of communicating information to human musicians, MIDI is a way of transmitting musical information to computers.

It is only natural that these methods of transmission change over time, and it is important that we clearly recognize that there are things we lose during these changes. While, during the Meiji Restoration, Japan learned from different cultures around the world and gained much in the process, it is also true that the culture lost some of the traditional Japanese methods of transmission.

Culture is very important. In many cases, we may believe that everything we are taught in textbooks is true and not know much about anything else. But recently, there have been many instances when we've realized that what we were taught was not the whole truth. So I think the most important thing for us is education. Education is not about teaching something new and expecting to effect immediate change. Things start to become clearer only over time.

Gradual improvement comes when a variety of matters become public and their realities become evident. I think we still need quite a bit of time for this to happen.

As Japan digested foreign culture during the Meiji era, it built on the things it incorporated. In other words, the people improved upon foreign cultures and made them blend into Japanese culture through their attention to delicateness. On the other hand, as Japan grew as a national power, the entire nation became arrogant, and even incorporated as samples the methodologies of imperialism and aggression against other countries. As a result, the nation was defeated in World War II and occupied by the United States. The people who were engaged in rebuilding the nation were 100 percent steeped in American influence. So the changes brought about by this second major period were immeasurable.

The third major change was America. After the war, American culture came to Japan through military occupation and brought about changes different from those that resulted from the influences of China and the Meiji Restoration. Without much conscious awareness, the Japanese familiarized themselves with and enjoyed these changes. Yet while the importation of this culture resulted in great enlightenment, it is also true that many aspects of Japanese culture that I believe to be critical were lost.

This influence is evident to this day in many aspects of Japanese life. About a third of the words used in the TV shows Japanese people watch are imported from English. If we include abbreviations and the flood of "katakana-ized" English words (a term used in Japanese to denote words of foreign origin), one might wonder where certain programs originated. For example, it is difficult to make out what language the people are speaking on the NHK program *Cool Japan*. Their discussions are not that difficult for Japanese viewers to follow because translated subtitles appear when a guest from, say, the UK speaks English, and the Japanese MC usually follows up on the guest's comments. This method of production can essentially be exported to any country and I actually feel that this is what the producers have in mind.

TV news programs repeat the same news over and over and have now reached a point where they play an active role in teaching viewers how certain English words are used in certain contexts. I think these things are hugely influential. Even if we were to set aside the issue of Americanization for a moment, because English has become the de facto standard language used in all parts of the world, including in business and on the Internet, one can safely say that people will not get very far unless they study English and enable themselves to communicate with people from other countries.

Have We Got Our Bearings Right?

I am also often asked—or rather challenged—to make forecasts, but the only wish I have is to be able to read tomorrow's newspaper today. Then I would know all the winning horses, which means I would never again have to buy a losing ticket, making me a rich man in no time flat. This would surely take all the fun out of baseball and other sports, but my version of tomorrow's newspaper is conveniently absent the sports pages, so this is something I wouldn't have to worry about. In terms of business, any business, my belief is that, short of waiting for tomorrow's newspaper to come today, the only way to predict tomorrow's news is to make it.

News outlets rely on the trustworthiness of their writers and have a great responsibility for the accuracy of the news that leaves their printing presses. In any line of work, it is crucial that we maintain our bearings on a mid- to long-term basis, so we can carry out our work in a responsible manner. While it can be very difficult to maintain one's bearings when making decisions, I think I've managed to do this in my own style. For example, when making a business forecast for the next ten years, instead of speaking like a commentator, all you have to do is speak of your plans that you have developed based on your own convictions. And when you put in hard work day after day to achieve a goal, the results will follow in one form or another. There will be challenges in continuing to move forward because you are acting on your own words, but these types of forecasts are rarely too wide of the mark. It's okay if you don't reach your goals when you planned to. Sometimes you reach them even earlier than you planned.

Take for example the world of musical instruments, the world that I am involved in. I was asked to "make a forecast on electronic pianos" in an interview for the September 1976 issue of *Music Trends*, a music industry magazine. I became quite the laughing stock when I stated, "Electronic pianos will eventually make up 50 percent of the piano market." At the time, only a limited number of manufacturers were selling electronic pianos for home use, and there is no doubt that my forecast was quite optimistic. Even I thought that maybe I had overstated myself. By the time I was interviewed again by the same magazine in October 1985, production volume had grown considerably and the laughing had dwindled down to a smirk. Eventually, fifteen years after the first interview, my prediction of a 50 percent market share became a reality. By then, the number of electronic pianos sold had surpassed that of acoustic pianos and was on its way to exceeding them in terms of actual total revenue as well.

This was thanks not only to the company I founded, Roland, but also to other companies that entered the electronic piano market. So our competitors had a part in fulfilling my prediction. There is no prosperity where there is no competition. In the end, Roland came to be known as the first company to produce electronic pianos for home use. It is a lot of hard work to believe in your forecasts and work toward them, but I think an even more difficult thing to do is to be able to listen to people when they point out your mistakes, and take their advice to heart. Up until the postwar period when the country became Americanized, Japan had a lot of samples to learn from, and catching up with others was simply a matter of mastering these numerous samples. But now, look as we may around the world for samples, we find none for Japan.

This applies to other countries around the world as well. The United States has lost its ability to be creative and original in business. China too. These countries have not been able to find resolutions to many of their cultural and business issues. In Europe, the peace brought about by sharing a common currency, the euro, is now coming to a crossroads. This is because the Europeans got caught up in the financial war, of which the Lehman Brothers crisis was a symptomatic representation. So they are also at a loss as to what to do. Armed conflict has become an ongoing reality in the Middle East.

All of these countries are at a loss as to what to do. All countries and regions, including the Americas, Europe, and Asia, are going through an age where no samples are available. It is clear that any potential resolutions to the particular issues these regions face would have little in common, and that such resolutions are still a long way away.

Essentially, we can find our way only by adopting the idea that there are not going to be any samples in the next age, so we are all going to have to determine our own direction and act on our decision. This is not a time to be looking for samples, but to set our own course and move in that direction.

When I was twenty-eight, I decided to make my lifework something that had to do with music. Many years earlier, I had graduated from the mechanical department of a technical school, but since I had no intention of working on machines for the rest of my life, I told myself, "I can do anything I want," and started making musical instruments. Is it wise to determine the course of one's life based on what one has learned by the age of fourteen or fifteen? There may be nothing wrong with that, but whatever the case may be, there is no end to opportunities when one adopts the idea, "I can do anything I want."

In any field, advancement comes about as a result of others dropping out, not because we come out ahead in competition. My thinking is: "Number one is number one, and that is okay." We did not come to where we are today by gleaning from other samples. I think this understanding of the "age without samples" is a very important one to have.

The nature of musical instruments is such that you can bang on anything, even a pot or pan, and as long as the player's rhythm is good, that pot or pan can be a great instrument. So, a keyboard instrument can create great music only if it produces great sounds as imagined by the player. More so if the player is a virtuoso. This is why the keyboard instruments I have built were based on feedback from a wide range of people. The only question I made sure not to ask was what type of instrument they wanted. This is because, while it goes without saying that user feedback is valuable, users are not equipped to propose something completely new, something that goes beyond mere improvement.

What kinds of products will sell in an age where no samples are available? For example, if you look at the scale of automobile companies such as Toyota and their research facilities, it would be impossible to conceive of going into the traditional automobile business at this stage in the industry's development. Even a well-funded company would probably incur huge losses. It is very difficult to enter any market by basing your product on an existing sample. But in the case of electric vehicles, a small to midsized company would at least be able to enter the market. Therefore, when we think of starting something in an "age without samples," it is imperative that we conceive of something unique and work toward that vision. And this cannot be done by simply gleaning from common sense or existing knowledge.

There is no point in imitating others in an "age without samples." We must think for ourselves and design our days, our years, and consider how we want to live our lives by holding a vision of where we would like to be five years from now. I think the only way to live in this "age without samples" is to take excellent care of our current business needs while always maintaining a forward-looking perspective. We have more than enough bad samples, so we don't have to copy those. I think all we need to do is find the most successful way for ourselves to do things, and have a positive outlook.

As I mentioned above, recent TV programs contain so much English that one might be puzzled as to whether they are Japanese or not. Many of the names of companies listed on the stock exchange are written in katakana, and many of these names appear to have no meaning. Such is the influence of America in Japan in this day and age, and there is nothing we can do about this. And while it is true that these developments have been meaningful and have enabled much progress, when we look back at Japanese history and consider how the culture has transformed as a result of this influence, we see that we have reached a point where we ourselves must become the initiators of actions. There are no samples, no matter where you look. We must all determine our own direction based on our own wisdom and what we have learned up to this point. This is the kind of attitude that will be indispensible as we consider the next age.

In terms of music, one could say that Japan had no samples prior to the Meiji era. Then in the Meiji era, melodies that were completely foreign to Japan came in from Europe. This was when the Ministry of Education designated four standard subjects: Japanese, math, science, and music. This was a very important decision.

The Japanese were introduced to the heptatonic scale of the West after they had used a pentatonic scale for centuries without giving it much thought. And one hundred-some years since then, Japan has produced talented conductors, violinists, and many other musicians. However, in the realm of music, techno-pop is about the only musical culture that has made its way from Japan into other countries. It should be noted that the Japanese language has been a handicap in that it isn't spoken throughout the world, so the Japanese have become a minority in media and products that use language. This is one reason that techno-pop and also manga, which is based on illustrations, have become successful forms to represent Japan.

Japan has been influenced by a broad range of civilizations. Its level of refinement is the highest among Asian countries, and the Japanese have made great things from what they took in. Take for example the pagodas in Horyu-ji, or the shapes of temples. The shapes of Japanese temples are the most elegant of temples anywhere, and the five-story pagoda has amazing architectural features. The Japanese have an excellent sensitivity to detail. They have improved things one by one, and made them blend in harmoniously with Japanese sensibilities.

In this sense, because we are in an "age without samples," I believe the Japanese should do new things based on the excellent features of Japan.

What Is Required in the Age Without Samples

How then should we discover new opportunities in an age without samples? I would like to take musical instruments as an example, as this is my line of business.

Let's say you decide to make a piano. To do that, you'll need the iron frame that supports its structure, the felt for its hammers, the strings, and the lumber that makes up its keys and body. It is an absolute requisite that the wood used in pianos be well dried, so you will have to store the lumber in a large storage area and let it dry for many years. On the other hand, if you were to load all of a piano's sounds on an LSI computer chip, you would not have to go through this trouble. Those who had been making acoustic pianos would have to accept changes that went beyond their imaginations. This was the reasoning behind my conceiving of Roland's V-Piano concept. But no matter how many upgrades you might make to its inner workings, you would have no chance for success unless the audience recognized the sound produced by this device as that of a piano. Many people are using V-Pianos in concert these days. This is where we are now.

I don't expect my methodologies to be accepted by everyone. This is because, for one thing, the acoustic piano is an instrument that has reached its pinnacle of perfection. You will notice that you could say the same thing about organs, if you were to evaluate their sound-producing components. The same goes for accordions. In terms of the order in which you want to carry out development, keyboard instruments have the most potential. They are followed by percussive instruments in second place, and stringed instruments in third. Horns produce enough volume without amplification as the player uses his or her mouth to play them, and they do not produce harmonies. Keyboard instruments have fixed pitches and are based on a fixed set of rules. So in this respect, keyboard instruments have the most potential in the electronic realm, and I believe you will get the most efficiency by introducing percussive instruments next, followed by stringed instruments, and then horns.

In the past, only a limited number of people were able to enjoy music. In the baroque period in Europe, twenty to thirty members of the nobility and aristocracy would get together in court to enjoy a performance. Now, we have stadium concerts that play to tens of thousands of people. In these situations, the sound needs to be amplified because otherwise it cannot reach the very back of the audience. And this has brought about the development of highly sophisticated sound-reinforcement equipment.

Organizers of large concerts now show what is happening on stage on large screens, and also record the concert on video. Considering the technology from that perspective, you'll notice that products that incorporate both audio and video, prioritizing neither element above the other, have great potential.

These audio and video technologies have now become indispensable for music. While traditional thinking considered videos unrelated to musical instrument sales, video has actually become an important sales theme in a very short span of time. My hope is that the combination of audio and video will spur a revolution. So far, no style of musical instrument has emerged that lives up to this.

With the advancement of electronic technologies, users can easily create videos and share them with others around the world, and this has expanded the scope of opportunities. This is precisely where A-PRO comes in. A-PRO is a name I invented and stands for video (*eizo* in Japanese, pronounced AY-zo) which is then processed (PRO) in real time and transmitted over the airwaves.

What True Venture Businesses Are Made Of

In the past, people who wanted to make music their business had a hard time, but this is no longer true. I think a characteristic of the current time is that there are huge opportunities in each and every field of endeavor. But we have a hard time seeing these opportunities because we see no samples. For example, it's been over eighty years since the first electronic musical instruments were invented, but only in the past couple of decades has this industry grown to prominence. Electronic instruments are composed of mechanical hardware and the software that controls it. But these two elements on their own are far from enough to create something that could pass for a musical instrument, and we have come to realize that these machines can become musical instruments only when they are infused with artistic and human sensibilities. This element is what I call *artware*. My theory is that these machines become musical instruments only when all three of these elements—hardware, software, and artware—come together.

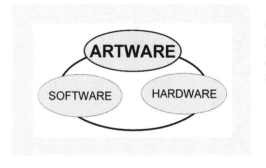

There have been many venture business booms in the past, the first one originating in Silicon Valley in the 1980s . Steve Jobs and Bill Gates both emerged from this movement and became darlings of this era. This inspired Japanese businesspeople, creating a venture boom in Japan as well; I remember a newspaper publisher organizing a venture business event in my hometown of Hamamatsu.

The majority of companies that attended that event have since gone out of business; Roland is the only one still around. All the companies that entered fiercely competitive industries in which you either make it or break it in one or two years went out of business. In the musical instrument business, it takes much longer to make it or break it and the profits are not as huge, but our company is still going strong. This is because musical instruments are constrained by many rules. For example, you can't force musicians to change the musical scales or how they play. Because of such rules, you can't just modify things willy-nilly. On the other hand, we were able to incorporate the strengths of electronics to improve our products and grow our customer base little by little. Because of these peculiarities, we do not always stay abreast of rapid changes in technology, but it is precisely because we were not able to keep up with the latest fads that we are still around. This is why I never felt that we needed to "win" or "prevail." That isn't the goal.

When you look at other industries, you start to notice that venture businesses cannot succeed based only on clever ideas or new technologies. Only those that have something to contribute to culture tend to stick around, and many of the ones that have stuck around are companies that make musical instruments and games.

Looking around at our current situation, you'll find there are still numerous companies that claim to be ventures. However, 80 percent of these are engaged in services, consulting, nursing care, or nonprofit operations. There are too many people who could care less what theme they have set for themselves, and simply want to get rich by starting up a venture company and eventually having their stock go public. You'll also notice that fewer companies than you would think make physical products. Venture companies do not value such "down-to-earth" types of businesses.

This is not to say that functions such as management, consulting, and nursing, all indispensible to society, are meaningless. It is just that venture businesses are primarily perceived as idea-based businesses that give investors the opportunity to make a lot of money in a short period of time, and therefore such idea-based ventures tend to be investors' businesses of choice. However, this is hardly assurance for success.

This much is true. It is difficult to build a venture business based on making physical products. You cannot be mimicking other products, and you must develop shapes and forms that go beyond expectations, ideas that disrupt traditional norms, and the technology to realize these forms and ideas. My view is that this is what true venture businesses should be doing; that is, overcoming these hurdles to launch new products and consequently pioneer new fields and create new industries. It may sound difficult, but the seeds of venture businesses are all around us, for example as we see in the Roomba vacuum cleaner and the plastic wrapping for rice balls sold in Japanese convenience stores. It seems to me that we have a shortage of these kinds of ideas for originating something new, and the spirit to create new industries. This has very little to do with whether your technological capabilities are low or high.

In response to that, I can hear some ask, "Well then, what have you achieved so far?" All I can say is that where I am today is a natural result of the many years of hard work that I put in without really knowing much about anything. And I still have some new projects in mind that I'd like to start.

When we look at the "age without samples" from a historical perspective, we notice that we are now in a time when the world is overflowing with business opportunities. I wanted to communicate this fact to everyone who plays an active role in society. This was actually my greatest motivator in writing this book.

I think that in five years, what I am trying to communicate will become much more apparent. My belief is that we will all be able to determine what we must do in the "age without samples" by appraising the current state of affairs, and regarding ourselves and the world around us, with a levelheaded outlook.

2

Samples and Originals

As I have described in chapter one, "An Age without Samples," Japan has undergone many changes by incorporating, digesting, and then carrying on the legacy of foreign cultures. In my life, each time I witnessed a tradition originally imported and then absorbed by Japanese culture, I have found it fascinating and stimulating.

The Explorations of Shuinsen

Exchanges between Japan and China began as early as the fifth or sixth century. Historic documents record that the first kenzuishi, or diplomatic delegation to the Sui dynasty of China, set sail in the early 600s AD. This delegation was renamed kentoshi after the ruling Chinese dynasty changed from Sui to Tang, and continued to send a large number of monks to China. Of course, there must have been individuals other than monks on these ships, but their names were not recorded. This was the time when *The Analects of Confucius*, which still forms the basis of ethics and morals in Japan; Sun Tzu's *The Art of War*; a large number of Buddhist scriptures; the so-called nine Chinese classics; books on military strategy; and the Ritsuryo (legal) code were brought back to Japan. And since that time, *The Art of War* has also been published in many other countries as a guide for studying business strategy. During the Warring States period, Japanese warlords studied these military strategies and, without exception, had strategists ("staff officers" in current parlance) who were well versed in Chinese documents and military strategies working by their side.

These kentoshi spent a considerable number of years in China and diligently engaged in Buddhist practice and transcribed Buddhist texts. I once saw a TV program that attempted to illustrate the hazards of the journey these delegates undertook, based on research into actual sailing routes, using reproductions of the types of ships they sailed in. It was clear that these journeys were major undertakings, quite unimaginable from a modern standpoint. The yearning these people had for foreign cultures was stronger than anything that we, with our ability to travel freely abroad, can conceive of today. The decision to embark on this journey required a great commitment, since safe return to Japan was not guaranteed, to say nothing of the immense difficulty the travelers faced in safely bringing back the numerous books and scrolls. It appears they had to be willing to risk their lives.

In the Edo period, the shogunate issued overseas trading licenses—what we would call passports today—and the ships that were granted these trading licenses were called *goshuinsen* or *shuinsen*. This brought about a great increase in the number of people who sailed to Southeast Asia for trading purposes. At the time, the only port that was allowed to have exchanges with the outside world was Nagasaki, and feudal lords were not allowed to trade. The Edo shogunate took these stringent measures to ensure the stability of the feudal system by making sure that the feudal clans could not accumulate economic strength.

From Portugal, Japan saw an almost simultaneous influx of the latest hardware—rifles—and software, in the form of Christian culture. By then, Japan had already incorporated Buddhism, Chinese culture, and the Ritsuryo (legal) system, thanks to the kenzuishi and kentoshi, and the shuinsens had traveled to many parts of Asia through which they had brought home European culture, which already had a presence in these regions. Riding on these two major tides, a large amount of "software" came to Japan in exchange for vast amounts of gold and silver. In the late nineteenth century, the Tokugawa feudal system, which had gone on for three centuries, and the strict policy of isolationism were lifted, and Japan entered a new era. Based on information brought home during these times by those who traveled on the diplomatic mission to America on the warship *Kanrin Maru*, and those who were dispatched to Europe by the Meiji government to develop the Japanese constitution, it is obvious that these were the formative years of the basic framework of modern Japan. After World War II, Japan recovered from the rubble and established the culture it enjoys today. These accomplishments were not made solely during the seventy years after the war but owe much to the accumulation of software that the country had imported, incorporated, and further developed throughout the centuries up to that point.

During the postwar occupation by the US armed forces, an internal quiet revolution was driven forward in a heavy-handed way that would be unthinkable today, resulting in the collapse of old institutions, the disbandment of the zaibatsus (family-run conglomerates), and the privatization of land ownership, all of which brought about great change in Japan. By "quiet" I mean that no blood was shed by the Japanese population—in other words, there was no civil war. But as a fifteen-year-old at the time the war ended, I saw the chaotic postwar situation as nothing other than a major revolution occurring before my very eyes. Given these conditions, I feel very fortunate that the country was able to make a new start based on the cultural foundations that had been its legacy for centuries. Food was scarce and we all had a hard time economically, but we also had the influx of fashion, music, cinema, and new technologies. Thinking back to those days, I remember being keenly interested in and influenced by all of these factors, except for fashion.

In particular, I delved deeply into radio, the main source of music in those days. Japan's recovery, which started with importing technologies and licensing foreign patents and such, was dramatic to say the least. Many companies, including Matsushita Denki (now Panasonic) and Hayakawa Denki (presently Sharp), which had been around since before the war, and other companies that were in the heavy electronics business, such as Toshiba, Hitachi, and Mitsubishi, now began to enter the light electrical appliance market. In terms of quality, the quality-control technologies such as those recognized by the Deming Prize were not just a concept but a revolutionary idea that approached the sanctity of religion. All of this was great stimulation for individuals such as myself who were involved in manufacturing.

Our predecessors were amazingly quick to incorporate foreign trends. Looking back, it appears that the cultures brought back by the kentoshi and shuinsen had a major impact on the Meiji Restoration and Japan's postwar industrial prosperity. There is something there that goes beyond mere copying. Much of the artwork that was imported at the time is still with us today, but I believe that the cultural software imported in the form of books and scripture was much more significant.

The word *software* has a very clear-cut meaning in the realm of computers, with numerous programs being developed in the area of operating systems and a diverse range of applications. Here again, Japan has become an importer of software. I believe the significance of classical literature becomes much clearer when considered from the software perspective. Unfortunately, Japan lags behind other countries in areas where systems thinking is required. Although Japan may need some more time, I believe new software unique to Japan will be developed once the imports have been incorporated into the Japanese style and digested. The spirit and mental fortitude the Japanese displayed not only in keeping themselves from being washed away by the deluge of Western culture in the Meiji era, but in actively driving pumpwells into this deluge to absorb what it had to offer their ends, would have been impossible if not for the tradition of accumulation and absorption beginning with classical literature in the time of the kentoshi.

Elementary School Songs

Kanji came to Japan, which had developed from Hiragana via Chinese culture and Buddhism. This was later followed by English, as well as Arabic numerals and the Greek alphabet, all of which arrived at roughly the same time. For example, Greek letters are used to denote alpha and beta versions of software, and in the area of electronic circuits, we have what engineers refer to as delta modulation. The angles of cutting blades are determined by theta control, and the circular constant is denoted by pi.

The French have translated words such as *TV* and *computer* into French, but the Japanese imported them phonetically with the use of katakana. Japan also has many examples of words imported from the Portuguese and Dutch languages, which arrived earlier than English. I believe that the fact that the Japanese were able to carry out the uniquely Chinese way of performing the four arithmetic operations without the use of Arabic numerals owes to the invention of the abacus. The abacus was also imported to Japan and has evolved to suit the Japanese culture. The difference in the way store clerks calculate change in Japan and Western countries may have to do with the fact that the Japanese calculate with the abacus and not with equations.

Music also arrived from the continent along with Buddhism, which eventually led to the creation of uniquely Japanese music as it fused with ancient Japanese cultures. By the Meiji Restoration, the instruments used to perform this music had also evolved to suit Japanese styles. The Meiji government determined its education policy and schools began teaching the primary subjects around 1879. Music education started alongside the other subjects, but because Japanese music was based on a pentatonic scale, I believe this transition to heptatonic and twelve-tone scales must have been a very difficult one. It is quite certain that Japan had exchanges with Europe via the Silk Road, and it is clear from musical instruments housed in the Shosoin Repository, a large storage facility of the central and regional government, that Japan had been influenced by stringed instruments that originated in Central Asia and Persia. But there is no way of knowing what type of music was played. As impressive as European music was, it did not make its way to Japan, perhaps because the Arab and Indian cultures proved to be insurmountable barriers. In the latter half of the sixteenth century, the Jesuits brought church music to Japan. They brought with them organs and harpsichords, and even taught students how to play them at seminaries in Kyushu and Azuchi. The chances that the warrior Nobunaga Oda, who overthrew the shogunate and unified much of Japan, actually listened to some of this music are very high. Unfortunately, however, because of the policy of isolation and persecution of Christians taken by the Tokugawa shogunate, Western music gradually died out without leaving much of an influence on Japanese music. Since music in Japan was transmitted primarily orally and not through notation, harmony had not developed by the time of the Meiji Restoration. It is clear that there were heated debates regarding the pentatonic and heptatonic scales in the early Meiji era. It was truly eye-opening to read the composer and historian Ikuma Dan's book *Encounter with Different Cultures*, in which he explains in detail the transition from pentatonic to heptatonic and then on to the twelve-tone scale.

Do Re Mi So La by Hiroo Sakata, who was not a historian but a well-known writer of novels and children's songs, was a very useful book in understanding this transitionary period. This was a history based on examples as seen from the eyes of a musician and composer. It was a flat-out fun read that gave a good description of the situation of those times. It was through this book that I learned that I actually had numerous ties to Mr. Sakata. The Minami Osaka Church in Abeno, Osaka, which housed the electronic organ that I repaired, was built by Mr. Sakata's father. Mr. Sakata's older brother was the president of Sakata Shokai and organist of that church. The first song he played to test the repaired organ was not a hymn but "Harbor Light." I still remember listening to this song in the empty space of that church.

▼ Ace Tone TO-32. First full church organ with two rows of sixty-one keys.

This became my impetus for launching Ace Electronic Industries, to make electronic organs, and the composer Toraji Onaka agreed to play the company's first organ prototype. We were under quite a bit of pressure just knowing that the organ would be tested by the person who wrote the song "Yashi no Mi," whose lyrics were penned by Toson Shimazaki, and who was also the organist of the Reinanzaka Church in Tokyo. We were to bring the organ to Minami Osaka Church so that we could test it in a place with good acoustics. Toraji Onaka was the younger brother of Hiroo Sakata's mother—so, his uncle. Wearing a woolen cap, he was all smiles as he began playing the organ. He played one hymn and that was the end of the test. I knew that we had failed. He had nothing to say about the mechanism of the organ itself, but remarked, "It would be better if it had a gentler tone," to Ace Electronics president Kazuo Sakata, who was also present at the test. These words had great gravity for me, as I had been planning to bring this prototype to production without making any changes to its specs. But what he said was completely true. First and foremost, organs must feel good to play hymns on. So we decided to redesign it. Although we did not have another chance to have Mr. Onaka test our organ, that first test with him is the instance I always look back on when I'm involved in creating tones. It was much like being witness to one's own child's school entrance exam.

By the way, I don't think there is a Japanese person who has never sung the children's song "Satchan." which is in a pentatonic scale, but for me personally, Satchan is not just any girl when you realize that the song's lyrics were written by Hiroo Sakata and the melody by Megumi Onaka (Toraji Onaka's son).

I have many great memories with "Yashi no Mi," which was broadcast by NHK Osaka in 1936 as a national children's song. My grandfather taught Japanese and *kanbun* (Chinese literature) for a period of time. The grandfather I remember had already retired, and I remember him sitting with knees folded, taking a Japanese bound book from a box made of paulownia wood, and reading it in a straight posture. He didn't seem interested in music, and he was completely uninterested in the popular songs that came from the gramophone shop (not called a "record store" in those days) two doors down. But he didn't complain about them being noisy or level any criticism against them either. I was very surprised, however, when I heard my grandfather gently humming along to "Yashi no Mi," which was playing on the radio, and ran to tell my grandmother. I remember my grandmother saying, also surprised, "Well, it's written by Toson"— and that was the last time I heard my grandfather singing. One time, when I was still in elementary school, I was singing "Yashi no Mi" as I was making a model. Suddenly, my grandfather called to me, and when I looked up he told me, "You should understand the meaning of the words 'Nare wa somo nami ni ikutsuki' ['How long have you been traveling the waves?'] and separate the words in your heart when you sing them." I remember these words clearly, as he rarely ever chided me about anything in my daily life. It was after I entered intermediate school that I learned that "Toson" was Toson Shimazaki.

Music Is an International Language

The music of the seventeenth and eighteenth centuries that we currently listen to was not composed on the perfected musical instruments we have today. Similarly, it is easy to imagine that the solo and ensemble parts, even though the notations remain unchanged from the original, must have sounded very different when performed with the musical instruments of the time. With that in mind, I believe the time is ripe to take a fresh look at the combination of software, i.e., notation, and hardware, i.e., musical instruments. Music can sound dramatically different depending on what is going on in the musician's mind and his or her interpretation while performing it. This has been the topic of many debates and while I do not have enough knowledge to contribute to the debate, there was one realization that had a huge impact on my thinking in recent years after I developed an electronic harpsichord and positive organ with one row of keys.

The temperaments, or adjustment of tuning intervals, that were used when these instruments were first developed were not universal, and there were at least four or five different major temperaments. The music was composed on various temperaments as well. Because the majority of keyboard instruments today are based on equal temperament, some songs will sound different from the original. The way to accommodate the composers' intent would be to play their compositions on instruments tuned to temperaments thought to be the best suited for each composition, but this would mean having multiple instruments on hand. It might be possible to have two harpsichords at a concert, but not two organs. This is in fact one of the reasons equal temperament has become the universal temperament. This spurred a synergistic effect in the development of keyboard instruments; moreover, equal temperament was also needed to enable musicians to travel anywhere in the world and play their music.

With electronic instruments, it is quite easy to accommodate different tunings. I believe such features will make the new breed of electronic instruments very useful to musicians who play the classics.

Having established a methodology for notation, which led to the notation we use today, European music of the nineteenth century took the lead as the international language of music. Harmony and song structure developed in northern Europe based on church music, and the south created music infused with the gaiety of the Latin peoples. Composition methods that involve theme development and calculated structure are possible only with an established method of notation. I believe this also spurred the evolution of keyboard instruments and contributed to the distinction of roles and positions among composers, performers, and conductors.

However, notation does not contain all the necessary information, as illustrated in the fact that ten different musicians would produce ten different styles of music even if they were reproducing music based on the universal European notation. My feeling is that only about half of the music is actually contained in the notation.

Once a melody is laid down on a chart, it becomes easier to develop and change it, or come up with combinations of harmonies with other instruments or other tones, or use different instruments for different parts. This enhanced the composers' ability to structure their music, giving rise to the symphonies that we are familiar with today. This becomes possible—that is, we are able to enjoy these beautiful harmonies—thanks only to the separation of the roles of composer and performer, the emergence of conductors as the ones who give direction on musical expression, and an established method of notation.

In contrast to this, the music of the East, particularly Japanese music, appears to have transitioned quite abruptly in the Genroku era (1688–1704) from *kagura* to *kabuki* and *ongyoku*. Needless to say, there was a complex process involved, but I will not go into this here as it is described in detail in elsewhere. In Japan, music was traditionally transmitted from master to apprentice through oral means, and I believe there were many traditions that simply disappeared in the chaotic Warring States period. Neither does there appear to have been much intermixing between Noh songs, folk songs sung during festivals and other civic events, and work songs.

▼ Roland Classic Series electronic cembalo C-30.

As far as the ability to faithfully reproduce a musical piece, while the person-to-person method of transmission may seem to be on shaky grounds compared to the notation method of Europe, the former method has quite surprisingly succeeded in vividly communicating human emotions and nuances down through the ages. For this reason, melody became the center of Eastern music and harmony did not emerge. While *gagaku* is a form of orchestra, it has come thus far without making an impact on the music of Japan.

Either way, music with a long legacy is a common world language. And notation is a common world software program. I believe this is the reason the names of musical pieces and their composers from the sixteenth and seventeenth centuries have been passed down to our present age. From this perspective, it is unfortunate that the composers and lyricists of Japanese tunes are unknown in the majority of cases. If the composer is not known, then the issue of copyright becomes moot. Puccini became the first composer to receive royalties, thanks to the establishment of copyright for notation. Notation, a common global language, is indispensable in enabling multitudes of people to enjoy music.

There is a good reason why keyboard instruments and fretted guitars dominate a large part of the musical instrument market: both are readily able to produce the pitches written on a score. While there may be musicians who dislike equal temperament, for the time being, the other temperaments must be left up to non-fretted instruments that allow the musician to choose the pitch of notes. While electronic instruments already have the potential to break through the constraints of temperaments, this cannot be realized without the cooperation not only of theorists but of musicians, the ones who will actually be playing the instruments. The musical notations that survive today are invaluable assets of humanity, and it is a great joy that music is an international language. There are no "cold wars" in this world of international language.

Nostalgic Melodies

I believe that Japanese music education, which started in the Meiji era, is something the Japanese can be very proud of. Without the reformations that began in the Meiji era, the country would not have been able to incorporate Western music in such a short amount of time to come to where it is today. Needless to say, without that, Japan's musical instrument industry would not have taken off either. Music was only a smart part of the environment that I grew up in, but there was no denying that I was in the midst of the massive change that music was undergoing.

In Japan, where the written language was distinctly different from the spoken, song lyrics were also written in the literary style. Three volumes called "Collection of Elementary School Songs" were printed between 1881 and 1884, during which time the Ministry of Education founded a music research department and appointed Shuji Isawa as its general director. This department was founded with the help of American music educator Luther Whiting Mason. I was actually not aware that Japan and America already had musical ties in the early Meiji era until I began studying this material.

Perhaps because Mason was heavily influenced by British music, the "Collection of Elementary School Songs" volumes contain many Scottish and Irish folk songs. Traditional Japanese scales contained five notes, which made up the *yo* and *in* pentatonic scales. Of these, the yo pentatonic is used often in Scottish and Irish folk songs. "Hotaru no Hikari," "Niwa no Chigusa," "Aogeba Totoshi," and many other tunes fall into this group. However, the lyrics in those days were almost always written in literary style, and it was only after the colloquial-style songs movement starting in 1897 that lyricists began writing new types of lyrics. This began with nursery tunes such as "Momotaro," "Usagi to Kame," "Daikoku Sama," and "Hanasaka Jiji," which were written in pentatonic scales; scales that the Japanese were familiar with.

"Kindergarten Songs" was one group of colloquial-style songs, and seventeen out of all twenty of these were composed by Rentaro Taki, including songs like "Hatopoppo" and "Oshogatsu," which all Japanese are very familiar with. Other famous songs include "Hana," "Hakone Hachiri," and "Kojo no Tsuki."

This movement of colloquial-style songs began in the literary realm, and its influence can be seen in the changes the lyrics underwent. As I started elementary school in 1936, we still sang songs with literary-style lyrics during singing class. On National Foundation Day (or Empire Day, as it was called then), which came on February 11, we would sing, "Kumo ni sobieru Takachiho no, takane oroshi ni, kusa mo ki mo, nabiki fusiken ohmiyo wo, aogu kyo koso, tanoshi kere."

While I did not know that I would end up living in Takachiho, which was mentioned in those lyrics, for four years after the war, I remember the lyrics and melody of this song clearly to this day. Other songs that I and others in my generation sang in literary style include "Tetsudo Shoka," "Umi," "Furusato," "Haru no Ogawa," and "Oboro Zukiyo." After the war, books such as the Christian Bible were also translated into colloquial style, but many of the songs still retained their original style. For example, in the song "Cho Cho" (originally titled "Kocho" based on a Spanish folk song), which everyone from Japan has sung at least once, and which is still sung by kindergarteners around the country, there is a passage that goes, "Sakura no hano no, hana kara hana e," which was originally sung, "Sakura no hana no, sakayuru miyo ni." This was when "cho cho" was written "tefu tefu." While not in a pentatonic scale, the wonderful melody of this song, which has become a timeless favorite for many, is made up of the five notes do, re, mi, fa, and sol.

While music education first had students singing in unison, it soon became clear that instruments were needed that could play notes at distinct pitches. Organs were best suited for this purpose as they could be used for accompaniment as well. And thanks to their reasonable price, organs made at the Yamaha Fukin Seizosho (Yamaha Organ Manufacturers), launched by Torakusu Yamaha in 1888, were sold throughout the country. Still, accompaniment in those days was different from what we would consider to be accompaniment today, and consisted of the teacher playing a monophonic melody to which the students sang in unison. These foundations were laid by Shūji Isawa, mentioned above.

The fortieth episode of the travel documentary series based on novelist and essayist Ryotaro Shiba's *Kaido wo Yuku* featured a journey through Taiwan, and I remember being surprised that the program touched on a story about Shuji Isawa. After the First Sino-Japanese War, Taiwan became a territory of Japan in 1895, when Isawa was forty-four years old. Isawa volunteered to work with the governor's office, was appointed director of academic affairs, and relocated to Taiwan. Once there, he built an elementary school on the Shizangan plain. It must have taken a great deal of passion and commitment to relocate to Taiwan with a vision to build his ideal school. At the time, however, there was still much social unrest, and half of the six staff members who traveled with him were killed, derailing his plan before it saw fruition. Music education in Japan was initiated by such figures, who had a strong sense of mission.

Just for the sake of information, I would like to list songs that were created on a pentatonic scale and those that were written in literary style, ten songs each, from among the many elementary school songs, children's songs, and folk songs written in those days.

Songs written on pentatonic scales were: "Momotaro," "Yuyake Koyake," "Toryanse," "Nanatsu no Ko," "Dendenmushi," "Akatombo," "Satchan," "Sakura," "Tetsudo Shoka," and "Kokyo no Sora."

Songs whose lyrics were written in literary style were: "Ware wa Umi no Ko," "Hana," "Kojo no Tsuki," "Hakone Hachiri," "Hamabe no Uta," "Schubert Lullaby," "Yashi no Mi," "Ryoshu," "Kokyo," "Aogeba Totoshi."

"Hotaru no Hikari" (known in the West as "Auld Lang Syne") is a pentatonic Scottish folk song given literary-style lyrics, and is also a hymn. Pentatonic scales were used in many other folk songs, horsekeepers' songs, and traditional celebration songs, including "Itsuki no Komoriuta," "Hietsuki Bushi," and "Kuroda Bushi." The composers of "Satchan" and "Yashi no Mi" were father and son, so we've had the good fortune of enjoying the musical gifts of a family over two generations.

The Suzuki Method

Matsumoto, a city located in the region traditionally known as Shinshu, is known for its pure air, but it was not for its pristine air that the thirtieth general meeting of the Japan Musical Instruments Association was held here in 1980. The Shinshu region is known throughout the world for the many precision manufacturing companies that call it home, and also as a major production center for stringed instruments. Everyone also knows that the people of this prefecture are passionate about education and highly engaged in cultural activities. The annual Saito Kinen Festival, held here in Matsumoto to honor the cellist Hideo Saito, who trained many conductors including Seiji Ozawa, brings performers connected in one way or another to Saito from around the world. The Harmony Hall in the Matsumoto Municipal Music and Culture Center houses a large pipe organ. An organ fan club has formed and the hall is open to the public.

This makes Matsumoto the ideal city for people connected in one way or another to musical instruments to come together. Roland has its Matsumoto factory in the industrial district adjacent to airport, and I often ride on the Chuo Line to make business trips to the factory. At Matsumoto Station, I occasionally see children with violin cases walking with a parent, and I know there is only one place they could be going. There is no one in the world who has anything to do with violins who has not heard of the Suzuki method, a mode of training provided to children from a very young age, which has produced many excellent violinists. Matsumoto is also home to the headquarters of the Suzuki method, the Talent Education Research Institute.

One theory goes that stringed instruments originated among the equestrian people of Mongolia and spread eastward and westward from there. The strings were made of sheep gut, and the use of horsehair in bows is a remnant of those days. A Mongolian instrument called the *morin khuur* appears to be the prototype of the cello; if this is the case, it may have been brought to Europe during Genghis Khan's forays there. It was only in the seventeenth and eighteenth centuries that the violin took the shape we are familiar with today—a relatively recent development—and the use of horsehair in violin bows is not unrelated to the Mongolian influence. Japan saw an influx of *biwa* and *kokyu* via China, Korea, and Okinawa. The *shamisen* clearly has its roots in the Chinese *sanxian* and Okinawan *sanshin*. With dog or cat skin replacing the snake skin, and played with a *bachi*, or plectrum, the shamisen was transformed into a uniquely Japanese instrument. While shamisen performance styles suit traditional Japanese attire well and confer on the player a certain stylishness, this pales in the face of the refined style of violins. The violin is a frictional stringed instrument capable of making sustained notes, giving the player a richer range of expression.

While many people aspire to play the violin, it is too late once the right brain has lost its pliability. Training from a young age is indispensable for musicians whose instruments' pitch must be determined by the player, and this is one of the greatest challenges of these types of instruments. Neither the shamisen nor the violin has frets. The player is required to determine the pitch with his or her own ears. Looking back at the transition to Western music that began in the Meiji era, the violin might have been a more natural choice. However, it was reasonable that keyboard instruments with their fixed pitches were chosen for elementary school classrooms around the country.

The musical education for young children implemented by Shinichi Suzuki, the founder of the Suzuki method, was revolutionary. I had the good fortune to listen to two of Mr. Suzuki's lectures. He related to us that he had visited the zoo for days on end to observe the behavior of apes, and realized that there was no right- or left-handedness among apes. He said in his matter-of-fact way, "We should not be trying to correct left-handed children to become right-handed, but should be helping them to become ambidextrous without them thinking about it. It took me many days to make this very simple realization. My method of education is the implementation of this idea." Citing a specific example, he said, "All we have to do is have the children play the same tune until they are able to express their sensibilities as freely as they do when they walk or run," and went on to clearly explain, "There is no such thing as talent that you are born with. A person's abilities are developed by his or her environment." The Suzuki method is now used all around the world, and it is probably better known abroad than in Japan.

In the 1980s, I heard that Mr. Suzuki had begun a program for piano education as well, and quickly decided to arrange a meeting with him. I thought it would be best to ask Yuichiro Yokouchi, president of the instrument-manufacturing company FujiGen, which had its headquarters and factory in Matsumoto, to set up a date. I was surprised at how quickly we heard back that Mr. Suzuki would meet us, and I was able to persuade Mr. Yokouchi to accompany me to the meeting as well. I brought along with me our brand-new HP-70 electric piano in hopes that Mr. Suzuki would be open to using it on a trial basis in his classes. I explained the benefits of the piano, such as how its volume could be controlled easily and that students could play through headphones, making it an ideal instrument for learning in groups.

Mr. Suzuki was very interested and remarked, "The kids will love this . . ." and called one of his piano teachers. The teacher checked the keyboard touch carefully and was not very impressed, pointing out that the touch was "different from acoustic pianos." Regardless, Mr. Suzuki asked his staff members, "Do you think we can use this in our recitals? What is our schedule looking like?" And then the conversation got even more specific as he asked me, "How much is the entire set, including piano, headphones, and bench?" All of this happened within a span of about fifteen minutes during which there was absolutely no small talk.

My intention had been to meet with Mr. Suzuki, show him the piano, ask him if he would be interested in using it on a trial basis in his classes, and then leave. But he said, "I like this piano and would like to purchase it. President Kakehashi himself has come here to describe the product, so I want to pay the proper retail price." And before we knew it, he had already signed a check for the retail price of the piano and handed it over to me. This was completely unexpected. Mr. Yokouchi and I looked at each other stunned. At the time, Roland was selling its products through retailers so it had never sold its products at more than wholesale. I may have been the first and last person from Roland to sell a product with all of its accessories at "retail price."

▲ Shinichi Suzuki.

About fifteen years from that day, on January 27, 1998, I read an obituary in the newspaper announcing the sad news of Mr. Suzuki's passing:

> Shinichi Suzuki: Deceased of cardiac failure at his personal residence in Matsumoto, Nagano, at 6:00 a.m. on the 26th. Mr. Suzuki, born in Nagoya, was 99 years of age. His funeral wake will be held from 5:30 p.m. on the 27th, with funeral and memorial services to be held from 1:00 pm on the 28th at the Catholic Matsumoto Church at 9-32 Marunouchi, Matsumoto. The funeral host is his wife Mrs. Waltraud Suzuki. In 1921, Mr. Suzuki studied violin performance in Berlin. Upon returning to Japan in 1931 he formed the Suzuki Quartet, a four-member chamber ensemble group that included violin. In 1948, he formed the Talent Education Research Institute. Based on his idea that "there is no such thing as talent that you are born with; every child can grow his or her talent; it all depends on how they are taught," his "Suzuki method," a method of teaching through music, spread throughout the world. In addition to 120 branches in Japan, he has established branches in 34 countries. Toshiya Eto, dean of Toho Gakuen, was one of his students. (From the *Sankei Shimbun*, January 27, 1998.)

▲ From left to right: Carolyn Leslie, myself, and Don Leslie.

His death was reported not only in Japan but also in many overseas outlets such as *USA Today*, *Time*, *The San Francisco Chronicle*, and *Asia Week*. Currently, a variety of material from a broad range of countries on Mr. Suzuki and the Suzuki method is available on the Internet. I feel only respect for his vision and ability to put ideas into action. A century after Japan first began importing "music as software" in the Meiji era, I was very fortunate to have the opportunity to meet Mr. Suzuki, who exported "music as software" from Japan and achieved so many great milestones. He was someone who took in the huge number of samples that he saw around him and then added Japanese culture to the mix to create a wonderfully unique method.

The Leslie Speaker

In addition to the changes in the world of software, major changes were in motion in the realm of hardware as well. All electronic instruments express their sounds through loudspeakers. Hammond organs, a breed of electronic instrument invented in 1934, also require loudspeakers. The Leslie speaker, which caused a revolution in the world of electronic musical instruments, was invented by Donald Leslie in the 1940s. To this day, the sublime combination of Hammond organ and Leslie speaker is considered to be the best in the world and continues to be highly popular, especially in the area of jazz organ. While we are now able to reproduce these tones through electronic means, they are the same tones that made the Leslie speaker so popular for so many years. Thanks to my line of business, I was close with Don Leslie, who unfortunately passed away in 2004. I was very fortunate to have been able to produce and donate the *Don Leslie Story*, a video based on material that his wife, Carolyn Leslie, was kind enough to lend me.

3

My First Venture Business

THE FIRST YEAR WE WERE ABLE TO EXHIBIT OUR PRODUCTS AT THE National Association of Music Merchants (NAMM) Show, a musical instrument trade show in the United States, was 1964. The first year we took part in the Frankfurt Musikmesse was 1967. At these trade shows, in countries where electronic instruments had already begun to gain momentum, we were able to glimpse what was actually going on in these markets and were finally able to see our direction for making musical instruments. By this time, however, twenty years had already passed since I opened my first business, the Kakehashi Clock Shop, immediately after the war. Counting back from today as I write this book, more than sixty-five years have passed since then.

The Years Before and After the End of the War

I was an intermediate school student as World War II was nearing its end. On March 13, 1945, the house that I had just moved into after a mandatory evacuation was burned to the ground during the bombing of Osaka. Everything seemed so evanescent. All the model trains I had made, as well as the photo books and scrapbooks of steam and electric locomotives I had compiled since my elementary school years, were burned to ashes. This was a collection I was never going to be able to put together again. Even as I stood in the rubble, looking at whatever remained of my collection, I remember not feeling any regret or chagrin, but feeling rather refreshed. My interest in models continued but I never restarted a collection.

By that time, my grandparents, who had taken care of me since my parents passed away when I was two years old, had already moved to Fukasumi in Takachiho-cho, Miyazaki Prefecture, my grandmother's birthplace. In a span of just one month, I had parted with my grandparents, been forced to evacuate and relocate, and had the house that I lived in burned to the ground by a bombing raid. For about five months from that date until August 15 when the war ended, I stayed with the family of one of my classmates, Yoshiharu Sakai. I can't thank the Sakai family enough for taking me in during those chaotic times. Considering the scarcity of food at the time, I was very lucky.

In those days, air raid sirens would ring out almost nightly, at which point we would make our way to the bunker. But we soon got used to this and we increasingly opted to stay in bed until the bombs actually started falling. But still, we were all sleep-deprived and short of food, so I remember it was a very hard commute to the Hitachi shipyard in Sakurajima near Osaka port, where I was working as a mobilized labor student. At the shipyard I was assigned to the milling machine section of the engineering department, where we made mechanical parts. We made parts for oil tankers, coastal defense ships, and special submersibles. The work proceeded according to order slips and drawings, and each of us started out under the supervision of expert workers as we operated—with barely passing proficiency—the machines to which we were assigned, one machine per worker. I found the mechanical practicum that I had taken in the technical school very useful in this regard, and a year later, I was making sophisticated parts. I remember one day Yoshio Tabata was on site on an entertainment visit, and sang songs such as "Kaeri Bune" amid the piles of steel plates in our factory. I remember those days as if they were just yesterday, but those of us with such memories are getting fewer in number. I worked alongside Koreans who had been forcibly relocated there, but I did not feel anything out of place as they worked in the same environment as those of us who had to work instead of go to school.

We were instructed to give top priority to jobs whose slips had "SS" stamped on them, which we began to see more and more of. Rumors went around that those parts with the "SS" mark were for special submersibles and we learned that their construction had begun in the factory next door. One day during lunch break, I went with three of my colleagues of the same school year to take a nervous peek at the special submersibles being built in an area enclosed by plywood partitions. For some reason, there were no guards on the lookout during lunch break. These special submersibles did not have their warheads attached, but we were able to see them in their entirety. They were very crudely built, and I remember thinking it bizarre that the rudder was simply weld-cut and not given any finish treatment. They were designed for the pilot to ride astride the engine to steer the craft, and there was a cramped, small dome welded onto the craft's cylindrical body. While a periscope was attached to the dome, which had room for only one, it was not designed to move up or down. Without a periscope that could move up or down, the only way to make observations of the surface was to actually float or submerge the craft itself. Instantly, I knew that these were being built solely for *tokko* (suicide) missions.

We had read glorified reports in newspapers of tokko aircraft squadrons, but it was quite a shock to see a tokko submersible with my own eyes. It was clear that what we had seen was a secret military weapon so I remember that I didn't talk about this with any of my colleagues for fear that the story would spread as a rumor. Every time a slip marked "SS" came my way, my heart would sink from the memory of seeing that submersible. A photo of a special submersible called a Kaiten was shown on a TV program some years ago, but this looked much larger than the ones we saw. The ones at the factory may have seemed small because they had their warheads removed, but they were definitely not Kaitens. We were never told what those crafts were called, and I suspect they were never used in battle. A few of my fellow students had already been assigned to aviation corps after finishing Naval Aviation Preparatory School, and this left a deep scar in my heart.

On August 14, the day before the end of the war, an ordnance factory that was producing weapons in a location east of Osaka Castle was bombed. This was a dramatic change from all the bombing raids up to that point, which were typically nighttime incendiary bomb raids. I was watching from a distance of about two and a half miles northwest of Osaka Station and I remember seeing the shock waves expand every time a bomb fell, creating ripples in the air just as on the surface of the water when a pebble is dropped into a pond.

Thinking of it now, I believe that by this day, which was the day before the actual war-end announcement, the government must have reached an agreement with the US forces to end the war. So every time I travel on the Osaka Loop Line near Kyobashi Station, I wonder why such an intense bombing raid was carried out that day. My guess is that the Americans wanted to make sure there would be no revolts by the surrendering Japanese when they came in to occupy the country. The factory director of the Hitachi shipyard where we were assigned died in this bombing raid. This location was the setting of Sakyo Komatsu's first sci-fi novel, *Nihon Apache*. Now, the area is crowded with high-rise buildings and there is nothing that would remind us of those days.

I later had the opportunity to meet Sakyo Komatsu. This was at the February 6, 1982 Conference for Osaka Prefectural Residents on Osaka's Economic Development, organized by then Osaka governor Sakae Kishi. The event featured appearances by Komatsu as well as fashion designer Hiroko Koshino, both of whom contributed their own exhibits. I asked the jazz pianist Oscar Peterson if he would be willing to come do a concert. He agreed very cordially so we were able to invite him as our special guest. His performance of "Caravan" was received to a huge round of applause.

What was the sense of liberation like after the war? When I think back now, many memories come to mind. The bombing raids stopped, the content of newspaper reports changed, music was everywhere, American fashion flooded into Japan, and there was all the food you could eat as long as you could pay for it. These are some of the things that come to my mind as having given me a sense of liberation. But the biggest thing for me was music. I think the biggest impact for me was listening to types of music that I had never heard before.

Most of the music we had during the wartime years broadly fell into the category of military songs. While some of them still stir a sense of nostalgia in me, all the music was militaristic and very little of it is connected to fond memories. That said, during my elementary school years, right up to the time World War II broke out, Japanese society still enjoyed the afterglow of what was called the Taisho Democracy era. There were times when all foreign music was referred to as jazz, but what I do remember is that we had access to music from many countries around the world. Radio broadcasting began in 1925, and our family was one of the early adopters of this medium, though radio did not have much of a place in my day-to-day life. While talkie cinema came on the scene between 1937 and 1939, I also remember going to silent movies voiced by a reciter.

Cinema was instrumental in the rise of French popular music in Japan, and people also listened to a lot of *kayokyoku*—standard Japanese pop. While I had little interest in the popular music of the day—the type of music I would hear almost daily coming from the gramophone shop two doors down from where we lived—I do remember "people's songs" such as "Yashi no Mi" and "Haru no Uta" coming over the radio. Some of these are still around today, and we

▼ Panel discussion at the Third Conference for Osaka Prefectural Residents on Osaka's Economic Development, 1982. From right to left: Oscar Peterson, an unidentified person, Sakyo Komatsu, Hiroko Koshino, and myself.

have had the opportunity to listen to them when they were featured on TV. My feelings toward military songs, which I could not relate to at the time, have also changed over the years. Songs like "Wakawashi no Uta" and "Doki no Sakura," which we sang with ragged but strong voices on the banks of the Yodogawa River as we sent off our fellow students before they were transferred to the Naval Aviation Preparatory School, to me are not military songs but continue to be nostalgic songs of farewell. I never had the chance to listen to an orchestra or jazz performance until 1946. All I had seen was the performance of military bands on newsreels.

During the war, in 1943, about a thousand pieces of music imported from the United States and Britain were designated as highly inappropriate and banned from public performance. People were even banned from playing recordings of these pieces. A list of banned American and British records was compiled and enforcement began. I did not know which songs were on this list at the time, but I recently reviewed the list and was surprised to learn that it covered light music, jazz, and even semi-classical music. The choice of songs was completely unintelligible; even songs by Stephen Foster and folk songs were included. Record store inventories were seized and disposed of. Private citizens were also required to dispose of their records. What this tells us is that, only sixty years after it was first introduced, Western music had become popular enough in Japan to warrant a prohibition. Radio was also regulated. During wartime, when airwave control was at its peak, the fabrication or ownership of shortwave radio was prohibited as an act of espionage, so there was no way of listening to news and music broadcast on foreign programs. Besides seeing and hearing live music, radio was still the only medium for music. And I spent my youth with no exposure to live music.

All the more intense was the inundation of music after the war, so much so that we were barely able to keep up. We relied on radio broadcasts for music until a new record was released. At the time, there were still no private radio stations, so the only reliable source of music was all-wave receivers, which were capable of receiving everything from US Armed Forces broadcasts to shortwave. This is hard to imagine now when we have access to a rich range of media including private broadcasts, FM, TV, and satellite, but we were all very happy with these all-wave receivers as we could choose the airwaves we wanted to listen to as opposed to just having NHK 1 and 2. Since radio was the only medium, if you wanted to listen to music, you had to have one of these all-wave receivers.

Of course, there were no program listings that would point us to a frequency that we might want to listen to, so we would turn the dial on the radio to search for stations one by one and jot down the frequency of any station that caught our fancy. Once radio magazines came out, we had access to program details and this was a great help as it increased our options in one fell swoop.

While all-wave receivers were available commercially, they were imported from abroad and quite expensive. So building an all-wave receiver became an opportune challenge for me, and I built a large number of them during the chaotic postwar period. This eventually went beyond the realm of hobby and turned into a semi-profession. So by 1947, my life became quite hectic as I was repairing old clocks and radios to earn enough money to make a living and purchase radio parts, which I would use to build new radios that I could turn around and sell for a profit.

My First Venture Business

I remained in Osaka for seven months after the end of war until my intermediate school graduation, when I applied to Sakai Engineering College (present Osaka Prefecture University) to pursue chemistry, my field of interest at the time. The entrance exams were given at the end of February, with about three hundred applicants to the chemistry department. Fifty-three of them passed the test, of which I fortunately was one. However, two students failed the final health exams and I was one of those, too. An X-ray had found a shadow in my lungs.

Looking back now, I don't know how I thought I would get through school with no potential source of money for tuition or living expenses. In April, eight months after the end of the war, I decided to go to Takachiho, Miyazaki, where my grandparents had relocated earlier. However, things were very unsettled in those days, and I remember the simple act of purchasing a train ticket to Kyushu being quite an ordeal. By making this decision, I was moving from Osaka, which was undergoing intense postwar change, to a location completely removed from all that.

The food situation in the town of Takachiho, thanks to its location in the mountains, was much better than in Osaka. People came from many neighboring areas and were very warm, so it was a comfortable place for me to live. Since I had been prone to illness and was not in the best physical condition, it was a great environment for me to revitalize myself.

That said, this small town located in the middle of the island of Kyushu had no industry to speak of and I could not find any work. The best thing available was construction work and a part-time surveyor position with the town. A person I knew remarked, "If you've graduated from a technical school, you should be able to do surveying work," and got me the job, for which I was paid my first day's wage. The three of us—the person in charge of the district, the person in charge of the survey, and me, the survey technician—would walk through all districts near Takachiho, charged with renewing the land ledger, which had not been revised since the Meiji era. Thanks to this job, which I did part-time for four months, I got to know many people in the area. I was very grateful for this opportunity as these relationships proved to be a great help in many ways when I later opened my clock and radio repair business in Takachiho.

I also worked as a part-time laborer building a new bridge across Takachiho Gorge, a tourist destination. This bridge still exists but is no longer used for transportation and now simply functions as a tourist site. The main road now goes across a new bridge farther upstream, and the old bridge that I worked on can be seen down the ravine from this new bridge. The date of completion embossed on the old bridge says March 1947. I earned fifteen yen an hour, but if I ate lunch, three yen would be subtracted from my pay, leaving me with twelve. This was a very small amount of money, but we did not have the luxury of being picky and you had to consider yourself lucky if you had a job at all in those days.

While I was engaged in these jobs in survey and construction, I was searching for a line of work that would suit me, and that was when clock repair caught my eye. The demand for clock repair was high as no new clocks were being sold, so if you had a broken clock you had to have it repaired. I would stand outside of a clock-repair store for one or even two hours at night after my survey or construction work, looking in on the repair process through the store's window.

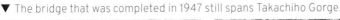
▼ The bridge that was completed in 1947 still spans Takachiho Gorge.

Then one day, the owner came out and said, "Do you want to apprentice with me and learn?" So I would go at nights to learn clock repair. Once I began, I quickly gained a general understanding of the mechanism thanks to my training in the machine section in intermediate school. Once I was able to do an overhaul cleaning, I felt that I knew enough about wall clocks and table clocks, so I timidly told the owner that I wanted to learn about watches. But to this request, he gave me one stern shout of denial.

The practice of clock and watch apprenticeship had been around from before the war and generally involved three years of working on wall and table clocks, then on to learning more about the business by polishing cases and making deliveries, and then gradually moving up to watches over a period of about five years overall. Add to this two years of gratitude service (in which the apprentice continues to serve the master as a token of gratitude for apprenticeship), and the period of apprenticeship adds up to about seven years. To ask to learn about watches after only two months of work was completely out of the norm. Come to think of it now, it was no surprise that my request was denied because, actually, the seven years of apprenticeship were only had for learning the skills but took into account the time it would take to become familiar with customer interaction, learn how to purchase supplies, and establish a relationship with the guild.

But at the time, I was too young to understand this master-apprentice system, and I was also hot-blooded. I had no intention of putting another two or three years into what I thought I had mastered, so I bought a collection of lessons on clock repair that was advertised in the paper and decided to teach myself. Although these lessons were quite a shabby affair—a very simple thing printed on a mimeograph—they were enough to give me a general idea of watches.

I had the opportunity to see this collection of lessons again fifty-five years

◀ The Kakehashi Clock Shop, which I opened in 1947 in Takachiho, Miyazaki. As a sixteen-year-old shop owner, I was still growing my hair in an effort to look like a mature adult.

later in the year 2000. This was when I was taking a stroll through Kanda, Tokyo, with my grandkid, visiting the many used bookstores in the area. As I casually glanced into one shop, I saw the mimeographed collection of lessons on display in a showcase. Instantly, I was taken back to those times, and felt a great sense of nostalgia as well as an awareness of the passage of time.

Since there was no shortage of watches that I could practice my repairing skills on, I made the decision right there and then to open my own shop. Although the town had a population of only twelve thousand, it already had three watch shops. So it was natural that the existing ones would not be amused at my opening up shop. In addition to that, it was a long time before the guild would accept me as a member, as I was this young fellow who had just been a trainee a little while ago and had suddenly opened his own shop.

Although you had to be a guild member to receive rations of volatile oil, I had no other means of making a living, so I rented a two-tatami-mat space to open my shop. With a handwritten sign on the door, the Kakehashi Clock Shop opened in mid-1947.

The income from watch repair was actually quite good so I enjoyed the work. At the time, a variety of types of watches came in for repair, such as small women's watches nicknamed *nankin mushi* and larger pocket watches. I was also surprised to learn that many people owned Swiss-made watches. Most of the watches were at a point where they needed overhaul cleaning. Held in different regard from the fashion and accessory items they are considered to be today, watches in those days were the most precious of status symbol items.

What I learned from repairing watches was that the more expensive the watch, the easier it was to repair. Overhaul cleaning made up 80 percent of the repair work; this involved washing off old oil from the parts, lubricating them with new oil, and then reassembling them. In almost all cases, the watches would continue to work just fine after an overhaul. As for watches made in Japan during the war years, however, iron pieces (details of the material are unknown) were used to make the parts of the escapement that were subjected to friction, ankle notch, and the pin where the balance and ankle came together. These parts naturally had more wear on them compared to parts that used rubies, and would no longer behave as designed. Replacing these iron pieces was a very complicated affair, partly owing to my lack of experience, so I would have to assemble these watches and hope for the best. Such was the quality level of Japan-made watches in those days. The cheap watches were a lot of work. Regardless, the guild had set a strange pricing scheme by which repairers could charge 50 percent more for upmarket watches.

While my clock-repair business went well and I no longer had trouble earning a living, my interest in radios for listening to music continued to grow, and I soon realized the potential of radio-related technologies. The nature of clock repair was such that your final objective was to bring the watch or clock back to the condition it had been in when it shipped from the factory, nothing more. There was a certain joy in seeing the balance move after a repair, but that paled in comparison to the allure of radio. Once I realized that, I reduced the amount of time I spent repairing clocks and shifted my focus to repairing radios. Reports in radio-related magazines on the developments in radio and the proliferation of radios at the time, as well as the deregulation of the shortwave band, were all very alluring to me.

However, I was living in the mountains in central Kyushu, and this made it very difficult to purchase radio parts. I had to place my orders with parts wholesalers in Kanda or take two-day part-purchasing trips to Kumamoto, the closest large city on Kyushu. To repair radios, you needed old parts as well as new ones. I purchased old radios and disassembled them for parts that I might later be able to use for repairs. If I had five or six old radios, I could make one radio by adding just a few new parts. A category of parts in those days notorious for low quality was capacitors. There wasn't much else I could do but replace them. The majority of radio failures, however, resulted from broken electrolytic capacitors and vacuum tubes, and this made repairs easy.

Vacuum tubes used in those days had a magnesium film called sputter inside them to increase the degree of vacuum. I found that nearly half the tubes could be brought back to life by heating this silvery glistening part with a candle flame, which would in turn cause the magnesium to reabsorb oxygen and increase the degree of vacuum in the tube. I revived many vacuum tubes using this method and used these refurbished tubes for repairs. Radios that provided good receptivity were the so-called five-tube supers. These radios came with five vacuum tubes and had an oscillator with a higher frequency than that of the incoming radio wave, so instead of directly amplifying the radio wave, it would create beats in conjunction with the incoming waves. These were called intermediate frequencies, and by using a lower frequency than that of the incoming radio wave, you could stabilize the amplification and increase receptivity. Soon after the war, a new type of receptor based on the superheterodyne system (super for short) emerged, which provided dramatically better performance than earlier radios. This system was indispensable particularly for making all-wave-type radios.

So I ended up building several tens of radios and then selling them one after the other, which allowed me to perfect my craft. My work gradually shifted from clocks to radios, and in about four years' time, more than half of my work had to do with radios. During the months when the local farmers who had helped me out in different areas of my life were busy with harvesting and planting, I would be busy helping them out and having a good time doing so. My fingers would shake for about two days after I engaged in physical labor so I could not do any clock repairs, but it was a very important experience for me to have this opportunity to engage in farmwork and familiarize myself with the land. There was a period of about one full year when I worked on farms from morning to night. The physical labor was tougher than I had imagined, but I look back nostalgically at the daily work of drawing water into the paddies before rice planting, steering oxen for rice nurseries, and weeding the paddies. I also believe this helped me to develop physical strength at a time when I was still growing.

Radios and amplifiers were still new in those days, and they were more than enough to absorb my interest. Four years had gone by in the blink of an eye. In those days, there was a law that prohibited people from relocating to large cities such as Tokyo and Osaka because the food situation in the cities was so bad. When I heard that this prohibition was about to be lifted, I quickly decided to sell everything at the Kakehashi Clock Shop and move to Osaka. I finished repairs on all items that I had on hand and sold my inventory at bargain prices. It was quite an ordeal to convert all of that to cash and return to Osaka, but I managed to do so in about two weeks.

There was only one reason for me to return to Osaka. It was to go to university, not in the chemistry department but in a department related to electronics. Thanks to the decisive step I took to convert everything to cash, the amount I had managed to accumulate in four years of working on clocks and radios was just enough to get me through four years of university. So one month after I heard the news of the city relocation law being lifted, I was preparing for my university entrance exams in Osaka. For four years since 1946 I had lived in the mountains in Kyushu, away from the city, a very important experience for me. Even though I was born in Osaka, I now felt I had a place I could call home. This was during my youth, from age sixteen to twenty.

▲ At the main entrance of Kaizuka Sengokuso National Sanatorium.

Sengokuso University

Until the war intervened, there were five grades in the preparatory schools. During the war the system was altered to cut the curriculum to four years so the students could be mobilized to work after early graduation. I was one of those who spent only four years in prep school under the altered system. Once the war was over, we realized that we did not meet the requirements for entering universities or taking entrance exams in accordance with the restored educational system. To obtain qualification, I had to either enter a high school as defined under the new system or take a high school equivalency test. So I transferred to Nishinoda Technical High School, which by that time had been converted to a high school under the new system. But because this was a technical high school, the majority of classroom time was spent on technical lessons, diagram drawing, and other specialized areas, with relatively little time spent on English, math, or physics. This meant that I would be wasting too much of my time on subjects unrelated to the entrance exams, so I decided to transfer to a night school where I could concentrate on the subjects I needed to complete to be eligible for the exams. Based on the convenience of the commute and other factors, I took a transfer enrollment exam at Kitano High School. The mood of the chaotic postwar period lingered in the Kitano night school. A number of my classmates had been enrolled in the naval academy or military college during the war and were also there to qualify for university exams. We were all of different ages, partly because this was a night school, but we all had a great time.

▼ Here I am (second from left) with my friends at Sengokuso.

I was very fond of Kitano High School and had a fulfilling experience there, but in January, just a few months before graduation, I began coughing blood and was diagnosed with tuberculosis. I immediately took a full physical exam and it was recommended that I be hospitalized. All sanatoria and similar facilities were full at the time and I was placed on a waiting list. Six months later, I was finally admitted to a sanatorium called Sengokuso in the city of Kaizuka, south of Osaka. My teacher at the high school recommended that I apply for a leave of absence, but since there was little chance that I would make a quick recovery, I decided to leave the school. I was very disappointed at the time, but looking back, I think it was the right decision.

When I was first admitted at Sengokuso, I still had enough strength to carry my own luggage, but in about six months, my condition had deteriorated considerably. I became lethargic, lost the energy to move around the way I wanted to, and my condition got worse by the day. Ultimately, I underwent a treatment in which they stabilized my lung activity using an artificial pneumothorax procedure on both sides of my lungs. This was a very indirect treatment with a very direct effect on the patient. The treatment involved creating a layer of air in the chest cavity to reduce the lungs' activity in order to control symptoms. The treatment helped to stabilize my symptoms. Because both my lungs were affected, a condition that precluded me from having thoracic surgery, it was all the more frustrating for me to see patients undergo this surgery and be discharged within a year. However, I was ultimately fortunate not to have undergone this surgery.

Most of the funds I had saved up for university went to cover my long hospitalization, and I had to do part-time work to earn the money I needed for food and other expenses at the hospital. However, I was happy that I could use my rest time and the time after lights-out to listen to music. I placed a six-tube super on the table by my bed and listened to it through a headset.

Treatments at tuberculosis sanatoria at the time consisted primarily of clean air, rest, and good nutrition, with the active treatments being pneumothorax and thoracic surgeries. Lobectomy operations were still in their testing stages. The only drugs we took were calcium by intravenous injection and para-aminosalicylic acid (PAS), an antituberculous drug. The only exams we took were

▼ This is a fourteen-inch TV receiver I built as a prototype when I was hospitalized. It has no channel selector because there was only one station.

the weekly blood sedimentation tests and X-rays. All the calcium shots did was make your body warm for a moment, and I believe the doctors, nurses, and patients knew this was just a feel-good treatment. I had those shots several times and they felt somewhat futile. While atmosphere and rest treatments could be valuable depending on the patient's attitude, the most important issue was nutrition. Taking into account the food situation at the time, one could not complain about the food being served at Sengokuso. I believe the hospital director's most challenging task at the time might very well have been the securing of food supplies for the patients.

There were seven hundred of us hospitalized at Sengokuso. As a matter of course, there were communists amongst us, one of whom published a newsletter titled *The X-Ray*. Instead of political articles, it devoted space to demands for better conditions, particularly improved food service, and gossip. I was dumbfounded at such demands that ignored the social conditions of the time. I could only sympathize with what the hospital director and staff must have been feeling. As a means of self-sufficiency, able patients grew vegetables and potatoes on vacant patches of ground on the premises, and purchased eggs, butter, and dried fish at the kiosk to supplement their nutrition. While I was lucky enough to be able to pay for these items with the money I earned from repairing clocks and radios, food was the primary concern for other patients. In addition to this, the question of how they would make a living after they were released from the hospital was a major issue for patients who were unsure of their physical strength. This being the case, I volunteered to teach radio assembly and clock repair to patients who wanted to learn. As a result, there were a few people who opened electrical appliance and even clock shops after they left the hospital. Light electrical appliance manufacturers were busy expanding their factories but had trouble supporting their customers when private radio stations began broadcasting in 1951, so radio repair and assembly was a good job for someone just out of the hospital.

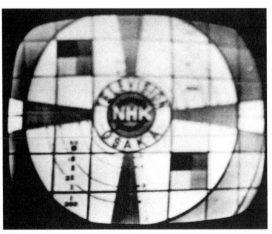

▲ This is a test pattern I received on my handmade TV. The resolution seen here is not as good as the actual image since the photograph is out of focus.

Around this time, radio-related magazines increasingly began to publish articles about TV. While TVs were already available in the United States, TV production and broadcasting was still a fantasy in Japan. Still, some companies were beginning to make prototypes. I had read about the principles of TV and studied circuit diagrams in magazine articles, but most of it had gone over my head as it all seemed so unrealistic. My interest was instantly piqued however, when I heard the news that NHK would be beginning TV test wave broadcasts, so I went back and reread all the articles that I had previously only glanced over. I wanted to be able to receive this test broadcast, whatever it took.

I wanted to make a TV, but many of the parts were not readily available. And the primary parts, even if they were available, were very expensive. Since I could not afford to buy them, I decided to make the bulk of the parts myself. I planned to do this in a small corner of my hospital room with my limited tools and material.

The most expensive component was the cathode ray tube, or picture tube. At the time, a tube made by the UK manufacturer Mullard cost about ¥40,000. This was quite expensive, considering that in those days the typical office worker earned ¥5,000 to ¥6,000 a month. But I was bold enough to borrow the money from my aunt, and became the owner of a ¥40,000 cathode ray tube. This sum would be difficult to repay even if I fully recovered, but now that I had purchased the most expensive component, I had to make my TV. The project picked up speed. I purchased other parts in Nipponbashi, a shopping area in Osaka.

Test broadcasts were aired once a week for two to three hours at a time. Most of the broadcasts aired test patterns, but sometimes they would show a movie. Eagerly anticipating these airings, I would adjust my setup ahead of time and wait for them to begin. During the short broadcasts, I would fine-tune the circuits as I watched the picture. These fine-tunings were a lot of fun to do because I had already made rough adjustments using measuring instruments. On top of that, the results of this fine-tuning were immediately reflected on the screen, and this was a completely new experience for me.

This was a time when the only broadcasts available were the test broadcasts, and TVs themselves were still very rare. So even if all the tube showed was a motionless test pattern, the six-bed hospital room where I set up my TV overflowed with people who wanted to view it. This made things difficult for my roommates. Eventually, I was instructed by the nurses' office to do my adjustments somewhere else. Since I lacked the proper measuring instruments, the picture's horizontal resolution—the measure of picture quality—was limited to about 220 lines. In 1953, broadcasting increased to four hours a day, and TV production began with manufacturers aiming for a price point of ¥10,000 per inch. When they were first launched, a black-and-white fourteen-inch tabletop TV set cost ¥175,000.

▲ Kakehashi Musen opened its doors at Fumi no Sato, Abeno-ku, Osaka. This was a sixty-five-square-foot electrical appliance retail store.

Since I planned to enroll in university once I was better, I made it a point to continue studying English, a popular subject at the time. But I showed no sign of recovery even after three years, and it was very frustrating to see my physical strength wither away. All of us in the hospital would get excited each time a new drug was announced. Of these drugs, hydrazide and streptomycin were assessed as being the most promising, prompting some patients to request postponements to scheduled surgeries. However, these new drugs were difficult to come by, and if you considered their black market price of ¥10,000 per dose and the fact that you had to take about forty doses, they were essentially a fantasy for us. But I was lucky: since my fever would not subside, and I had come down with an onset of diarrhea, and my physical strength was declining rapidly, I was chosen for a trial administration of streptomycin. Thus began my regimen of two half-gram shots per day.

The effects were dramatic from the very first day. On the second day, my appetite came back, my fever came down, and the diarrhea stopped. I regained the energy to resume my studies and everything started to look rosy. By the time I finished my twentieth shot, my body weight began to increase for the first time since I had been admitted at Sengokuso. By the time I had finished all forty shots, I was able to plan for what I wanted to do after I left the hospital, and things started to get quite busy.

By then, my weight, which had dropped from 130 pounds to about 80, had increased to 100. Still, I knew it would take much more time for me to regain my strength. At around that time, I received a letter from one of my schoolmates at Kitano High School, mentioning that he would be graduating soon. The fact that I had been hospitalized for four years sunk in upon reading this letter. When I thought ahead to what I wanted to do after I left the hospital, I came to realize how unrealistic it would be for me to re-enroll in university. I decided to consider the hospital my university, and my discharge my graduation from Sengokuso University. I had paid no tuition, taken no exams, written no dissertation, yet I would graduate, and they would even have the occasional alumni reunion.

I would be a self-proclaimed graduate of the Department of Electronics, Sengoku University, with a focus in music. General-discipline universities such as these are a true rarity.

Although I hit the job-hunting circuit immediately after my "graduation," no company would hire me, as they had not heard of my university. Everywhere I applied, I was asked to hand in an actual-size X-ray photo. Such was the prevalence of tuberculosis at the time. I believe they thought that a skinny fellow with a pale bluish complexion would not

▲ This is my first organ prototype, which I made as a side project when I opened my musical instrument store. It had no model number.

even be able to haul things around. Things being as they were, I decided to open a small electrical appliance store in Fumi no Sato, Abeno-ku, Osaka, and name it Kakehashi Musen. The Kakehashi Clock Shop had shed its old skin and taken a new name, this one represented partially in katakana characters. However, all the cash I had on hand went toward renovation and telephone access. This meant that I had no money to purchase products to display in the store for three months, so I started out as a repair shop. So the word *musen* in my shop name had the meaning of "no money," rather than the intended meaning of "radio." Upon being discharged from the hospital, I married Masako Kondo, and she kept her job, so we started out as a two-income household. So within a year of leaving the hospital, I had married my wife and opened a retail store, and we had our first son, Masayuki. I am deeply grateful to Dr. Selman Waksman, who discovered streptomycin. I was also very lucky not to suffer any hearing loss, one of streptomycin's known side effects, so I could go on to work with musical instruments.

While the retail business could get quite busy as there were no fixed hours, it also offered quite a bit of free time, so I was able to listen to a lot of baroque music. And as I listened to records that featured organ music, I began to think how wonderful it would be if I could play the organ myself. The problem was that I had no organ. I had built a prototype of a monophonic electronic instrument before, but the organ was so big that the thought of building an organ prototype did not even cross my mind. One day, I saw a small portable organ in a photo book of pipe organs. While I thought I might be able to build one of this size on my own, I still had no place to put it even if I did. Of course, I had no space to build one in either. And even if I wanted to attempt to build one myself, it would be impossible even to gather the materials. I was naive enough to ponder building one myself even though I had never actually seen one firsthand.

One day, I had the opportunity to see the pipe organ in the Eiko-kan building at Doshisha University. I was amazed at the complexity of the mechanism's console and pipe room, but I also noticed that the sound-generating mechanism was actually quite simple and easy to grasp. If I were to use electronic oscillators instead of pipes, I could make a smaller organ and players could even use headphones with it. I thought that the electronic route had everything going for it, so I began designing one. I assembled it using keys for reed organs and telephone relay contacts as the key switches. I used transistors as the sound generator, and I now had my first prototype: an organ with a forty-nine-key single-level keyboard and twelve pedals—which, from a circuit standpoint, was essentially forty-nine monophonic instruments put together. Unfortunately, the tone of the instrument sounded nothing like an organ. Sometime later, when I repaired the organ at the Minami Osaka Church, I saw a real electronic organ for the first time (it was a Lowrey Organo). I was stunned by its elegant design. But had I not built my first prototype, I doubt this encounter would have become the catalyst it was for me to start working on organs in earnest.

I sometimes think I owe my drive to start a variety of businesses to the solid upbringing provided by my grandparents, who raised me. Both of my parents had died by the time I was two years old. My father died first and my mother passed away a year later. So though I did not know my parents, I was raised in a very warm environment and provided for by my grandfather and grandmother, who were born in 1868 and 1878, respectively. I realize now that they could not have been rich, as they were living on their pension, but they let me build models, my hobby, and I was never scolded even if I went to the cinema by myself.

Right next to our house was a wall where ads were posted, and every time there was an ad for a film, triangular pieces of paper, admission tickets, were attached to the edge of the poster. At a time when children were generally not allowed to go to theaters unaccompanied by their parents, I had the good fortune of being able to use these tickets to go watch movies for free. After a while, the theater operator would let me in even without a ticket, though our relationship didn't go as far as the one portrayed in the Italian film *Cinema Paradiso*, in which the main character befriends a film technician who gives him actual film reels.

In any case, these happy childhood experiences may have prompted my first steps toward making appliances and musical instruments.

First Test Broadcast

Up until 1950, the only radio broadcasts that we got in Japan were NHK 1 and 2, which broadcast in Japanese, and the American radio station for the occupying troops, which broadcast in English. Finally, in 1951, private radio broadcast started. In the Kansai region, the first station to begin broadcasting was Shin-Nihon Hoso (presently Mainichi Hoso) out of Osaka. I remember setting up my receiver to the frequency this station was scheduled to broadcast on and waiting for the broadcast to start. The first piece of music played on Shin-Nihon Hoso was *Symphonie Espagnole* by Édouard Lalo. At the time, we had few opportunities to listen to such music, so almost all of the classical music was new to my ears, and I naturally did not know the titles of any of the pieces. I think I remember this one only because the radio announcer stated the title of the piece over the very airwaves I had been aching to receive. I believe I have heard the piece once or twice since, and although it was not a piece that I became familiar with, the fact that I remember its title to this day is probably a testament to the huge impact this event had on me. The records say that the first test broadcast from a private station was sent out on July 8, 1951, from 8:00 to 10:30 p.m.

The radio station and producer must have gone through much deliberation in choosing which piece of music to play in their very first broadcast, so it would be interesting to know why they chose Lalo's *Symphonie Espagnole* for this occasion. While an LP of his music was released that same year from a Japanese record company, I find it hard to imagine that Lalo's music, which was not particularly popular among a Japanese audience, had already been pressed at that time. Full broadcast started on September 1, and on September 2, a live broadcast of a Japan-US friendly baseball match was covered live from Koshien Stadium. I'm not sure if what I had heard was a test or full broadcast.

This is a radio I made while I was waiting to be admitted to Sengokuso. I fondly listened to this radio in the hospital.

My understanding at the time was simply that we now had many more programs as private stations came on air in addition to NHK, the national broadcaster. I could not even begin to imagine the changes that would eventually come about with the advent of private broadcasting.

On a side note, twenty-six years after I heard the first test broadcast, when the Berlin Wall was still intact, Roland had the opportunity to display products in

▲ A photo of a Beethoven portrait that I hung above my bed in Sengokuso and eventually in my office at Roland. (The photo is pockmarked with countless thumbtack holes.)

West Berlin. In Copenhagen, we boarded a train that drove right onto a ferry and we landed on East German soil late at night while we were asleep. We stayed on the same train, which took us into West Berlin, where armed soldiers with German shepherds made their inspection rounds before daybreak. They woke me up, after which they proceeded to turn my mattress over and inspect my passport. The inspection was very brusque, and clearly drove home, whether I liked it or not, that we were about to cross the border into Soviet territory. Our hotel in West Berlin, of course, was run by a Western company. We were able to view both communist and Western programs on the TVs in our rooms. Although there were still a few national broadcasting companies around the world, the contrast between Western news programs and communist propaganda was quite surreal. The fact that we were able to see these programs in West Berlin, located in the heart of East Germany, meant that as long as you were able to remove certain controls from your TV receiver, you would be able to access Western programs, and this in turn meant that it was impossible to control information. I remember the war years in Japan when shortwave receivers were prohibited. The ten-foot-high, sixteen-foot-long antenna I made for my crystal radio when I was in elementary school had also been a target of investigations a couple of times.

As receivers with channel selectors were presumably also available in East Germany, I don't think the airwaves were controllable. Thus the people of East Germany must have been watching the same Western programs that we were watching in our hotel rooms. Soon after our visit, the Berlin Wall came down. This was an event that I should've naturally been able to intuit. But even though I had spent three days in Berlin, I had not even imagined something like this might happen. I recognized that it was a great mistake to take for granted our freedom to choose the broadcasts we wish to view. Our present-day freedom to access information was built upon many political struggles and the blood of countless victims. The reason I was able to receive private radio airwaves and test TV broadcasts that first aired while I was hospitalized was because I was ill and had free time. Come to think of it now, I was witness to the first or second page in the history of the information revolution that is ongoing to this day. As such, these were very important experiences for me.

▲ Mr. Shimomura, who gave me this photo, and I go back forty years to when we were at the sanatorium together.

Joint Venture

Development Starts with Sales

NO MATTER WHICH COUNTRY YOU ARE FROM OR WHAT TYPE OF BUSIness you are in, everyone has a good idea of the sequence of events for starting up a company, which begins with someone developing a new product and proceeding from there with taking the necessary business steps. What may be less known is that the very first issue that comes up for the new business is how to create sales. Up until the 1970s, small musical instrument manufacturers and wholesalers provided distribution and financing for products made by individual craftspeople and therefore played an important role in the musical instrument industry. This resulted in a three-step distribution system by which wholesalers would carry large inventories, which they would then sell to retailers. Importers also played an important role. Pianos and other large products were sold under a two-step system by which manufacturers would set up distributors in different regions around the country. While wholesalers in the electrical appliance and electronics markets were gradually disintermediated as distribution became more streamlined and market size continued to grow, they still have an important role to play in the musical instrument industry. Particularly in the United States, we see examples of manufacturers, such as Chicago Musical Instruments, growing their businesses through the acquisition of distributors (wholesalers). This is the complete opposite of the traditional sequence of steps in which manufacturers would sell products to the wholesaler.

Mergers and acquisitions (by which businesses are acquired through the acquisition of their stocks) by large corporations were stimulated by the advent of electronic instruments and became widespread in the seventies and eighties. This brought about dramatic changes in the American industry, as well as new developments in the instruments themselves, and the movement of human resources had a vitalizing effect on the market. In postwar Japan, pianos maintained their high level of quality, and production growth was spurred by strong demand rooted in the public's keen interest in education. However, beginning around 1972 when the dollar-yen exchange rate began to rise, Korean manufacturers grew stronger and increased their exports, resulting in a downturn in Japanese piano production. Although light electrical appliance manufacturers began making electronic musical instruments in hopes of benefitting from growth in this market, manufacturers such as Victor, National, Brother, Columbia, and Hitachi were ultimately frustrated and exited the market.

As a matter of course, these developments had a major effect on distribution. While the traditional wholesale system was a major player in the distribution of traditional acoustic instruments such horns, strings, and percussions, it was not able to exert the same clout in the distribution of electronic instruments, or deliver in the area of technical services. This affected Roland as much as any other manufacturer. The more new products we launched, the larger these contradictions became. These problems became particularly pronounced in the United States, Canada, and Australia, and we found ourselves in a position where we could no longer delay. With this situation as a backdrop, we formed our first joint company in Australia, and then in the United States and Canada. While we had some previous experience from forming a joint company with Hammond during my Ace Electronic Industries years, expanding our business into other countries and then forming joint companies locally was a completely different matter. So we had to be extremely careful about how we set out our basic principles. If we were to form joint companies each with a different set of conditions, it would become difficult to coordinate between these companies. We would not be able to run our business in an open manner and this would surely lead to confusion down the road. So we had to go back to the drawing board to rethink how to run our businesses overseas.

- The president of the joint company had to be from the country where the company was located, and was responsible for day-to-day business, human resources, and business transactions.

- Partners had to have equal equity share in the company. If there were three parties, each party must have one-third of the equity.

- The company had to be independently operated, including financing.

- The partner we chose had to be younger than myself.

These were the four points we included in our basic principles of forming joint companies. Although our legal counsel advised that decision-making can become difficult when equity is shared equally and suggested setting equity at 51/49 or 60/40, I insisted on 50/50, even after taking into account all the potential negatives that could occur as a result of just that 1 percent difference. While running overseas companies is complicated by a variety of issues including exchange rate fluctuations, relationships with the competition, and factory ownership, we were fortunate to have been able to maintain this principle of mutual trust as equal partners and avoid any unpleasant incidents. The first joint company that we formed is about to celebrate its thirty-eighth anniversary.

However, as the companies grew, their capital reserves also increased proportionately. So when it became difficult for companies to maintain a 50/50 relationship in terms of real percentages, we had to take the step of separating capital from management. The use of stock options is one way of supplementing our efforts and we reached a point where we had to consider this course of action. Currently, the only companies with which we still maintain a 50/50 relationship are Roland Taiwan, Roland Asia Pacific, and our distributor in Switzerland. Some of these companies are at a stage of transitioning to the next generation, and all of them have been blessed with good potential successors. However, while we started out by choosing partners younger than myself, we are now facing the problem of some presidents of joint companies being older than the current president of Roland in Japan. While this may represent a deviation from our basic principles, our principle of having a local individual at the helm remains unchanged, and we still follow the original 50/50 spirit.

▼ Roland US's first company building.

We also identified a goal and formulated three slogans. The goal and slogans are similar to a country's constitution in that these are rarely changed. All the rules other than these slogans make up the laws, and must be revised accordingly to suit the times.

Roland's goal:

"We design the future."

Roland's slogans:

"Inspire the enjoyment of creativity."

"Be the BEST rather than the BIGGEST."

"Cooperative enthusiasm for all stakeholders."

Cultural Differences Are a Given

The Japanese market, with its high population density, has characteristics that are unique among other countries in the world. While the total land area of Japan is roughly the same as that of California, its land mass is home to a population nearly half the size of the population of the United States. Furthermore, its population has considerably less mobility compared to the US population, possibly because 70 percent of Japan's total land area consists of mountain or hilly regions unsuitable for living, and the Japanese have a long history as a farming people. Those involved in newer trends, such as music and fashion, tend to concentrate in and around Tokyo. People who make music a profession can find work only in Tokyo. Although the educational musical instrument market grew considerably even during the economically challenging postwar years, supported by the population's keen interest in education, the electronic musical instrument industry lagged far behind, making this market the polar opposite of the American market. The reason I mention this in the past tense is that the Japanese market has now come to resemble the American and European markets in many respects. While the market was previously centered in Tokyo, chain retailers who implement full-fledged merchandising are opening their doors in cities in other parts of the country, with multiple companies competing against each other. Large-scale retailers of electrical appliances now have floor space dedicated to musical instruments and hire knowledgeable staff to compete against musical instrument retailers. In particular, markets for products in the lower price ranges have grown to much larger scales than the markets dedicated musical instrument retailers cater to. Needless to say, the same is happening online. Sadly though, this means that musical instruments have now become commodified. This also means that we are up against cost competition, and once we reach this point, even the winners can see their business declining.

It would not be an overstatement to say that the rapid postwar growth of Japan's unique market was a result of the fierce competition between the country's two major piano companies, Yamaha and Kawai. The production of acoustic pianos including grand pianos peaked at 387,000 per year in 1980. The proportion of these pianos sold domestically was exceptionally large, with 306,000 being sold in the Japanese market and 81,000 being exported. The American market peaked at 275,600 pianos per year in 1979 and less than 100,000 pianos were sold in 1994. Few people know that more pianos were being sold in the Japanese market than in the US market, although the former is only half the size of the latter. At around the same time, the production of Japanese electronic organs peaked at 379,000 per year in 1981 and quickly approached US production levels.

There is no shortage of war stories that illustrate the intensity of competition between Yamaha and Kawai that drove this growth in Japan. Eventually, the two companies went on to take separate slices of the Japanese market, with Nippon Gakki Seizo (presently Yamaha) implementing a special agent system and Kawai Musical Instruments Manufacturing operating outlets run directly by the company. This monopolistic state, which was created for the distribution of pianos and was a rarity among other countries in the world, created a market that was very difficult for newcomers to enter. The only path Roland could take was to move ahead in the area of electronic instruments, an endeavor neither of these companies had yet embarked on. And the only way to achieve this was to establish our foundations in overseas markets, which were beginning to mature, and gradually work our way back to the domestic market. More than 50 percent of Roland's sales came from exports, but there was another reason for this. With exports, deals were being settled with LCs, or letters of credit, which meant that we would receive cash upon shipping our products. It was very difficult to persuade buyers in the Japanese market to settle in cash. It was no surprise that Roland—which had a starting capital of only ¥33 million and no track record to speak of—would have a difficult time borrowing operating capital. The only other way was to ask our distributors to settle in cash, but to do that, first we had to make products to sell them. We were able to secure ninety-day notes from our parts suppliers. Unless we made complete products, shipped them, and received cash within ninety days, we would run short of capital. Although the tension was nonstop, I look back now and realize that these were very important experiences. I am truly grateful to our suppliers and associates who extended these ninety-day notes to a company that had no track record. They were all companies that I had worked with during my years with Ace Electronic

Industries. What I learned here was that, regardless of the size of the company, running your company will get very difficult unless you base your operations on the principle of holding zero inventory.

Since we would launch new products one after the other, the basis of our operations for making the best use of this ninety-day window was to determine the types of products that we were sure would sell overseas and could potentially be accepted in the domestic market. We had to operate in this mode for four or five years, but it ultimately took us about eight years before we were able to reach a balance between receiving conditions and payments. It was during this time that I learned the lessons of cash management on an instinctive level. There used to be a one- to two-year time lag before electronic instruments that began to sell overseas would catch on in Japan. This time lag was important to us in that it gave us time to smooth out our production and prepare production plans. This time lag is a thing of the past, however, as information on new products travels around the world instantly. As the boundaries between industries dissolve, we are entering an age in which totally unexpected products are released in industries other than the musical instrument industry. Conversely, this also means that products that were traditionally not within the purview of musical instrument companies are now within our grasp. It also means that new entries to the musical instrument market will find it to be a very easy and vulnerable market. Boundaries no longer exist in the age of the Internet. This is our major challenge.

A huge part of what makes musical instruments different from other products is that the person who purchases an instrument has to put in practice to enjoy it. So it's only natural that education is at the basis of the musical instrument industry. It is a very fortunate thing for everyone in Japan that music education is mandatory for elementary and junior high school students. Initiatives led by piano manufacturers to open music classes all around the country also greatly contributed to the proliferation of music. These are examples of success that have no parallels in other countries. Electronic musical instruments come with functions that can be utilized in a variety of ways in the area of education. Not many instruments aside from electronic keyboards are able to produce a stable pitch at all times. The housing situation in Japan is such that it has become difficult for people to play their instruments, not only at night but even during daytime. Japan is the only country with a market for soundproofed rooms for pianos, which is an idea that many in other countries will find inconceivable. The market's reaction to soundproofing was very different in the United States and Japan, since the respective housing situations were so different. Having said that, the housing situation in other countries is also beginning to change and noise is starting to become an issue.

One Winter in Europe

The Japanese yen appreciated sharply between 1979 and 1982, and this pushed Roland's European general agent, Brodr. Jorgensen of Denmark, close to the brink of bankruptcy. We were faced with a situation where we could lose our European distribution depending on how we moved forward. These events transpired over a period of four months from the time we received our first telex on October 24, 1982. When we received this telex in Vancouver, Canada, we were still not sure of the whole picture, so we continued our business trip on to Australia. Looking back, these were very inconvenient times, as we had no tools such as the Internet or e-mail that would allow us to gather information instantly. In Melbourne, I met with Geoffrey Brash, a longtime friend and our partner in Roland Australia, who gave me an important piece of advice. Later, as we came to the point of making the final decision in our talks with Jorgensen, I remembered his counsel, "Make sure to keep your priorities straight in your decision-making," and this helped us navigate through the situation. I was very glad we had gone through with our visit to Australia.

After making emergency arrangements and preparations for production adjustments, I flew to Denmark in early November. Jorgensen's main bank was located in Hamburg so we began making frequent visits there to ascertain the entire picture. We had acquired a ¥200 million line of credit from Daiwa Bank (presently Resona) before our departure because we didn't know what the situation was with Jorgensen and we had to move quickly. The Hamburg winter was cold and felt even more so given the circumstances of our visit. This became a prolonged business visit of three months as we worked to come up with a rough roadmap before the Frankfurt Musikmesse, which was scheduled for early February. Although we returned to Japan for Christmas and New Year's, we visited many European countries for our negotiations with the receiver and to set up our new company. While this crisis ultimately turned out to be a blessing, the process was a long series of difficult decisions. Even when I look back these many years later, I can still feel the thrill of going through the process of understanding the receiver's position and discerning where to reach an agreement. Ultimately, we were able to take care of the situation with ¥30 million, so we were very grateful for the leeway we had in handling it thanks to the line of credit from Daiwa Bank. It was through this ordeal that I realized how important it was to have good credit with our bank.

This became the catalyst for us to set up joint companies in various other regions, and we did so in Scandinavia, Germany, the UK, and Switzerland in rapid succession. In other countries, we continued to work with companies with whom we had distribution relations and set them up as agencies. There were many other similar situations in which we presented our case to banks and asked for their support, but I remember being surprised at how different each of their responses were.

In this way, we were able to fight back against the first wave of yen appreciation. From 1980 to 1985, the yen depreciated to about ¥240 to ¥260 to the dollar and remained relatively stable. But there was a possibility that it would rise again so we could not afford to be overly optimistic. In fact, the yen would eventually appreciate to levels where ¥100 was worth more than a dollar.

The winter of 1983 in Europe was truly very cold. The three months I spent there taught me many lessons that I still carry to this day. First of all, as a manufacturer of export products, it was natural to think that one way to circumvent risks that result from exchange rate fluctuations was to produce our products in our target markets. At the time, while Japanese exports in industries such as light electrical appliances, automobiles, and some machinery and tools were competitive in international markets, products from other industries were not as strong. But the climate at the time was such that you would draw a great deal of attention even if you had just one or two products that had a strong competitive edge, and the way in which Japanese companies exported their products, often likened to torrential rainfalls, also became a point of contention. I believe one of the driving forces for Europe and the EC coming together to form a single economic bloc was the desire to protect their markets against such practices. The United States also used the trade tariff barrier card to apply pressure to Japan in a variety of aspects of their negotiations. While the primary targets were semiconductors, automobiles, and various light electrical products, other products such as machine tools and tools in general were also included. Japanese products such as pianos and guitars, which offered a good balance of quality and price, also drew much attention and were included on this list. Even today, musical instruments can be imported to Japan tariff-free, but Japanese musical instruments exported to the United States and Europe are subjected to tariffs. While these tariff rates will likely change as the Trans-Pacific Strategic Economic Partnership Agreement negotiations move forward, these changes will be minor compared to exchange rate fluctuations, so tariffs will not be such a major problem for musical instruments.

Under these circumstances, until 1985, the basic arrangement at Roland continued to be to produce all products in Japan and price them in yen for export to different regions. Currently, we have production facilities in four countries including Japan, and we still maintain our policy of setting the export price in the local currency of the producing country. Nowadays, we see an increasing number of Japanese companies setting the prices of their export products in

▲ Roland Scandinavia's first office.

yen, but this practice was quite uncommon in those days. Since yen was not even a key international currency, it would have been difficult for most companies to do this. I think we were able to do it because almost all of our exports were sent to our joint companies. If producers (i.e., Japanese companies) were to set the price of their exports in US dollars, this would be good for American consumers because the price would stabilize, but fluctuations would be inevitable in other countries. Manufacturers must always work toward reducing their costs through production streamlining, no matter how small the amount. On top of that, pricing exports in the importing country's currency becomes extremely risky unless a margin of safety is applied to absorb exchange rate fluctuations.

Indeed, there have been countless examples of trading firms pricing their products in dollars and incurring massive losses when the amount of yen they received shrank. In this context, the pricing strategy at Roland Japan, which was responsible for product design and manufacturing, started out with our efforts to maintain appropriate margins by cutting costs wherever we could so that we would be able to offer the best prices through ongoing development, and have the joint companies take on the risk of exchange rate fluctuations. We were fortunate in that the joint companies understood our situation even during periods when the yen appreciated and consequently resulted in significant price changes in destination markets. This need to make price changes applied not only to Roland but to other manufacturers as well. And because there was a lag between the time the exchange rate changed and when price adjustments needed to be made, and also because we had to keep an eye on how our competitors responded to the situation, these actions would not have been possible without great effort and understanding on the part of the local companies we were working with.

For such a system to work, the people responsible for manufacturing must constantly supply products that have a competitive edge. But in the long term, we must reduce these types of exchange rate risks as much as possible, and the only way to achieve this is to employ operations that are less affected by exchange rate fluctuations. In other words, we need to have production facilities in regions other than Japan. Thus began our search for candidate locations. For the North American market, we did not need to look any farther than Mexico, but things were a bit more complicated in Europe as it is divided into many countries, each with their own national culture, language, and customs laws. This made it very difficult to decide which country to do business in. Among the various concerns, some issues—such as how important it would be that there were daily flights between a particular country and Japan—could not be gauged until we had actually started our operations. When we considered the importation of parts from Japan and the purchasing of other materials, another prerequisite was that the region have an international distribution port. The labor situation would also have to be relatively straightforward, and our Japanese employees and their families who were to be transferred to these countries would have to find their daily lives in the region comfortable enough so that they were able to deliver their best performance throughout their stay. The most crucial issue was language. One major point was that the people in the region should be able to communicate in English.

The trend of a stronger yen rapidly reversed in 2013, calling into question the rationale for transferring our manufacturing outside of Japan. There must be a business model that continues to manufacture products in Japan regardless of what the exchange rate is doing. Specifically, the solution is to take the components, sourced in Japan, to the destination market country and perform assembly, the final process of manufacturing, in that country. Markets in destination countries welcome such arrangements since the assembly of products in their country becomes a source of pride among the people doing it. Furthermore, this allows the manufacturer to mitigate the effects of exchange rate fluctuations. Needless to say, there is no single method that will satisfy all of our needs, so we must watch the situation closely and act decisively if needed.

One Spring in Europe

By the late 1970s, Japanese industry had passed the point of debating whether or not to transfer production overseas. Examples abounded of companies that actually moved their production to regions that offered labor cost advantages such as Southeast Asia (Thailand, Singapore, Malaysia), Taiwan, or Korea, and such moves were beginning in the musical instrument business as well. With respect to these developments, we were faced with the reality that we could expect to mass-produce very few—indeed almost none—of the products related to musical instruments. Our industry is a typical example of a high-mix, low-volume industry, so it would take too much time to start up our factories if we were to transfer our operations to, say, Southeast Asia and begin by training the locals from scratch. And there would be no advantage in having a production base in Southeast Asia if we could not expect to have local demand for a portion of what we produced as opposed to exporting our entire production output. When we think along those lines, the list of products that meet the conditions for producing in regions with labor cost advantages is short.

So we had two options: Should we transfer to Southeast Asia where labor costs were low? Or should we set up factories in North America and the EU, the consumption centers of electronic musical instruments? While no obstacles such as tariff barriers existed at the time, whichever we chose, our choice had to be the most advantageous over the long term. My decision was that, based on the nature of musical instruments, we should shelve, at least for the moment, Southeast Asia, where low labor costs can be taken advantage of only with mass-produced products, and set up our production in the United States and Europe. Ultimately, this came down to our priorities. Was it the labor cost, or the market's understanding of musical instruments? Boiled down, it came down to the question of labor cost versus culture.

Of course, there were uncertainties at the time in terms of establishing a factory in the European market. While EU integration was being discussed, we all thought that it would be far off into the future, probably farther into the twenty-first century. At present, the EU has already become a reality and there are no economic borders within Europe. In those days, northern Europe did not seem very suitable for manufacturing as labor costs were high. Germany was known for having the highest labor costs in Europe, and Spain was problematic in terms of the supply of basic materials. We received much input from Antonio Punti, president of Vieta Audio Electrónica, our agency in Spain at that time, and had to conclude that it would be difficult to manufacture musical instruments in Spain. From a Japanese perspective, France is predominantly associated with fashion and wine, and it was difficult to think of manufacturing musical instruments in the country. Language was also an issue so we had to exclude France as well. The countries remaining on our list were the UK and the Benelux countries where English is spoken. Roland UK was already operating in UK, and based on our previous experience with assembling amplifiers there, we were somewhat reluctant to start up a new manufacturing operation in the UK. If we were to go ahead, it seemed that one of the Benelux countries would be a good choice.

It was just around this time that Bruno Barbini, president of our joint company Roland Italy, asked us several times to meet a friend of his who manufactured synthesizers and was seeking to speak with Roland. However, because we had no practical knowledge of Italian manufacturing, it never occurred to us to start up a manufacturing operation in Italy.

▲ At the entrance of the new factory at Roland Europe (RES).

Two years later, Bruno Barbini came to our show booth in Chicago with Carlo Lucarelli with no appointment to meet with us. Although at first it seemed out of the question that we would begin manufacturing in Italy, Carlo Lucarelli's detailed explanations of future industrial trends in Italy and, above all, his analysis of his own company were enough to make us think twice about his proposal. In any case, we recognized that the impressions we held of various countries were very abstract and outdated, often based on perceptions that were over half a century old. I was no exception to this tendency. Our image of Italy was very biased, and primarily revolved around notions such as trains not operating on time, postal service delays, and the mafia operating behind the scenes. Equally, I suspect many foreigners when asked of their image of Japan would still only be able to come up with Mount Fuji, geisha, and kamikaze. My preconceived notions about Italy were wiped clean in two hours. And two years after we mulled over different potential factory sites and conditions, Italy became one of our prominent candidates, backed by a specific plan. This is how Roland Europe S.p.A. (RES) came to be founded in November 1987. We often visit RES after the musical instrument show in Frankfurt in March, when we always feel the warmth of spring as we cross the Alps.

We currently have factories in Italy, the United States, and Taiwan. Our factories in Japan are in Hamamatsu and Matsumoto, and we are seeing increasingly more exchanges between engineers in Japan and other countries. As we collaborate with these joint companies, we are also made to realize at times that there are huge differences between traditional Japanese ideas and ideas prevalent in other countries. Problems sometimes occur even if we understand the other party and make sure to work things out with each other in our work. In these instances, differences based on divergent views and historic experiences cannot be resolved by reasoning. For example, when deciding on a location for a factory to make violins and accordions, it would be unthinkable to manufacture in a country other than Italy, due to their deep experience. And as business issues arises, communicate well with the factory partners in Italy so each can proceed with their work.

One Summer in Taiwan

It is actually a very difficult thing to operate a factory in a country with a different culture, history, and customs. While Roland currently works with twenty joint companies worldwide, China, Taiwan, the United States, and Italy are the only countries where we have more than one joint company. Of these countries, the situation in Taiwan was somewhat special when we started out in the 1980s. The Taiwan dollar was more or less linked to the US dollar and moved in similar fashion, and the electronics industry in Taiwan was very active at the time. There was also a great deal of technology being transferred from Japanese companies, and many Japanese-brand products lined store shelves. Another unique positive about Taiwan was the culture's affinity with Japanese people, and we were eager to locate one of our factories in the country. While labor costs in Taiwan were cheaper than those in Japan, they were already quite high compared to those in Thailand, Malaysia, Korea, and other Southeast Asian countries. Based on Taiwan's central location to our markets, and the possibility of establishing a factory that would directly reflect market conditions, we thought it wise to establish factories in the United States and Europe, and position Taiwan as a center that would supply parts, half-finished products, and finished products to other countries. I still believe that this decision was correct. Currently, our competitors have moved most of their production of small keyboard instruments to Indonesia and Malaysia. Some of our competitors have set up production in China and are enjoying success. At the time, however, Roland did not have the resources to do both. The only remaining way for us to compete was to focus on our R&D efforts so that we were able to lead the industry in quality and new sounds. And what was more, the market was increasingly demanding proactive and market-leading R&D.

Many centuries ago, the Portuguese who first sailed to Taiwan called it Formosa (from *ilha formosa*, "beautiful island"), and this name was used to denote Taiwan on foreign maps. For the Japanese, Taiwan is the only name that comes to mind. The Ming dynasty's influence on Taiwan began around the fifteenth century, and records show that the name Taiwan was in use by the sixteenth century. Japan neighbors Korea, China, and Taiwan across seas to its north and southwest. Taiwan is very close to Okinawa, the southernmost island of Japan. Taiwan also has important historic ties with Japan.

In the seventeenth century, the Dutch landed in the area currently known as Tainan and occupied it as their center of trade with the Far East. Records show that the Chinese military leader Cheng-kung Cheng, whose mother was Japanese, reinstated the Ming dynasty and fought the Dutch to end their occupation. These events are well known from the play *Kokusenya Kassen* ("The Battles of Coxinga") by the eighteenth-century dramatist Chikamatsu Monzaemon. Cheng-kung Cheng is still regarded as a hero by the Chinese and Taiwanese people, as well as by the Japanese. Japan and the Qing dynasty of China fought the First Sino-Japanese War from 1894 to 1895, and Taiwan became a territory of Japan under the Treaty of Shimonoseki. Japan governed Taiwan for fifty years, until occupation ended with the end of World War II. Though during different periods, both Korea and Taiwan were once colonies of Japan, and the consequences of this colonization can be felt to varying degrees in the countries' politics, economies, and cultures, often causing friction. However, whereas Korea made the shift to use Hangul letters exclusively, Taiwan continues to use traditional Chinese text, or kanji. One of the reasons the Japanese feel an affinity with Taiwan may have to do with our ability to decipher most of the signs as we walk through its towns.

I have made more than ten trips to mainland China, primarily to Beijing, and the text that they currently use there has been simplified, making it very difficult for me to understand. While a part of me can understand why a country with such a long history would choose to replace their complex kanji with simplified text, the question of whether people educated with this simplified system will be able to read Chinese classics is a big one. I asked some people in the younger generations if they could read traditional text and their answer was no. I believe you would have to be at least seventy years old to be able to read traditional kanji text. Since it is difficult to imagine that the huge number of classical writings have all been republished in simplified text, and taking into account that there was a time under Chairman Mao's rule when books were burned and intellectuals were purged from their positions, it would seem that vast amounts of Chinese cultural heritage have been lost. That said, I have no doubt that many writings and elements of cultural heritage are being stored in neighboring countries among the Huaqiao, ethnic Chinese residing outside of China, and feel a sense of relief knowing that the restoration of old books has begun in mainland China.

Perhaps it is because I can read their writing that I feel more at ease strolling through the towns of Taiwan. Soon after we started Roland, I had the chance to meet with Yin-Shang Shaw from Taiwan, by introduction of Gene Trademan, president of Great West, our agency in Canada. Mr. Shaw's company, Audision Electronic Industrial Corp., made microphones and microphone stands, among other products. They had also finished a prototype of a preamplifier, and had just begun their operations with a focus on audio input equipment. The first time I visited Mr. Shaw's factory, I recalled the early days of Roland, and felt a great sense of affinity. Mr. Shaw was also a very good business person, and we began purchasing microphone stands from his company. This was the starting point, and as we got to know each other better, we began thinking of forming a joint company to manufacture products—primarily analog products—for Roland. Partly because we got along so well, our talks went smoothly, and we eventually decided to establish a company and build a new factory. The two of us visited many potential locations for the factory, including Kaohsiung in the south, industrial parks near Taichung, and Taoyuan, near the current Taipei airport. Eventually, we decided on Nankang at the northern edge of Taipei.

The president of the real estate company we worked with was a woman, and I got the impression that there were more women working in business in Taiwan than in Japan. She stood fast throughout our negotiations, which was difficult at times, and eventually we purchased the factory at very close to the asking price. The moment we signed the agreement, we heard the sound of fireworks outside. When we asked her what this was all about, she said, "This is in celebration of our deal working out." Although I felt relief at finally reaching an agreement, as I listened to these fireworks, I also felt that we had been outwitted.

Thanks to Mr. Shaw's hard work and persistence in quality improvements, and to the assistance of Katsumi Yamamoto, then president of Boss Corporation, Taiwan now plays a critical role as a supply center for Roland and Boss products. This was how Roland Taiwan started in 1986. The company's official name in Taiwan is Roland Taiwan Electronic Music Corporation.

Aside from our dealings with Mr. Shaw, I visited Taiwan on several occasions at around the time PC sales were growing in the market because our supplier of video displays was located there. We had started selling these displays under the Amdek brand. This business was primarily led by Go Sugiura, the son-in-law of Kazuo Sakata, president of Sakata Shokai. Amdek stood for Analog, Music, Digital, Electronics, and Computer. We began by thinking of names that started with *A*, then wrote a program in Basic that would produce various sequences of letters beginning with *A*. We printed out the results, which filled about two

▲ At the signing ceremony of the founding of Roland's manufacturing joint company in Taiwan.

sheets of A4 paper. AMDEC stood out, but we thought the spelling did not have enough impact with a *C* at the end, so we used *K* to represent the act of making a kit and partly because *K* was the initial of my last name, Kakehashi.

In any case, we launched our Amdek business, which consisted of four pillars or product families: video displays, drafting plotters, effects assembly kits, and computer music sound modules. Amdek displays sold very well in the United States and quickly became the first choice in the market. However, faced with fierce cost competition, we decided to withdraw from the display business and transfer ownership of the Amdek brand to Mr. Sugiura. As for the other product groups, the timing was not yet ripe for computer music sound modules, and the assembly kit idea did not match the needs of the time. So we decided to focus on the development of plotters, change the company's name to Roland DG, and enter the computer peripherals market.

One of the people I got to know during my search for video displays was Chue-Shek Lee, president of Taiwan Sanyo Electric. While it was not easy to export products to Taiwan in the 1970s, tape echo machines sold exceptionally well. One of the major developments in popular entertainment in Taiwan was singing performances held at luxurious tea shops that young people flocked to. And echo machines, which softened the singers' voices, were indispensable at these shows. As Roland Space Echo (RE-201) became a hit product, I next met Shin-Fa

Ho. I remember being surprised at how my network of acquaintances in Taiwan had grown when I heard that Mr. Ho was to become a relative of Mr. Lee.

At the time, Shin-Shun Tu was stationed permanently in Japan as the person responsible for purchasing parts in Japan for Taiwan Sanyo, so I sought his help in making contacts in Taiwan. It was with the help of both Mr. Ho and Mr. Tu that our exports to Taiwan began. I remember thinking that this was the best combination of people, because when read phonetically in Japanese, Mr. Tu's name would be *toh*, or *toh san* with Japanese honorifics, and Mr. Ho's name would be *kah*, or *kah san*, which respectively mean father and mother in Japanese. This is how the company currently known as Roland Taiwan Enterprise Co. Ltd. got its start. Mr. Ho is president and shareholder of Roland Taiwan Enterprise.

In the beginning, many Japanese companies moved portions of their operations to Taiwan partially because labor costs were lower than in Japan, but eventually, when labor costs increased, many of those companies relocated their production from Taiwan to Malaysia or Thailand. On the other hand, Taiwan's technological capabilities also grew with the rise in its labor costs. Taiwan has long maintained the world's top share in the production of motherboards, which are essential for personal computers, and their semiconductor businesses are also doing very well. Within this environment, our other company in Taiwan, Roland Taiwan Electronic Music Corporation, which is responsible for manufacturing, also plays a crucial role in our efforts to provide products with good added value.

The Tropic of Cancer passes through Taiwan, which means the country is in the subtropical climate zone. For some reason, my visits to Taiwan tend to fall between the months of June and September, so my impression of Taiwan is that it is always summer there.

Thus far, I have covered as far as Taiwan in terms of what we are doing at our joint companies. We currently also have a distributor in Hong Kong, and a factory in Suzhou, China. This factory, however, is becoming difficult to operate. The reason for this is that we are having more difficulty ensuring the safety of our Japanese staff, to the point where many are reluctant to make even short business trips to the location. This makes it impossible for us to fully leverage the functions of this joint company, which in turn makes it difficult for us to run our factory. Our business in China remains important to us, but we have come to a point where we must make major changes in how we send our Japanese staff to the country. The only solution is to switch to a system where our Japanese employees make repeated long-term temporary visits. Needless to say, we will continue our policy of having a local individual at the helm of the company as we work toward improving the situation.

One Autumn in Australia

The seasons in the Southern Hemisphere are the opposite of those in Japan, the United States, Europe, and other regions in the Northern Hemisphere. Australia consists of a vast landmass with major cities such as Brisbane, Sydney, Melbourne, and Adelaide clustered relatively close to each other on the east coast. There is Perth on the western side of the continent, and the central region in between consists primarily of vast desert land. There is a great distance between Brisbane toward the north and Melbourne in the south. This means that there is a great difference in the climates of these two cities. The climate and seasons in Melbourne are close to what one would find on the Pacific coast of Japan, making this area easier for Japanese people to adapt to. It is also a source of pride for us Japanese that Hiroyuki Iwaki was a lifetime Conductor Laureate at the Melbourne Symphony Orchestra.

Australia as a country was founded as a colony of the UK, and at one point adopted the White Australia policy to restrict immigration from places other than Europe. Whether for this reason or not, there appear to be fewer racial problems compared to the United States. On the other hand, however, the small population relative to its landmass may be a hindering factor to the country's growth. Australia has developed its unique culture on a foundation of British culture with a massive influx of American influence in areas such as fashion and music. This may be one of the reasons that many Australian bands are enjoying success in America.

Australian markets for electrical appliances, as well as for musical instruments, are somewhat peculiar. There are very few domestic manufacturers that make these products, and some industries have no domestic manufacturers at all. Therefore, competition among international manufacturers for the Australian market tends to be intense, and product superiority or lack thereof tends to stand out more in Australia. This is because products can be compared on a very clear-cut playing field, as all products in any given category are subject to the same import tariffs, freight costs, and other factors.

Comparing Australia's electronic musical instrument market to the United States, we notice that in the United States there are a large number of excellent musical instrument manufacturers that cater to its huge market. Also, because the United States is home to a variety of distinct musical cultures originating in regions such as Nashville, New York, and the West Coast, it has very powerful markets not only in the area of musical instruments but also in music publishing, records, and videos. These soft aspects of the music business have been accumulating even more clout in the age of the Internet. For this reason, it is not

▲ Roland Australia made its start at this dealer convention held at Sydney Opera House.

easy to do business in the US market. In Australia, however, the prices and performance of all imported products are compared on a level playing field because there is little or no competition with domestic manufacturers. Another characteristic is that upmarket products tend to sell well in Australia relative to what one would expect from the country's population. So Australia is conferred with some interesting features as a test market. This was one of the reasons that Roland Corporation Australia Pty. Ltd. became Roland's very first joint venture.

This joint company was formed by partnering with Geoffrey Brash, one of our agents and a personal friend of mine since my Ace Electronic Industries years. We decided to find another partner to start up a company, with each holding one-third of the shares. At the time, we had to make a number of bold decisions, in part because our product line was not as large as it is today. I am particularly grateful for the bold decisions made by Mr. Brash, our Australian partner.

We decided to rent a conference room on April 1, 1976, to hold our company founding announcement party. With a view of Sydney Harbor and the ships going by, Sydney Opera House was the ideal location to hold this event. However, because our company had just been founded and our product lineup was still small, we moved the date of the party to April 2, thinking that some might suspect that this was some sort of April Fools' prank. This was not something we were seriously uneasy about, but we did have some concerns about the date.

▲ John Egan, president of Roland Australia, and myself.

It was around this time that John Egan took the helm at Roland Australia. His personal character and experience were crucial to the growth and performance of the company.

The company did well and we eventually came to a point where we could hold dealer conventions every year, the third of which we held at Newport, on the outskirts of Sydney. Everyone stayed up late the night before, preparing for our first demo of the GR guitar synthesizer. But in a moment of lapsed attention, our GR guitar was stolen from the boat where we had stored it. This caused a huge fracas as we had only one sample, which meant that we might have to go ahead with our dealer convention without the guitar, the highlight of the convention. We wasted no time in contacting the local police and newspaper to ask them to help us find the guitar. We made sure that the press included in their reports the fact that this was a special guitar that needed an oscillator unit to produce a sound, and that you could not play it through a regular guitar amp. We asked that anyone with information about the guitar contact us.

Response was immediate, and after a complicated negotiation process with the thief, we got our guitar back in time for the dealer convention. The story of the stolen GR guitar was carried in the July 18, 1977, issue of the *Sun*. Thanks to the safe return of the guitar to our possession, the story of the theft grew bigger, and we ended up being featured on TV channel 9 and in another follow-up newspaper article. In response to a reporter asking me how much the guitar

It doesn't work—you can have it back...

THIS is the $1 million guitar (left) plucked from Newport during the weekend.

The guitar was stolen from a national music dealers' convention where it was the star of the show.

The only one of its kind in the world, the instrument can produce the sound of a human voice, whistle, make bird calls and even rude noises.

But for the thief, it stayed silent.

Without a "little black box" the guitar cannot strike a single note.

After spending a day trying to play the instrument, the thief deiided to return it to the

owners, the Roland Corporation of Japan.

"It doesn't work—you can have it back," he told the relieved owners.

The thief phoned the Newport Inn and spoke to Roland Corporation officials after reading of the guitar in The Sun-Herald.

They went to a nearby home and recovered the instrument after promising not to take further action.

The guitar is now back with its inventor, Mr Taro Kakehashi, who spent $1 million and more than two years making it.

CESSNOCK JAIL 'A JOKE'

By MURRAY TREMBATH

POLICE today described Cessnock Jail as "a joke" following the escape of another five prisoners on Saturday.

The prisoners did not return after running in a 16km race from Cessnock Town Hall, around

Mr Taro Kakehashi with the $1 million guitar.

▲ An article in the *Sun* reported on the return of GR-500, the "million-dollar guitar."

cost, I answered, "Close to one million dollars." In my mind, this included the development costs, but the papers reported this as if it were a dream guitar which itself cost a million dollars. It took me completely by surprise that news of this theft would be reported on TV, and the event gave me a real-world sense of the media's power of information dissemination.

Nineteen years later, in 1996, the latest GR guitar model made its debut at the NAMM show as a "dream guitar." Since Roland Australia made its start on the beautiful sunny "autumn" day of April 2, we decided to celebrate its twentieth anniversary in Sydney again in 1997. We invited our major dealers on a cruise aboard a huge chartered yacht in Sydney Harbor. It was a very memorable party, and this time we had a view of the opera house from aboard the yacht.

Jazz Concert in China

The Australian market is served by a large volume of imported products. Mr. Brash had also been importing pianos from China under the Lisner brand. The quality of the products at the time was still quite problematic, and his company had to put in a lot of work after the products arrived. Given this state of affairs, Mr. Brash asked me if I could visit the piano factory in Beijing to give them instructions on quality control, and thus I made my first visit to China in 1982. I accepted his request because, although I did not know much about acoustic pianos, I thought I could be of help in the area of factory operations and quality. At the time, all Chinese factories were nationally owned, and factories in industries that were designated as part of national strategy were fitted with the latest equipment. During my visit, I also asked to see a TV production factory for reference. While the facilities appeared to be four to five years behind those used in Japan, they were all very well equipped and production lines were humming along, producing TV sets for export to Germany. However, although I'm not sure whether the radio and piano industries were part of national strategy, the equipment used at those factories was all outdated and their operations were not even at a level to start thinking of quality control.

I found the language barrier considerable when giving instruction to the factory workers, so I wrote kanji letters that I knew on the blackboard to get my points across. For example, I would write the character for *dust*, write an *X* mark over it, and then retrieve a piece of paper trash from my pocket. Those listening would finally get my message. To explain to them that quality improvement is based on down-to-earth work, that there are no shortcuts, and that results don't happen overnight, I had Mrs. Brash act out "hop," "step," and "jump" motions. This was easy to understand for people who were expecting to jump from the very start, and was also an icebreaker in that it drew laughter from the crowd. The people at the factory listened intently and we had these meetings every year, during which I explained various aspects of the production process, but the quality of the pianos never improved. Mr. Brash was not going to give up, however. In 1983, he sent a jazz group to Beijing to expand his scope of activities from piano imports into the area of cultural exchange. This was a continental approach aimed at the Chinese people, who cherished personal relationships. There was no way I was going to miss the first postwar jazz concert in China, so I took part in this tour as well.

The group was a wonderful four-piece jazz band led by Don Burrows on clarinet. On trumpet was James Morrison. This was in 1983 when travelers would not know where their hotel would be until they arrived in Beijing and were assigned a hotel by a government tourism official. We were not able to get into a hotel in the city of Beijing and spent two nights on the outskirts of the city in an inn that appeared to be exclusively for Chinese people. The hotel room was very simple but had a TV, where we saw Japanese animation programs in which the characters spoke Japanese with no voice-overs. I do not remember the name of the hotel, but the photo we took out front includes a sign that reads Beijing Hokuren Hotel.

The following day, we planned to have an early lunch and set out for the venue to prepare for the concert. The lunch menu was all in Chinese and I was the only one who could at least make out the ingredients of the dishes and how they were cooked, so the ordering was left up to me. Even so, I asked if it was really okay for me to do the ordering as all the kanji were in simplified form and I therefore suspected that my hit rate would only be around 30 percent, but everyone there said that they would "eat anything." So we decided that the eleven people in our group would each order a single dish, and we would share these among us. The waitress did not understand English so we ordered by pointing at the menu. Thirty or forty minutes later our meal still had not arrived. We were a bit annoyed partly due to our empty bellies, so we took our minds off of it by joking that this was the Chinese way. Our meal finally arrived about an hour after we had placed our order. We were all surprised at the number of dishes that were brought to the table. In a very short time, the dishes filled two tables adjacent to ours, and they were still bringing more from the kitchen. We finally realized that there had been some kind of mistake so I ran to the kitchen and waved my hands for them to stop cooking any more food, to which they fortunately acceded without much of a fuss. There were already forty plates full of food on the tables. Apparently, they had mistaken our order as being eleven dishes for each of the eleven of us. Had we been late to notice, we would have had 121 plates full of food on our tables. Happy that we had been able to stop this at forty plates, we all laughed hard as we enjoyed a very hearty meal.

Fifteen minutes before the show, the hall was still empty with no audience in sight. Five minutes before the performance was to start, a group of apparently important people entered, leading a crowd of people who instantly filled the hall. The audience was very excited about the performance and the concert that night was a great success. While it is well known that jazz was performed in many nightclubs and dance halls in the settlement district of Shanghai since before World War II, I believe this was the first full-fledged modern jazz concert held in a concert hall in China. The concert was prominently reported on the next day in the *Beijing Evening News*. It was a very memorable concert.

Our First Purchase Order

A country that is similar to Australia in terms of its market size and characteristics is Canada. A major point of difference, however, is that Canada neighbors the United States, separated only by a border drawn in a straight line. Since the start of NAFTA, the country's economic ties with the United States have been getting stronger. The country code for making international phone calls to Canada is +1, the same as to the United States. In other words, this is the country code for North America. There is not much manufacturing going on in the country so its economy is largely based on tourism and trading, which makes it similar to Denmark in some ways. Canadian businesspeople are very astute in trading. Roland Canada was founded in Vancouver in partnership with Gene

Trademan, with whom we have worked for many years, and the company has grown thanks to the efforts of Laurie Gillespie.

The innards of electronic musical instruments are almost identical to those of computers. But the music market differs from the computer market in terms of business practices and speed, so we cannot run our businesses like computer manufacturers do. The only way we could create business opportunities in computer music and video-editing equipment—which were new to the market— was to create a new distribution channel. So we decided to establish Edirol Corporation North America to create a new sales network that would cover North America and center around computer music. Starting up something from scratch is a difficult thing to do, and not everyone is up to the task. So we sought the help of Laurie Gillespie, president of Roland Canada, to set up a venture business. To be president of a company in its startup stage, you need the fortitude not to lose your sense of humor no matter what obstacles you are faced with. The new company's office was located in Blaine, Washington, on the other side of the border, so Mr. Gillespie had to commute every day between Canada and the United States during the startup stage. While doing business across prefectural borders in Japan would be difficult enough, his commute had him crossing a national border. I am very grateful to Mr. Gillespie, who worked with us to start up both Roland Canada and Edirol. The video and audio technologies that we developed at Edirol continue to live on as part of Roland Systems Group (RSG).

For some reason, I have many memories of the company startup stages in Australia and Canada. Not even ten days after Roland was established in 1972, we traveled to Canada, the United States, and Europe with only hand-drawn diagrams and spec sheets. Our only product was a rhythm machine. If we were not able to win any orders, we would not be able to start up Roland. So we were very

Roland Canada. Tape-cutting ▶ ceremony at the company's office.

happy to get a three-month potential order from Gene Trademan in Canada, our first stop. This was Roland's first purchase order. Although we still had no sample or factory, we knew that this order would have a major impact on other potential customers. I immediately called our office in Japan and instructed them to look for a factory for lease and order the necessary materials. This is the only way you can get a business started with limited capital. I have many memories of Vancouver. It was in Vancouver that I received the telex alerting us to the crisis at Jorgensen in Europe.

We currently have twenty-one overseas joint ventures, the first one being in Australia. Looking back at the companies' histories from startup to the present day, I am very grateful that we have been blessed with great partners. From the get-go, our policy was to have an equal 50/50 capital investment ratio, and have a local businessperson take the helm of the company. A number of joint companies have already celebrated their thirtieth anniversaries and this policy remains unchanged. While some of our partners have since retired, and consequently some companies are now 100 percent owned by Roland Japan, our dealings with them remain unchanged.

▲ Roland US. Tape-cutting ceremony for the new office.

Our second joint company was Roland US, which was founded in 1978. The American market, the home of electronic musical instruments, was crucial in that success or failure in this market would have an impact on Roland as a whole. This joint company, which had its start at a meeting in Nagoya with Thomas Beckmen, grew to a ¥10 billion-plus company by 1990. At the time, the yen continued to appreciate unabatedly, and our respective views on how to move forward began to diverge as we approached the year 2000. This was when we decided to purchase all remaining shares and end our joint venture. Subsequently, the yen appreciated to levels that exceeded our expectations, and under the leadership of a new president, Dennis Houlihan, the company has grown to the largest in the Roland group with sales in excess of ¥20 billion.

Our second joint production company was founded in Italy. Mr. Lucarelli, president of Roland Europe, was awarded the highest recognition in Italian industry, the Cavaliere del Lavoro, in 1998 for his work. This represented a recognition by the Italian government of the success of our joint company and the high-tech industry in general.

Each year, we hold an international conference in Japan where the presidents of all of these overseas companies come together, and it is the active exchange of ideas between conference participants that gives Roland its driving force. As the standard language used at these conferences is English, I am very grateful for our partners who take great pains to understand my English. At this point in time, my relationships with the chairpersons, presidents, and directors of these joint companies span from at least ten years to as long as forty-plus years. I have many memories of the startup stages of each of these joint companies, memories which themselves could fill a book.

With the emergence of a new eurozone and the technological advancements being made in Asia, we are seeing dramatic changes in how we relocate production overseas, an undertaking we began in 1987. Our operations for the twenty-first century are just beginning. The new people we have had the good fortune to have join us in the Roland group are individuals I have known well in the musical instruments industry, and I think it would be impossible to find individuals in Japan capable of doing the same work as these highly competent presidents in each of the countries in which we operate. The basis of everything is full mutual trust. To do business in another country is to accept the culture of the host country. I believe Japanese culture has the ability to accept and digest foreign cultures, and present them in a new way to the world. It is no coincidence that an increasing number of Japanese people have risen to the forefront of art and technology over the past fifty years. My hope is to be able to contribute to new areas of music through joint ventures.

And then, in 2008, the history of joint companies changed forever with the Lehman crisis. Not only did the yen rate rise rapidly, but everything from management conditions to merchandise supply and communication underwent fundamental changes. The inability of the economy to adjust sufficiently to these changes has had a huge impact on all of us, and things have changed so dramatically that I find impossible to agree with. To overcome such a situation, there is no other path than to create something that has no samples. I believe that this is the best course of action to take.

Our joint ventures started out with sales and then extended into manufacturing. Over the years, there have been mergers and acquisitions. Joint companies are truly like marriages. There is no value if both of us are not happy every day. And unless both are willing to be patient, there will be strife. It would be a fortunate thing for such relationships to last a lifetime. This is what wonderful joint companies are like. But if we both agree that things are not working out, it is also important that we are able to cordially shake hands and go our different ways. This is what good business partnerships look like.

5

I Choose Music as My Life's Work

THE WORK AT KAKEHASHI MUSEN, A BUSINESS THAT I BEGAN IN 1954 in Abeno, Osaka, started out with assembling and repairing radios and TVs, then moved on to the retailing of household appliances such as washing machines and rice cookers. This electric appliance shop eventually grew larger and became Ace Denki Co. Ltd. Since I had already been quite deeply engaged in making electronic musical instruments as a hobby and had hopes of taking this a step beyond prototyping, we came to a fork in the road, where one path would have us continue our retail business and the other would take us into the manufacturing business.

In 1960, we founded Ace Electronic Industries. Our business performance stabilized in five or six years, and we reached a point where we could begin experimenting with keyboard instruments. Around the same time, we began importing Hammond organs, and since we had been exporting rhythm instruments, in 1968, we founded Hammond International Japan jointly with Hammond.

Through this process, we learned how difficult it was to transition from retail to manufacturing, a completely different playing field. Part of the reason was that there were no samples we could glean from anyone who had gone through a similar transition in the past.

Niche Market

It has often been noted that Japan has a short history with organs, which is only natural as Western music did not come to Japan until about 1880, and the country had no previous history with pipe organs. While they are surely no substitute, Tombo Gakki Seisakusho began selling accordions in 1928. The accordion, which was a reed instrument and could therefore produce sustained notes, gained a solid foothold of affinity with the Japanese people along with reed organs. As an elementary school student I owned two harmonicas—structurally the most simple of all reed instruments—which indicates the popularity of this instrument at the time.

Accordions were already being produced in large quantities in the 1930s, with ten thousand produced in 1930, and production growing annually from fifteen thousand in 1931 to seventeen thousand in 1932, twenty-four thousand in 1933, and thirty-two thousand in 1934. Even during the war in 1943, thirty-eight thousand were produced according to records, which also note that the manufacturing of these instruments became extremely difficult as brass and other materials used in the sound-producing components were hard to come by. The proliferation of music made possible by these reed organs, harmonicas, and accordions in Japanese homes has great significance in the history of music in Japan.

Prewar music classes in schools were based on singing and not on musical instruments. The school that I went to had no piano or organ in the classroom, so, for music classes, the entire class would walk to the music room where there was a piano and foot-operated organ. When we sang, we would all sing the melody in unison and there was no choral singing where we would sing different parts. After the war, each classroom came with an organ, and in 1969, annual reed organ production peaked at 560,000 units. The manufacture of blower organs, which were motor-driven as opposed to foot-operated, became a very attractive area of business not only for musical instrument manufacturers but for household appliance manufacturers, who supplied the motors. Manufacturers who specialized in musical instruments were increasing their production every year and organ lesson businesses were booming. This meant that a large number of households with elementary school children ended up with an organ in their home. Electrical appliance manufacturers eventually became dissatisfied with simply supplying motors and began manufacturing blower organs themselves. Though organs, first introduced to Japan in the late 1800s, transitioned from being foot-operated to being driven by electric motor, they were still reed organs, and electronic organs were not available anywhere.

Although I did have a vague sense that large corporations were attempting to enter the musical instrument industry, as proprietor of a simple appliance shop, these were simply machinations within the manufacturing industry that were far removed from myself. I had not even given thought to how wide that gap was. Although I was making prototypes of electronic instruments simply as a hobby with no intention of commercializing them, I did sense that there might be some opportunity in the field so I began investigating. Given the competition in the blower organ market, my thoughts were that electrical appliance makers were likely to have a difficult time mastering the musical know-how needed to manufacture musical instruments, and similarly, the musical instrument manufacturers were on a completely different technological footing that was not conducive to them mastering electronic technology. My thought was that the market for electronic musical instruments lay somewhere in between these two—a "niche market," in today's parlance. So I came to the very simplistic conclusion that electronic musical instruments would become this niche market, and decided right there and then, "Okay! This is going to be my life's work."

This was when I was twenty-eight years old, but I don't think this was too late. While I had only been going through technical material up to that point, I then began studying market information. I learned that the United States was also more advanced in this area. While electronic musical instruments lived in the lab from my earlier perspective, I learned from photos and such that electronic organs were already being sold in stores in the United States. I was shocked. While I must have come across similar photos when I was studying technical magazines, there was a freshness to them now as if I were seeing them for the first time. This was proof that no matter how high the quality of your studying material, it is of no use if you have no purpose. What I took to heart was that my first job as a manufacturer would be to gather as much information and knowledge as I could on the musical instrument market.

I thought that since no companies had been around in Japan in the late 1800s, that I could sample, then I should be able to find out how to build my business by studying how other electronic companies started out, how big their businesses were at startup, and how they grew. So I gathered company introduction packages from electronic component manufacturers that I was familiar with. The material from Trio (founded as Kasuga Radio, now Kenwood), Sansui, Pioneer, Akai Electric, and Kataoka Electric (presently Alps Electric) were very helpful in this respect. All of these companies made parts used in radio and TV assembly, and all were within a range of size that I could comprehend. Our appliance store already employed more than twenty people, had become Ace Electrical Appliances Co. Ltd., and was considered to be a medium-scale appliance retailer in those days. I decided that if I wanted to take the manufacturing route it would be now or never, so I asked my partner, Yoshinori Harada, to take ownership of Ace Electrical Appliances, and decided to concentrate on manufacturing in an electronic musical instruments department that I would set up as part of Taihei High-Frequency Research Institute, which was run by one of my friends, Hidemitsu Kanesada. This was in 1960, the start of Ace Electronic Industries.

We started by making spinet organs with two rows of keys, but in order to compete against reed organs fitted with blower motors and to sell organs in volume, we had to make one-keyboard organs that were priced affordably. We made prototypes and showed these to musical instrument wholesalers, who showed no interest at all in our organs. Our company's lack of reputation as a manufacturer and my own inexperience in the industry contributed to the wholesalers' reluctance to deal with us. At one point, I sought the advice of Mutsuro Hiyama, who was in charge of imports at Nippon Gakki Seizo at the time, to learn more about the musical instrument industry. He advised that because wholesalers in this industry had much more clout than their counterparts in the electronic products industries, unless we made products that the wholesalers would be able to carry, we would not be able to sell our products and they would not be well received in the market. So I concluded that things would move faster if we were to take our products to a company that had more sales clout, and decided to sell our products to National (presently Panasonic). It was at this point that I asked Kazuo Sakata, a shareholder of Ace Electronic Industries and president of Sakata Shokai, to bring our proposal to the attention of Shigekazu Nishimiya, who had just started up National House Industrial and was president of the company, and ask him to see our prototype. It was soon decided that they would sell this organ under the National brand. Our company just did not have the clout to release it under the Ace brand. It was after these developments that I asked Mr. Sakata, who was very knowledgeable about music and an organist himself, to invest in Ace Electronic Industries and become its president. He agreed and I became senior managing director of the company.

The factory was built by National Prefab House, and there we began production. The design team at National transformed my prototype design into a very attractive organ, and the first SX-601 National electronic organ was thus born in Suminoe, Osaka. The SX-601 sold very well, and National decided to move production operations to its Moriguchi factory as

The National SX-601, the first ▶ organ that we successfully sold. (Launched December 1963.)

the Suminoe factory could not meet demand. Consequently, Ace Electronic Industries concentrated solely on making keyboards, and its business changed into a supplier of keyboards to National. We also started supplying keyboards to JVC, a company affiliated with Matsushita (later Panasonic).

I have heard that Konosuke Matsushita commented on National's entry into the electronic musical instruments market, in Osaka dialect: "These things belong in the field of art and antiques, so they won't be huge sellers." At the time I thought his views were somewhat off the mark, as we were getting enough demand to warrant mass production, but looking back now and ruminating on his words, I've come to think that Mr. Matsushita was correct.

When the cost of labor began to rise in the United States in the 1960s, an increasing number of American companies began to import low-cost keyboard instruments from Italy. Hammond's major competitor, Chicago Musical Instruments, had acquired Lowrey Organs, Hammond's largest rival, and was importing organs from Italy. So it was critical that Hammond create organs that could compete against these products. If Ace Electronic Industries, official importer of Hammond organs to Japan, could produce organs, then Ace and Sakata Shokai could form a joint company with Hammond to export organs to countries other than the United States. Another major reason for this thinking was that Hammond did not have organs based on electronic oscillators. The role of the joint company would be to expand our share in overseas markets by adding competitive electronic organs to our product lineup, and this represented a great opportunity for Ace Electronic Industries to significantly increase its production volume.

From Clocks to Electronic Organs

Our Osaka factory was going to be too small to accommodate the production volumes we envisioned for our new joint company, so we decided to relocate to Hamamatsu to find a location for our new factory. With Kyowa Bank (presently Resona) mediating the deal, we decided to acquire Zenon Gakki Seizo, which had manufactured grand pianos, upright pianos, and blower organs in Hamamatsu in the past. The factory had been put on sale because the boom for blower organs had passed and their production volumes had fallen. Bob Olsen, VP of Hammond International, visited us on the occasion of this acquisition. He toured the factory with us in Hamamatsu.

The factory was already very old, and the office floor had holes in it. The building and its facilities were all in disrepair with no sign of upkeep. The conditions were worse than I had imagined, and I was concerned about what Mr. Olsen thought after the visit. Years later, I had the opportunity to ask him what he thought at the time, to which he replied, "I can't find the right words to describe it other than 'terrible condition'!" and laughed heartily. In any case, he did not object to the acquisition. The price was ¥200 million, but Zenon Gakki Seizo had more than ¥200 million in hidden losses. To refurbish this factory, Mr. Harada, senior managing director of Ace Electronic Industries, and four other employees would spend three days a week in Hamamatsu for about two years.

Once the acquisition papers were signed, we began cleaning up the office. There we found a wall clock that was disproportionately large for the office, and on its case was engraved "Tiger Yamaha Torakusu." Upon some research, we found out that the predecessor of Zenon Gakki Seizo was Tiger Gakki, whose predecessor was Yamaha Gakki Seizo. The name "Tiger" most likely came from the *tora*, Japanese for tiger, in Torakusu's name. During the Yamaha Gakki years, one of Torakusu's grandsons was running the company as its senior managing director. This information came to light only after we investigated the "History of Enshu Industry and Culture" and spoke to former employees, as no one had information on the company then. After the war, a large number of piano manufacturers started up in Hamamatsu, and there were several tens of companies in the area during the peak years, including cottage industry manufacturers, who were manufacturing products to fulfill the demand for pianos in postwar Japan. Tiger Gakki, or Zenon Gakki, was one such producer.

During the time when we were running the Kakehashi Musen, we had planned to manufacture a couple of products as a side business, including the ultrasound watch cleaner and watch tester that I had wanted myself when I was running my watch repair business. Watches made in Japan, the United States, and Switzerland had a balance (the heart of a mechanical watch comprising hairspring, balance staff, and balance screw) that moved at five cycles. Digital watches were still not around. Since everything was mechanical, you could hear the ticking sound when you brought the watch close to your ear. By amplifying this sound and comparing it with a five-cycle click produced by frequency-dividing the oscillation from a precise quartz oscillator, you could adjust the time difference to ten seconds or less. The difference between a good repair and a bad one hinged on this adjustment of time difference. The time-consuming nature of this adjustment process meant that it took at least two or three days to repair a watch after the customer brought it in.

A Swiss-made mechanical device called a Vibrograf that would output results on paper tape was available, but these machines were not something a small town watch shop operator could afford. So I prototyped the Watch Master, an electronic tabletop version of this idea that would display the results on a two-inch picture tube, and presented it to watch shops. They turned me down, saying, "If we were to test our watches on this thing, customers wouldn't even buy our new watches." Few watches in those days offered a daily error rate of less than ten seconds, so this comment made complete sense. While development in this area met an impasse, had I not had this experience with studying frequency-dividing circuitry to make this prototype, I might not have been able to understand the circuitry of organs.

Torakusu Yamaha was also someone who started out with watches and then moved on to organs. A brief biography of Yamaha is given in a book titled *Piano Story*, edited by Robert Palmieri. He was born in Wakayama Prefecture in 1851, relocated to Osaka in 1869, and became a live-in apprentice to a watch seller. He spent two years in Osaka, after which he relocated to Nagasaki, where he spent five years in a business operated by a British individual to further hone his skills and learn watchmaking. He later returned to Osaka from Nagasaki, aspiring to become a watchmaker, but could not launch his manufacturing venture due to lack of capital. So he opened a small retail shop that sold medical equipment and watches in Yamato Takada, Nara, near Osaka. This was when he was thirty years old. However, this business did not do well so he relocated, this time to Tokyo. He eventually moved on to repairing and manufacturing organs, and essentially single-handedly created the musical instrument industry in Japan. An interesting point to note is that, although he started out with watches in Osaka and then moved to Tokyo, at one time he relocated to Hamamatsu at the invitation of a hospital director. This connection was what led to Hamamatsu becoming the center of the musical instrument industry. While there are many versions of how these events transpired, this version seems to be the most accurate based on my research.

Germany had been a major production center of reed instruments such as accordions and harmonicas since before the war. Hohner harmonicas, played worldwide, were first made by Matthias Hohner, a twenty-four-year-old clockmaker based in Trossingen in South Germany. This business eventually grew into the company we know today.

The story of how Laurens Hammond, the founder of Hammond Organs, switched from manufacturing electric clocks to organs is also well known. I received a Hammond clock that runs on a synchronous motor as a gift from Eiji Kondo, a professor at the Matsumoto Dental University Graduate School and a researcher of electronic musical instruments. This clock continues to keep time quietly on my organ at home.

▲ A Hammond electric watch sits atop a Hammond M-3 organ.

My relationship with clocks and organs was different from what these great predecessors had, but based on my experience of running a watch and clock shop for three years, I have a certain understanding of the commonalities between these areas. At the time, these machines—in particular watches, which represented the pinnacle of precision mechanisms—were the ideal technology that captivated the imagination of many engineers. When I started to work on electronic musical instruments around 1950, there was no literature on the subject and I had no way of knowing that three of my great predecessors had started out working on watches before they moved on to musical instruments. After two years of teaching myself how to repair watches, I came to think that I knew all I needed to know about watches, and that repairs simply involved refurbishing watches to the condition they were in when they first shipped. Looking back now, I admit I was a bit arrogant, and I am embarrassed at how little I knew of the complexity of watches. Watches have a strange allure, and this is something I came to realize after I stopped working on them.

I was always listening to the radio while I repaired watches, and as I listened to all the foreign music that played on the radio, I became a huge fan of music. This was when I began to wonder if I could make any of the instruments that I heard producing the music. Violins seemed to be quite difficult to make, but the thought hit me that I could probably make an organ. This was when I chose music as my life's work. Upon learning later that my predecessors had also started out working on watches before making musical instruments, I was happy to know that I was not alone.

From Monophonic to Polyphonic

Around 1955, when I began to make electronic musical instruments as a hobby, keyboards that could be used on an electronic musical instrument were not commercially available, so instead of making an instrument that could play harmonies, my immediate goal was to make an instrument that a player could play melodies on. One of the electronic musical instruments at the time that could create melodies was the theremin. Based on what I read in articles, its circuitry appeared to be relatively simple, and was something I could easily wrap my head around given my daily experience with radios and TVs. The theremin was an instrument that had two antennas attached to an aluminum box containing its circuitry, and the player would control the melody with the right hand and the volume with the left hand by moving the hands closer or farther away from the antennas. But it was a difficult instrument to play as it was impossible to delineate the gaps between notes. In particular, it was very hard to hold an accurate pitch, so I decided that this was not the route to take as these problems were too difficult to overcome. In retrospect, my decision to give up was correct as I was not trained to play notes and determine the pitch with my own ears in the way players of fretless instruments such as violins and shamisens would have been.

Around 1967, I read a newspaper article that mentioned an electronic musical instrument on exhibit at the Soviet pavilion at the Osaka International Trade Show, and visited the show. This was a bit of unexpected news for me because most of my attention was directed toward the United States at the time. The instrument on exhibit was a monophonic electronic musical instrument with a keyboard. The tones of strings and reed instruments that this interesting instrument produced were wonderful, and the player was able to smoothly produce musical melodies on it. This was no surprise, coming from the same country the theremin had originated from. To my questions, "Is this commercially available?" and "If so, how much is it?" the attendant replied only that he could not say, but would have the embassy get back to me. Two days later, a Soviet trade representative came to visit our factory. The instrument, I learned, was called "Ekvodin." Our discussions at the factory started right off the bat with their asking price, which was presented in rubles. Since I had no idea what this would be in yen, I asked them to convert the price to US dollars, which came to about $28,000, far higher than any price I could have imagined. So I explained the market conditions in Japan and showed them the retail price of US-made monophonic musical instruments to illustrate how unrealistic their pricing was. However, I'm quite sure that this was not something a Soviet government employee would have been able to understand.

Needless to say, this discussion bore no fruit, but the next day I received a phone call letting me know that they would be willing to grant me a Japan-only license for $1,400. Although he had cut the price by 95 percent in less than twenty-four hours, I turned down the offer. It was clear that this sort of illogical "negotiation" did not bode well for a constructive relationship.

▲ Wataru Saito (1932–65).

If memory serves me correctly, it was around 1963 or 1964 that JOBK (now Osaka NHK) purchased an ondes martenot, an instrument developed in France. This was a very important monophonic electronic musical instrument. It has undergone many upgrades since then and there are still performers who specialize in playing this instrument. Back in the day, the connections of the speaker were complex, and this made the pitch unstable. I remember being contacted by NHK staff who had tried everything to no avail, and going in to help out with a number of their recordings. This was not an easy instrument to play; the performer needed to have a good ear to maintain the correct pitch. At the time, there were almost no musicians in the Kansai area willing to take up the challenge of playing a new electronic instrument, and since the process of tape editing after the recording was also a lot of work, the only person who would get involved was the organist Wataru Saito. Mr. Saito and I had been acquainted since the time he played on a demo for the Ace Tone, so I became the go-to person to tune his instrument before every recording session. Between sessions, I remember dropping in on him at other studios where they were recording, in front of an audience, *Otosan wa Ohitoyoshi*, a radio drama featuring Achako Hanabishi and Chieko Naniwa. It was very unfortunate that Mr. Saito passed away at such a young age. Many Japanese remember him from his frequent TV appearances as leader of the band Saito Wataru and the New Sounds.

The band had some stylistic similarities to the Three Suns, an American band that was big at the time, but Mr. Saito's arrangements were unique, and a perfect match for the TV era that had just begun. With an ensemble consisting of Hammond organ, guitar, and drums, the band infused a sense of novelty into their music, which was distinctly different from the Three Suns, a band that included an accordion. I concluded around this time that keyboard instruments, which would consistently produce the correct pitch when a key was pressed, were the best way to go, and decided to focus my development efforts there.

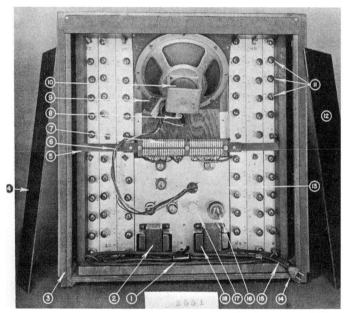

▲ The sound-producing components of the Organo, the first polyphonic organ I had the chance to hear.

One of the electronic organs I had the opportunity to repair was the Organo, made in the United States. Although I think this particular model had already been discontinued at the time, I was very surprised at the sound of this instrument played in a church, as well as its design and construction. It was capable of producing harmonies and even different tones, so this was two or even three steps ahead of what I had in mind, which was simply to produce melodies. Upon seeing the Organo, I felt as if the road from monophonic to harmony-producing instruments had opened up before me.

The Organo was made by Lowrey, an American company, and contained oscillators, an amplifier, and a speaker in an enclosure, which were connected to a switching unit by multicore cables. The idea behind this product was to set this switching unit on top of a piano keyboard to enable the player to play the piano keyboard to produce organ tones. An original iteration of the Organo was exhibited at the 1941 NAMM Show as "Orgiano." Records show that the instrument was demoed by Ethel Smith, an organist famous for her association with Hammond. Lowrey then relaunched the product after the war in 1949, this time under the name Organo. The product that I repaired was not the type where the unit would be set up on a piano, but where the switching unit was attached to a modified reed organ.

In retrospect, a cursory look at its sound generator and configuration would have told me that there was no way this organ would produce good tone, but what I actually heard at the church were the wonderful sounds of an organ. The sound of this small electronic organ in a live setting was better than the sound of a pipe organ on vinyl. Since I had never had the opportunity to hear an organ in a cathedral, this represented the wonderful world of organ music to me. However, even if I had had the opportunity to listen to a real pipe organ first, I don't think that is what would have inspired me to make an organ. I think what motivated me the most was that I could make electronic organs from parts that I was familiar with. What I take from this experience is that the image one gets from sound is a very strange thing in that even if you conclude from a technical standpoint that a particular sound should be not be producible, and indeed cannot be produced, your perspective has a way of changing depending on the venue, performer, audience, and general feeling of the place.

In a note at the end of *The Immortal Piano* by Avner Carmi and Hannah Carmi, Sumi Gunji, the book's Japanese translator, quotes Professor E. Leip, who made an interesting observation on these strange occurrences at the Europiano Congress in 1965: "Roughly speaking, 25 percent of the effects of the sound of the piano are created by the piano, 25 percent by the venue, 25 percent by the performer, and lastly (at least) 25 percent by the mood of the listener. Said another way, given the fact that the sound of a piano is in no way a simple matter even if one looks at it from a strictly physicalistic standpoint, the topic becomes infinitely more complex if we are to include the various other concomitant phenomena of human psychology in the mixture. Just as complex as human beings themselves . . ." As someone involved in the manufacture of musical instruments, this passage, which I first read over twenty years ago, is still unforgettable.

Rhythm Ace

The styles of folk music traditional to the various regions of the world are truly diverse and enjoyable. Once we began developing rhythm instruments, I came to enjoy these different musical traditions twice as much as I had before. The traditional musical styles of Europe, and those imported from European colonies in Asia and Africa, have unique flavors. In many regions of Africa, South America, and Asia, there is a wide range of music performed with only percussive instruments. Historically, American music was heavily influenced by the music of Native Americans, African music that arrived with the slave trade, and South American music. A melting pot of music, the likes of which cannot be found in any other country, developed in America during the late nineteenth and twentieth centuries as the cultures of immigrants from various regions of Europe blended with each other. People at traditional Japanese get-togethers will all clap to the beat in a similar fashion no matter which region they happen to be in, a practice that may be a remnant of the country's long history as a farming culture. The main element of Japanese folk songs is the melody, but the *taiko* drum rhythms are unique to each region and truly amazing. It is said that the clubs and teams that work to preserve traditional regional taiko styles vastly outnumber the prefectures in the country. This is the reason that the requirements of rhythm are a basic element of Japanese music.

In the 1960s, rhythm instruments began to emerge in the field of electronic musical instruments, which had gotten its start with organs. Wurlitzer launched the Side Man, which was a unit you could place beside your piano or organ that would play rhythm accompaniment. The instrument's timing was determined by a motor-driven disk and switches, and the sounds of the percussion instruments were produced by vacuum tubes. The unit was made of a combination of different parts used in the first generation of electronic instruments, i.e., mechanical hammers and vacuum tubes. While this product had some issues—it was difficult to start the rhythm in synchronization with the music you played on your piano or organ, and it was plagued with frequent contact failures—it was the first product out of the gate in the area of automated rhythm. The use of transistors was starting to catch on in the field of electronic organs, and this was a welcome development for rhythm instruments that needed to be made smaller. At the 1964 NAMM Show we exhibited the world's first transistorized rhythm instrument, the Rhythm Ace R-1, a simple machine that would produce the sound of a percussive instrument when the user manually hit a button.

▼ This Rhythm Ace R-1 was a manual rhythm instrument used by attaching it to an electronic organ.

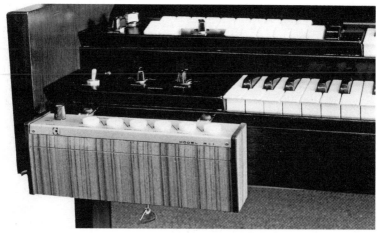

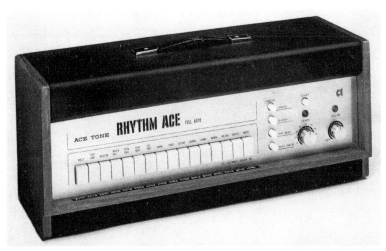

▲ Our first mass-produced automated rhythm machine, the Rhythm Ace FR-1.

Response to this product was good, but we sold only ten of them. All of the buyers were American organ manufacturers who were purchasing it for their research, and needless to say, we received no repeat orders. It became clear that its impact on performance would remain minimal unless it could automate rhythm, so this Rhythm Ace was never incorporated into electronic organs.

A least two bars, or measures, are needed to comprise a rhythm pattern. Even then, repetitions of the same pattern will feel monotonous and the rhythm will lack excitement. The basic way to create rhythms in two-four, three-four, four-four, eight-eight, and six-eight time using the electrical circuitry available in those days was to divide the time within a bar into twenty-four, which is the least common multiple of these time signatures in a single bar, and to create pulses that would electrically hit the sound generator at these timing intervals. However, because no satisfactory rhythm pattern could be created using these divisions of twenty-four, we ended up creating rhythm patterns using divisions of forty-eight. For example, in Viennese waltzes, the second beat does not come exactly one-third of the way through the bar, but is "pushed" slightly earlier. Consequently, this creates a longer interval until the third beat arrives. While even divisions of forty-eight were not sufficient to achieve the effect, using divisions of ninety-six meant that we would need to use twice as many parts, and this would raise the cost considerably. Since the series of pulses that determined the time-wise location of each instrument hit was being created in a circuit called a diode matrix, it was very difficult to make changes once the circuitry was defined and the printed circuit board was designed.

Finally in 1967, we were able to launch our first automated rhythm machine, the Rhythm Ace FR-1. Bossa nova began to gain popularity right before the release of the product, and we decided to include this pattern in our machine, but everyone we asked had a different opinion of what a "proper" bossa nova rhythm should be. We eventually ran out of time so we decided to include the rhythm pattern in "The Girl from Ipanema." I remember all of us feeling relieved when we learned later that this was fortunately one of the proper patterns of bossa nova. Today, we are able to create rhythm patterns using divisions of 120 for every quarter note, and changes can be made much more easily. Things are truly now a world away from what they were back then.

The Rhythm Ace FR-1 became a major turning point for me. One person had taken the FR-1, which we had on exhibit at the Hamburg show, and begun selling it. This was Erik Gramkow, who would later become president of Roland Scandinavia. His sales success became the impetus for expanding our sales network in Europe, and our relationship with him would eventually lead to our developing a direct relationship with Hammond.

In 1967, American organist Don Lewis rose to fame with a new style of music that combined the Hammond organ X-77 and the Rhythm Ace. As we were the importer and reseller of Hammond products in Japan, we invited Mr. Lewis to Japan and rented an Osaka cabaret, the Metro, to launch our promotion.

▲ The Hammond Piper prototype.

Hammond also decided to produce organs with a built-in rhythm machine, based on the idea that automated rhythm would become an indispensable part of organ performances, so we began selling our rhythm units to Hammond in an arrangement we now call original equipment manufacturing (OEM). This became the starting point for Hammond's Piper project, and the prototype of the automated rhythm machine unit for the new Piper product was to be made in Japan. The project was code-named Mustang. We made three prototypes, two of which we sent to Hammond headquarters in Chicago. These models were the very first organs with a one-row keyboard and built-in rhythm machine. The success of this project eventually led to the formation of our joint company, Hammond International Japan. Thus, the Rhythm Ace FR-1 became our first product to make an inroad into the heart of the American electronic musical instruments market. We also wanted to market this as a product on its own, so we asked Takuji Tomita, who had designed the Ace logo, to design that product.

Based on our success selling rhythm units to Hammond, we contacted five or six other companies, and Kimball Organ became the first after Hammond to incorporate our product. We thought we could also sell them as accompaniments for theater organs, so we visited Rodgers Organs in Portland, Oregon. This did not come to pass at the time as the production volume of classical organs, which Rodgers was making, was vastly smaller than that of home organs, and as the rhythm patterns they needed were different. I still remember the taxi ride on the rustic and sparsely populated country roads leading from the Portland airport to Hillsboro, where Rodgers had its factory. The area has now been transformed into a high-tech hub where Japanese companies such as NEC, Fujitsu, Hitachi, and Epson run facilities, and Intel operates a huge plant in front of the Rodgers factory. At the time, I did not even dream that we would end up acquiring Rodgers thirty years later.

It wasn't until 1978 that a rhythm machine that musicians themselves could program became available. This was the CompuRhythm CR-78, the world's first rhythm unit equipped with a microprocessor. This product had a huge impact and was widely acclaimed. Electronic musical instruments were a completely new genre in the musical instruments industry in Japan in the sixties; I can't remember how many times a new branch manager was assigned to the bank we were dealing with and I had to explain what electronic instruments were again. Additionally, every product we made at the time was subject to excise taxes, but because the tax system was defined based on existing categories of musical instruments, the definitions frequently did not apply to our new instruments, and in some cases our products were so novel that no definition applied. Because of this, we were once asked by an auditor, "So many of the products your company makes do not fall within any of the tax code definitions, to the point that one might think you were in the business of evading taxes. What is going on?" In many cases, we developed new product categories inspired by ideas we got from our conversations with musicians, instead of waiting for musicians to tell us what they wanted. Needless to say, we never did any investigation of the tax system before initiating new development processes.

Because the foreign markets were ahead of the Japanese market by over a decade, we could study overseas trends and use our findings as a basis for forecasting the future of the Japanese market several years down the road. Therefore, market research was of no use whatsoever in creating new product categories. There was a period of over ten years when the products we made would not sell very well in Japan but would do well overseas. This trend continues today, so if we were to hire a market research company before starting up a new category, their reports would conclude, almost without exception, "No market demand." We've had experience with these types of studies, and in our case, the only thing we can do is first make our product, then see what the musicians think, and repeat.

Products in novel categories can take several years and sometimes even longer than ten years to catch on, and the discernment to decide one way or the other is the true determinant of success or failure. Fortunately in recent years, we have begun to see products take off in Japan first. I often say, "We can't fail if we stick with it until we succeed." Success hinges solely on the conviction and commitment of staff members working on a project, more so than the perseverance to continue our development efforts. It is not an easy task to improve our batting average.

The Founding of Roland

A turning point can come from an unexpected turn of events. While we all worked hard to build our business at Ace Electronic Industries, the shares that our employees and I held in the company fell to between 10 and 20 percent of their original value. This happened because I had been running the business with no knowledge of business management. My own share of holdings had dropped because when we acquired Zenon Gakki Seizo, we formed a joint company with shares divided equally between Hammond and Ace. This equal merger was unthinkably strange, looking back now, and would become the root of a major problem three years down the road. Since business at Sakata Shokai—which was run by Mr. Sakata, who understood organs and was a supporter of ours—ran into difficult times, Sumitomo Chemical acquired the company, becoming one of the major shareholders of Ace Electronic Industries. Though it was unreasonable to expect people from a raw-materials-based industrial domain to understand the music business, the agony of having to work with them was unspeakable. Our decision-making criteria were so far apart, our conversations went nowhere. Regardless, our rhythm instruments and keyboards were selling well, and exporting these products overseas was a lot of fun. During the time we worked with Shiro Murai, manager of overseas sales at Sakata Shokai (presently representative director, chairman, and CEO of SIIX Corporation), to cultivate overseas markets, we could see our efforts bear fruit in tangible ways, and could even take proactive steps based on our forecasts. Everything about overseas markets was new and interesting to me as my expertise until then had only been in the area of technological development and the Japanese market. Our team, made up of a salesperson, Shiro Murai, and an engineer, myself, was on a tight schedule, visiting markets around the world. Our work also involved checking into ideas that "had no samples" by looking for what was and was not available, as opposed to looking for products that were selling well. Taking care of everything from sales to export, Mr. Murai made an immensely valuable contribution to our business.

The company was profitable, but we were not able to make any plans for the future. While I understood that rebuilding Sakata Shokai was our first priority, many events came to pass that I just could not accept as the person responsible for Ace Electronic Industries, a growing company that needed proactive investments. I had no other choice than to let go of, or rather leave, Ace Electronic Industries, which we had started up with much effort, and restart from scratch on my own.

▲ A statue of Roland in Bremen, Germany.

While the decision to leave a company that I had started and that was doing well was a difficult one to make, there were limits to the amount of frustration I could take on a daily basis, so the effort that I would have to put in after leaving was not an issue. This was the point when I bid farewell to Ace and Hammond. At the time, had I not had the clear conviction that making electronic musical instruments would be my life's work, I might have moved into another line of business. But since I had decided that this was what I would do, I was not about to renege on this decision. I also thought that the experience I had accumulated up to this point could not be easily acquired, and decided to take up the challenge of making electronic musical instruments again. My mind cleared once it occurred to me that this was a rare opportunity to design a company from scratch, after having acquired some experience in business management. So in March 1972, I resigned from Ace and started up my new company on April 18.

▲ Designer Takuji Tomita, who designed the Roland logo, circa 1970. The portrait of me on the cover of this book is also by Mr. Tomita.

Now I had to come up with a name for my new company. While there are many examples of companies named after the founder in the musical instruments industry, I had already graduated from using the Kakehashi name with my watch shop and electrical appliance business. Instead of using a Japanese name, which would inevitably contain many vowels, I thought it would sound better and be easier to remember if it contained two syllables and a voiced consonant. Also, because a company's name is often represented by its initial, I decided that the name should start with *R*, an initial shared by few names in the industry. Another important point was that the name should be pronounced more or less the same wherever you went in the world. One of the names that met these criteria was Roland. Upon learning that this was the name of a historic person, I looked it up in Webster's Dictionary and found that this person had been a brave knight of the Round Table and that his name was preceded by the honorific "Sir." I also registered the name Oliver, who I learned had been a great rival of Sir Roland. In the end, I stuck with Roland. I am often asked if I was inspired by the book *The Song of Roland*, but I only learned of this book four or five years after I started up the company. There is also a statue of an individual named Roland in front of the town hall in Bremen, but this was a different person altogether. There is another statue of Roland in Bad Bramstedt in North Germany.

Once I had settled on the name Roland, I was able to start without much second-guessing. In order to make the Roland image clear, the best thing to do was to determine the company's logo and print it on our letterhead and business cards. The designer Takuji Tomita, with whom I've worked since my Ace years, was kind enough to finish the logo in two weeks. The logo remains unchanged to this day and it has not lost any of its freshness. It's best to get corporate identity matters out of the way at the time of startup.

Companies tend to drive themselves when business is going well. While sales for Roland's first year reached approximately ¥100 million, by the time our fifth anniversary came around in 1977, we were creating plans for ¥10 billion in sales for our tenth anniversary, an outrageous target by some accounts. However, the yen-dollar exchange rate, which was ¥360 to the dollar when I started the company, momentarily rose to less than ¥180 to the dollar in 1979. This hit our business hard as a large percentage of our products for export were priced in yen. We began to experience headwinds including the bankruptcy of one of our agents in Europe. While the exchange rate improved considerably between 1980 and 1985, it continued to fluctuate widely around the ¥250 area.

Around the time that Bill Gates and Steve Jobs gained prominence, and "venture business" became the buzzword, I was invited by Simon Fraser University in Vancouver to lecture on venture companies in the musical instrument industry. This was at a time when Roland was growing rapidly, and I gave an hour-long lecture titled "Basic Rules for Venture Businesses" to an audience of students and professors. The points I made were that anyone who wants to start up a business must find a niche, clearly identify the directions for the company or new business, and determine a target, and also that one can build a large business as long as one has a solid foundation.

As I had experience on the order of ¥4 billion in sales annually at Ace Electronic Industries, I had no problem handling Roland's business management until its fifth fiscal year, 1977. Upon conducting a detailed review of our factories, employees, and cash management based on our ¥10 billion target, which was twice the annual sales then, I discovered that we would not be able to handle our operations with the same management methods we had been using. I was also thunderstruck upon realizing that our current sales were not of our own doing but were largely supported by a booming market.

As long as we kept our eyes on the American market—which was our sample— maintained our quality levels, and released products that were a step ahead of the competition, we were still able to generate healthy sales with the help of the still-low yen-dollar exchange rate. However, while I had been focusing most of my attention on keyboard instruments, I now became increasingly curious about the trend in which a variety of products were gradually going digital. While I had been thinking that the United States represented our sample in the realm of electronic musical instruments, I realized then that we should not be mimicking our samples, but should be making things that went beyond what one could find in America. While I had been thinking that our goal was to catch up with America, this was not the case in reality. We had entered an "age without samples."

It was obvious from the published patent bulletins that the industry was trending toward digitalization. And while I could understand transistors, as they were essentially semiconductors modeled on vacuum tubes, designing principles began to undergo a dramatic change as integrated circuits increasingly came into use. We had already embarked on our development of the guitar synthesizer, which we envisioned as another pillar in our product lineup in addition to keyboard synthesizers and rhythm instruments. With respect to the demands of overseas sales, domestic market growth, factory building, employee recruitment, new product planning, and cash management, we were already operating at levels far beyond what we could achieve with the human resources available at the time. While I and all of the executives who had been with the company since startup were handling these matters, things would come up one after another with no time for a break. Overseas sales entailed time-consuming business trips that robbed us of time for design work. Everyone filled more than one position and the company had no dedicated president, so in effect, we were compensating for these shortfalls by working long hours. We felt we were getting things done as we were busy running around, but we had no real idea of the bigger picture. Only by setting a ¥10 billion sales target, and certainly not by looking back and reflecting on our past, were we able to see the issues we were facing at the time. The company was running on its own, regardless of our capabilities. This was a first for all of us and had made us overconfident.

We knew that the company was running on its own, and also that it was violating speed limits, but we did not know how to apply the brakes. But by recognizing the situation we were in, we were able to take action. I decided that it would be much more forward-looking to hire people with expertise in their specialties than to slow down the pace of the company's growth. The first thing I did was to end my hands-on involvement in design. We also needed a specialist in accounting, an area in which none of us were expert. We also needed to split our sales division into different departments in charge of overseas and domestic sales. This much we knew, but two or three years went by as we remained in the dark as to how and where we might find these talents. Subsequently, although not everyone came at once, we were able to welcome Tadao Kikumoto to our engineering department and Itsuji Miyake as our managing director of accounting and administration (he has been senior managing director since 1989). This came to pass three years after I made a request to Sumio Abekawa, vice president of Daiwa Bank, that we wanted Mr. Miyake—who had been the branch manager of Daiwa Bank's Haginochaya branch, where Roland was doing business—to come to Roland. With these moves, Roland was beginning to take shape as a company, and thus we managed to overcome some of the same issues that venture companies still face today.

NAMM Show 1964

THE NAMM SHOW TODAY IS A LARGE-SCALE TRADE SHOW WITH PAR-ticipation from music-related companies from all around the world and booths featuring everything from computers to video. The 1964 show was originally a computer and electronics show, from which musical instruments branched off to become a musical instrument show. At the NAMM Show these days, computers and videos are drawn into the mix with musical instruments. By reading this chapter as a page in the history of the NAMM Show, I believe the reader will get a good idea of how new musical instruments were developed and became popular. I think the chapter has value as a historical reference and not simply as memoir.

Ever since my exposure to foreign music began when I was around fifteen years old, my yearning for other countries grew day by day. By the time I made my organ prototype in 1955, I had come to realize that I had to go to the United States to learn more about electronic organs, but there was not much I could do to realize this goal as proprietor of a small electrical appliances store. About ten years later, in 1964, in my Ace Electronics years, I was able to take part in the NAMM Show, and this became a huge turning point for me. The reality of the immense gap between the Japanese and US musical instrument industries, the state of art of electronic musical instruments, the scale of US wholesalers, and the low level at which we were operating—all matters that had not even crossed my mind till then—hit me like a ton of bricks during that short one-week period.

Chicago Musical Instruments Trade Show

The National Association of Music Merchants had been holding regular musical instrument trade shows every year before Independence Day in the United States. We were able to secure a booth for the 1964 show just before the show was to start, so I flew to the United States on very short notice. This was my

▲ At the Conrad Hilton Chicago, venue of the NAMM Show.

first trip to the United States, let alone to the NAMM Show, and I departed without having made any special preparations. Because there were few direct flights between Tokyo and the United States in the sixties, the most common route to Chicago included a stopover in Anchorage, Alaska. The moment I stepped out of O'Hare Airport, I was hit by a blast of hot air.

Without knowing left from right, I checked in at the Conrad Hilton Hotel, which was the venue of the show. I was surprised to learn that my hotel room would double as our exhibition booth. Everything was big, and you had to lean your body weight against the doors to open them. While just touring the show would have been a lot of work, I was at a complete loss as to how my first presentation at my exhibit might go.

It became obvious on the bus from the airport that people were not going to understand the English I had practiced. All the exhibitors' hotel rooms were doubling as their showrooms, not just mine. It took a bit of courage for me to enter any of these rooms since I was not there to purchase anything, and could not carry on a conversation in English.

On top of that, I had to be in the room, greet any visitors, and explain my products to them. I knew the products inside and out as I had designed them myself, but this was of no use if I could not communicate. The only products I had on exhibit were the Rhythm Ace R-1 rhythm box and the Canary S-2 solo musical instrument, both of which I had brought in my carry-on luggage. I was in the smallest room category for booths, but that did not matter as I had few products on exhibit. I had only two visitors to my room on the first and second days. One of them, a couple, looked around the room and asked me a question

I took to mean, "What do you make?" To this I proudly replied, "Rhythm Ace!" and pointed to the world's first transistorized rhythm box. Although I was able to get this much across, I don't think they understood what it did. So I showed them a photo of the unit attached to an electronic organ and they seemed to understand this.

But the conversation would not go any further. The couple smiled, said, "Good luck," and were about to leave the room, but I was not about to let my first customers in the United States go without a commemorative snapshot. I must have been quite nervous as I forgot to ask them their names or addresses. I was a complete failure as a salesperson. My second customer was Japanese, and I was surprised to see his business card. He was Shunkichi Shorosaka, director of Matsushita Electric's central research labs. I asked him for a photograph as well. These photos, of which there are three, including one of myself standing in my booth, have become the highlights of my photo album. In any case, I was not attracting any customers, so I decided to switch gears and began to actively invite customers to the booth. I took out my business cards, and wrote on the backs of them my booth number and the words "Transistor Rhythm Machine & Melody Keyboard." Then, after exhibit hours, I went around the rooms that seemed to be the booths of organ manufacturers and wholesalers and slid those business cards under their doors.

▼ Ace Tone's first booth at the 1964 NAMM Show. The booth was a converted single room.

Things were dramatically different on the third day. Representatives from over ten companies, some that I had not heard of before, visited my booth. My strategy worked, but attending to the visitors was another story. In some instances, the president of a company would come with an engineer. It was unheard of in Japan for top company executives to personally visit these booths. The list of visitors included Baldwin, Conn, Minshall, Wurlitzer, Hammond, Lowrey, Estey, Thomas, Kimball, Gulbransen, and Magnavox, including other companies whose names I did not recognize. In any case, I received eight orders for sample products. While this number seems small now, at the time it was a boost to my confidence. These orders did not go beyond sample orders, nor did they lead to ongoing business, but an important step forward for us was that we were able to reach an agreement with a company called Sorkin Music to be our agent. More than a decade later I would learn that Yuichiro Yokouchi, currently chairman of FujiGen, also began dealings with Sorkin at around the same time. This was immediately prior to the time guitar exportation from Japan, which began in 1960, would reach its heyday.

After my second or third year at the NAMM Show, I gradually came to understand that Chicago held a prominent place in the history of jazz in the United States. Wrigley, the famous chewing gum company, had a building in the central part of town, and there was a club called the London House across the river from the building. Although the club is no longer there, many famous jazz players used to perform there. I enjoyed visiting the club each time I came for the NAMM Show.

The show has since been relocated to Los Angeles. Now held in January and referred to as the "Winter NAMM," it continues to grow as the largest musical instruments trade show in the world. The show is now held in a large convention center instead of in hotel rooms, and it is open to the general public, making it a paradise of information on new products for dealers and artists alike.

Memorable Manufacturers

Once I got over my jet lag and was feeling a bit more relaxed, my curiosity about other companies began to grow. In the room next to mine, people were playing a "machine " that would play sounds prerecorded on tape. The sounds were produced by playing the instrument's keyboard. When the keys were pressed, tapes lined up behind the keyboard would start to run, playing the prerecorded sounds. Though you could press on the same key for no longer than eight seconds, this machine created beautiful tones. You could play vocal choruses, string ensembles, and even a variety of sound effects. I became acquainted with the exhibitor, and after listening to numerous demos, I started to notice some of the weaknesses of this "machine." Some of the things I noticed were tape noise, flutter, the resonance of the sound when you held down a chord, and that to get a different set of tones you had to change this big frame-like object to which the tapes were attached in an array. In any case, my head was spinning at the extensive work that must have gone into lining up as many tape reels as there were keys, ensuring that the tapes would run stably, devising a mechanism that would instantly wind the tape back when a key was released, and recording the correct pitch on tape.

The instrument had two rows of thirty-five keys each, and each row was fitted with a set of tapes with different sounds to reduce the need for tape replacement. This left me speechless. Judging from the size of the booth, the organization behind this instrument could not have been very large, and the energy that must have gone into designing and perfecting it exceeded anything I could imagine at the time. This instrument was called the Chamberlin after its inventor, Harry Chamberlin. Production of this instrument subsequently moved to the UK, where it re-emerged with a new name, the Mellotron. Sixteen years later, I would learn that the former president and sales manager at our joint company Roland UK, founded in 1981, had been the factory manager and production manager at Mellotron.

The booth next door down exhibited pipe organ components ranging from organ pedalboards to cabinets, none of which you could find anywhere in Japan. I was surprised at the sheer size of the market where you could specialize to this

▼ Our first keyboard instrument, the Canary S-2.

degree and still make a profit. These were all parts that I had wanted to acquire. I asked the person there if I could visit their factory, to which he pleasantly agreed. The company was Klann Inc. in Waynesboro, Virginia. He told me that the easiest way to get there was via Washington, D.C., and the piece of paper he handed me had "Chicago > Washington, D.C. > Staunton (Piedmont Airlines)" written on it and nothing else. This wasn't enough for me as this was my first visit to the United States. This was when I realized that Takashige Tsukishima, a classmate of mine from the technical high school, was on assignment from Nagoya University to the National Bureau of Standards in Washington, D.C.! I decided to ask for his help without actually getting his consent, and asked him to accompany me to New York. Come to think of it, I have yet to pay him for his interpretation services.

I was very interested in all the other booths as well, but I couldn't leave my booth without anyone looking after it, so I decided to lock my door after 3 p.m. and spend the rest of the day touring other booths. All the companies had very good demonstrators working for them. It was impossible to just glance through the entire show, but I was familiar with all of the songs that were being played in the demos. While Japan was behind the United States in terms of electronic musical instruments, there was no time lag in musical trends. Then, too, I think the primary target for keyboards in the United States at the time was buyers in their forties and older. The average age of organ users in the United States is quite high currently as well.

Also on exhibit was a theremin, an instrument that was always mentioned in historical discussions of electronic musical instruments but that I had seen only in photos. At the eighth Soviet Electrical Conference in 1920, Léon Theremin stood in front of a box fitted with two antennas and made gestures resembling those of a conductor, playing a melody by moving his hands closer or farther away from the antennas. He was able to demonstrate this electronic musical instrument that he had developed because he was a cellist. This theremin on exhibit here at the NAMM Show was not simply a reference exhibit but was actually for sale. If memory serves me, it was being demonstrated by Dr. Robert Moog, before he developed his famous modular synthesizer. While we did not know each other then, our relationship began after we had dinner together at the Frankfurt Messe in 1970, and I later had the chance to visit him at his factory in Buffalo as well as at his home in North Carolina. In February 2000, I was honored to be included in the Hollywood RockWalk—which celebrates musicians who have made major contributions to the development of jazz and rock music, and pioneers in the development of musical instruments—where my handprint tile was placed next to Dr. Moog's.

I was not able to view organs in detail as the booths of organ manufacturers had an atmosphere about them that made me feel too uncomfortable to enter. I was particularly impressed with the many exhibits of accordions. The major importers' booths were filled with them. Most were Italian-made, buyer-branded products and while I could also find accordions made in France and Germany, I could not find any made in the United States. Looking back now, I realize I saw only a small portion of the show, but

▲ The Canary S-2 was an all-in-one design and was easily portable.

my first NAMM Show experience ended before I knew it while I was still reeling from the confusion of being hurled into a completely different world from the one I knew.

Invader

The NAMM Show got larger year after year, and its venue was relocated from the hotel to a dedicated exhibit hall called McCormick Place. Each morning, we would receive a booklet titled "Upbeat Daily" at our hotel rooms. This booklet was essentially a free trade magazine that featured information on new products as well as scheduled events and demos. This booklet is still being published today. During the 1967 show, a friend let me know that I was featured in the second day's "Upbeat Daily." I ran up to my room to read a copy and was surprised at the first word that jumped out at me: "Invader." The thought "Why?" crossed my mind for an instant. There had been a time when piano exports from Japan were a big issue in the United States, and I wondered if electronic musical instruments were being targeted now.

At the time the yen-dollar exchange rate was about ¥270 to the dollar, so products made in Japan were much cheaper than they are today, and at one point in late 1978, the exchange rate would go below ¥180. However, because the exchange rate had been ¥360 to a dollar in 1972 when we started up the company, I didn't think that we would be criticized at the then current level of

¥270. This was a time when arcades in Japan were overflowing with games such as Pong and Breakout, which were now giving way to the immensely popular Space Invaders. This game was already available in the United States, and it wouldn't be strange if its name had become a fad. But upon reading more carefully, I saw that the word on the page was actually not "Invader" but "Innovator." This article depicted us in a very favorable light, so I was relieved as much as I was embarrassed at having misunderstood the message, even for an instant.

In the United States, the first thing that comes to people's minds when they assess a product is whether or not it is usable as a musical instrument. Issues of price or technical drawbacks come later. With this in mind, everything hinges on selecting the best demonstrator to show how easy and usable the product is. Product reviews by music journalists can be a concern, because at times they feature comparisons of products in totally different price ranges. But we must take this in stride as well because at least they are talking about musical instruments. Particularly in the field of electronic musical instruments, the question of price range can lose its meaning as prices have come down dramatically owing to advancements in semiconductors.

I have demoed products myself on two occasions in the past. The first time was in 1973, when we launched SH-1000, the first synthesizer made in Japan. Mr. Murai, president of Naniwa Musical Instruments, which was one of our dealers at the time, invited close to one hundred sales reps from different retailers to a ryokan—a Japanese hotel—in Takarazuka in the northern part of Osaka. We had been making final adjustments to the product right up to its launch so we had no time to train or brief a demo player, and therefore there was no way to demo the product other than to do it myself. SH-1000 was monophonic and delivered ten tones. In addition to that, you could create your own tone by adding sawtooth or pulse waves. I memorized two bars' worth of melodies that were suited for each tone and managed to survive the demo. I learned to my surprise that all the demos were being recorded. I would love to hear this again, but for better or worse, we have not been able to find the tape.

I did my second demo in 1975 at the first trade show in Australia, held in Sydney, when we had the opportunity to introduce Revo. This was a dedicated speaker system consisting of electronic circuitry that could add a revolving sound space to organ tones. We needed an organ to do the demo, and to give the audience a feel of a revolving sound space I needed to vary my speed as I played. To do that, I had to play a passage at least six bars long, and show them how I could control the speed with a switch while playing. I got away with playing only "Yesterday" for all demos for three days. Of the three songs in my repertoire, this was the only song that Australian audiences would know. The product did not sell very well, perhaps due to the quality of my demo, but I believe to this day that the demo was indeed a success as this became the starting point for us to establish our first joint company, Roland Australia. Those were the good old days. While it is difficult to become a good demonstrator, I would like to remain an "innovator" for as long as I can.

Hollywood Bowl

During my first NAMM Show, I felt quite stressed and nervous, and I also had very little time, so I spent most of it in my booth, never having a chance to go out to see the city, its museums, or even Old Town. But every night, various manufacturers sponsored great entertainment featuring wonderful artists at the hotel's lobby bar. These events were also a fun-filled opportunity for manufacturers to demo their products. Such being the case, I was soon on my way to Waynesboro via Washington, D.C., and then on to New York and eventually Los Angeles, without having seen almost anything of Chicago. On our approach to New York, I remember that the pilot was kind enough to fly over Manhattan to give us a view of the amazing skyscrapers as we made our approach to LaGuardia Airport. In New York, I stayed in a hotel that was not even a block away from a street lined with many music shops, but I never had an inkling of this during my stay. At the time, I had no friends who might have tipped me off.

▼ Hollywood Bowl.

By the time I reached Los Angeles, I had familiarized myself with the way things were done in this country and checking in at the hotel was less of a challenge. I was also starting to learn that the best shortcut to learning about a place was to walk around the town alone. At the time, the Japanese government allowed travelers to carry no more than $500 per trip so a big issue was how I was going to make it back to Japan with the little cash I had left. I remembered the advice I received from an older acquaintance that while first-class hotels were better, one could still stay in comfort and enjoy the nice atmosphere by staying in their cheapest rooms. So I booked a room at the Biltmore Hotel in Los Angeles. The cheapest room they had was for sixteen dollars, but even at that price, it would have been difficult for me to stay for two nights.

The cheaper the better, even if just by a dollar or two, considering the fact that I still had to stay for one night in Honolulu. So I haggled with the hotel clerk and managed to book a twelve-dollar room. What I found out about these price negotiations was that it wasn't much trouble to haggle for a lower price if I spoke English in the Osaka style. By that I mean the structure of the conversation rather than anything to do with the accent. I realized that blunt Osaka-style conversation was effective even in English. In any case, the only day that I had free time before my trip home was the next day. I went through newspaper ads to find an interesting destination, and I luckily found an ad for a concert featuring Duke Ellington, Oscar Peterson, and Ella Fitzgerald, so I decided to go. As it would have been impossible to see a concert in Japan with such a lineup of artists, this drove home that I was actually in America. So the next day I took several buses and arrived at the Hollywood Bowl while it was still light. Just as the name suggested, this was a very large outdoor theater situated in a valley, which was typical of California where the weather was good most of the time. I had not purchased my ticket yet so I started by choosing my seat. There were so many seats and the range of prices was also very wide. The highest price I could afford was four dollars, equivalent to the money I had saved at the hotel. The inside of the venue was amazing. My four-dollar seat was almost at the very back, and I could not see the faces of the performers onstage as they were too far away. Still, I enjoyed the music very much.

Given the distance, there must have been a lag in the time it took for the sound to reach my seat, but perhaps owing to the good PA, I did not perceive a gap between the sound and the musicians' performance. There was no way I was going to get a true feel for their live performance at this distance, but I remember feeling quite satisfied that I was able to hear them perform in the home of jazz.

To commemorate my visit, I purchased a nicely produced program of the concert. Twenty years later, when Oscar Peterson came to perform in Japan, I invited him on a tour of our Hamamatsu factory, after which I invited him to my home. That was when I asked him to autograph this brochure. I felt as if, finally, after twenty years, I had been able to move up from the very back of the audience to backstage. I had a very good time listening to his stories of Duke Ellington and Ella Fitzgerald in those days. Later, on October 28, 1999, Oscar Peterson visited Japan again to receive the music award at the eleventh Praemium Imperiale. The ceremony was held at the Meiji Memorial Hall in Tokyo and followed by a reception.

▲ This is the program from the Hollywood Bowl concert.
▼ Its cover is shown in the photo below. Oscar Peterson was kind enough to autograph it twenty years later.

Those who received awards that year were:

- Music: Oscar Peterson

- Painting: Anselm Kiefer

- Sculpture: Louise Bourgeois

- Architecture: Fumihiko Maki

- Theater/film: Pina Bausch

These were all individuals who had made great accomplishments in their fields. I was also invited to the ceremony as a friend of Oscar Peterson. Oscar played the piano at the reception as a representative of the awardees. The reception was a great success and his performance received a huge round of applause from all who were present, including many Japanese individuals in the music business. I stayed at the same hotel as Oscar the day before the ceremony and had a great conversation with him. I would have liked to be able to spend more time with him, however, as quite a bit of his time was taken up giving interviews to music magazines.

Shows Are a Source of Information

For someone who makes musical instruments, trade shows are a must-see. Although a box full of business cards and a charming attendant explaining products are common fixtures in booths at Japanese trade shows, the NAMM Show, where merchants used to exhibit their wares in hotel rooms, was a place where you could speak directly with company executives and actually do business. The booths at the NAMM Show have grown much bigger, and the emphasis now is more on "show" than on "trade." While this was inevitable as the musical instrument industry has grown much larger, I still look back fondly on the good old days. Ever since taking part in the NAMM Show in 1964, I have been at all shows including the Frankfurt Messe for about fifty years now. I believe I have managed this by making these shows my priority when I booked my other dates and by making sure that I was in top shape, although there have been times when I was not feeling very well or had to book other business dates.

These shows introduced us to new products from our competitors and information on other companies, but importantly, there was a certain atmosphere at these shows. And then there were the people. In the early years, we would usually arrive at the venue about two days before the show to set up our booth and exhibits and perform soundchecks. Once we were done for the day and returned to our hotel, we would have the chance to meet several of our acquaintances or friends. There were many people of my generation in the electronic musical instrument business, and partly because it was a relatively small industry, I was friends with most of the people from our competition, so I very much looked forward to these encounters. We would actively exchange information, as well as what we knew of new trends in technology. I think these kinds of exchanges were more difficult to have between Japanese companies. I was able to have very open discussions particularly with people working on the technological side of things. This was made possible by the convivial atmosphere at NAMM.

These shows are also a place where companies actively recruit new talent. Even if we knew a certain person, particularly if the person was in sales, we would have to check the name of the company on his or her name tag each time we met. This was because of the frequency with which people moved between different companies. In any case, in the United States you get none of the somber feeling around switching jobs that you get in Japan. Everything is open and up front. I could see very well how these practices helped vitalize the dynamism of the industry. In Japan, scouting someone directly from a competitor is essentially unheard of. Even now, former employees wait for a period of a few years before they transfer to a competitor in the same business. Roland employees come from a variety of manufacturers including Lowrey, Technics, JVC, Yamaha, and Kawai, so our roster of employees is quite diverse. Someday, we may see the same mobility of employees in Japan that we see in the United States.

The darlings of the market shift every five years or so, but none really go away. What I saw at the NAMM Show in 1964, which was the first NAMM Show for me, was that while organs were nearing their peak, accordions were still selling well. One unfortunate development in recent years has been that the number of piano manufacturers in the United States has fallen, as it has in Japan. One can see this same trend at the Frankfurt Messe as well. At these shows, traditional musical instruments such as pianos, stringed instruments, wind instruments, and percussive instruments are on exhibit in the same venue where companies set up booths selling software products on a single CD-ROM. With companies that sell lighting, DJ, and audio equipment added to the mix in recent years, the scale of these shows has also grown much larger. I think these are trends unique to the musical instrument industry. In this sense again, musical instrument trade shows continue to expand in a myriad of ways.

The NAMM Show has undergone many changes in response to the times, and has become the largest musical instrument trade show in the world. It would be very interesting to study how the NAMM Show has influenced and indeed provided fertile ground for electronic musical instruments over the past fifty or so years.

We have come a long way since the 1964 NAMM Show. On the retail side of things, we now have online sales, big box retailers, and specialty stores. The users have also changed dramatically, so we are a world apart from then. Currently, the musical instrument industry is struggling to survive in a landscape dominated by the telecommunications and home appliances industries. It is precisely for this reason that I believe that we should re-examine how we manufacture musical instruments by reflecting on the intrinsic nature of music. This is because, when we envision music's bright future, here again, we find ourselves in a new age where it is meaningless to look for samples.

7

The Birth of Electronic Musical Instruments

The Nascent Years of Electronic Musical Instruments in Japan

IN ANY FIELD OF ENDEAVOR, IT IS OFTEN THE CASE THAT GROUPS OF amateurs play pioneering roles. The area of electronic musical instruments was no exception, although things did not go beyond the level of a hobby as there were so few of us and we did not communicate. Around 1955, the only reference materials we had access to were monthly American magazines such as *Audio* and *Electronics*, which I would go to study at the Nakanoshima Chamber of Commerce Library. As for books, even if we placed an order for them immediately after finding out that they were in print, it would take at least five months until we received our order. I have never felt more thankful for technical literature than when I first laid my hands on books such as *The Electronic Musical Instrument Manual* and *The Electrical Production of Music*, both by Alan Douglas.

I did not know that *Electronic Musical Instruments* by Richard Dorf had been in print in the United States since 1954, and it was only after 1962 that I was able to acquire a copy. These three publications contained everything that I wanted to know at the time. While this brought an end to my groping in the dark, I was all but overwhelmed by the gap between the United States and Japan, so development at the time had to start with copying.

In those days, if I heard there was a pipe organ or electronic organ being used, I would go out to wherever that might be to study it. Two American-made Minshall organs had already been imported to Tokyo, so I visited a private residence in Omori, Tokyo, to study this organ. What I saw was an array of 12AX7 vacuum tubes, which I was familiar with from audio amplifiers and TVs.

When I first opened the cabinet, I thought that it was the same as the Organo organs I had had the opportunity to repair earlier, but upon closer inspection, I found that the organ covered all of its tones with only thirty-six 12AX7s, which was twenty-four fewer than what the Organo used. The circuit design of this organ was revolutionary. Later, I had the opportunity to repair a Minshall organ at the Seiko Gakuin in Tennoji, Osaka, and I concluded at the time that the Organo was a more stable organ. JVC also marketed a spinet organ, EO-4420, and I think this product was also heavily influenced by the Minshall and Organo. I was truly surprised by Minshall's novel circuitry design, which produced two tones an octave apart using only a small number of parts and a single triode tube.

A magazine called *Musen to Jikken* (*Radio and Experimentation*) focused on audio and radio at the time, but they gradually began to carry articles on electronic musical instruments. In the October 1959 issue, Takashi Izumi (a pen-name for Haruo Noriyasu) contributed an article titled "Making the Electrin, an Electric Violin," and the centerfold of the November issue featured the Pianet, a new instrument that was a rival of the Elepian, an electronic piano made by Nippon Columbia. The fifth installment of the magazine's Amateur Electronic Musical Instrument Seminar in its November 1960 issue included an article on electronic instruments titled "Visit and Play, Visit and See." Years later, I called Mr. Izumi, the author of the article, to see if he had a back issue as I had lost mine, but he unfortunately did not have one either. We had a great laugh as he replied, "I was only looking to the future at the time." I myself wrote a series called "Electronic Musical Instruments for Beginners" for seven consecutive issues starting with the February 1965 issue. Mr. Izumi, whom I got to know through Mr. Kataoka, the editor in chief of *Musen to Jikken*, was a regular contributor and eventually we worked together. Ichiro Kuroda, the maker of the Kurodatone, was another fellow organ enthusiast from those times. He was already working to commercialize a classic-style organ that employed the method developed by Wurlitzer of America, which involved using a reed as the sound generator.

The patent system of Japan at the time was irrational in that even if a particular electronic technology was already public knowledge in other countries, no one could dispute a patent filed in Japan unless they had documentation to prove their case. This meant that an importer of a new product could file for and be granted a patent. Even if the technology was known in other fields, if you filed your patent in the area of musical instruments, it would be granted. Although the current system will not accept such applications, the situation then created an uneasy sense of frustration among those involved in the research of electronic musical instruments. While patents were being filed for entire circuits and mechanisms of American-made organs, there was nothing we could do as long as this was legal. These types of patent applications still exist in the European patent bulletins. These documents give a view of the history of how patents developed and are also a very good read and available for free as downloadable files from the European Patent Office.

While these practices went against our ethics as engineers, because it was legal, it became common practice to file these applications as a form of protection. It was obvious to everyone that companies that were able to import new products from overseas before anyone else would have the advantage. Similar issues occur in developing countries today where local companies acquire the rights to entire brands and patents. The amount of criticism and misunderstanding that this outdated patent system drew from other countries cannot be overstated. The only way for amateurs and smaller companies to counter the situation was to immediately publicly document all the technology that they were aware of.

In October 1961, a book called *Denshi Gakki to Denki Gakki* (*Electronic and Electric Musical Instruments*) was published as a supplementary volume to the October issue of *Musen to Jikken*. So after, we agreed to publish an overview of the state of affairs up to that point, and *Denshi Gakki to Denki Gakki no Subete* (*Everything about Electronic and Electric Musical Instruments*) was published as a supplementary volume to *Musen to Jikken* and *Shoho no Radio* (*Radio for Beginners*) magazines, the primary contributors being Takashi Izumi, Kiyoshi Hama, and myself. These two publications became the first reference books for electronic musical instruments in Japan. When we look at the development of electronic musical instruments, the contribution made by these publications was significant. Six of the seventeen contributing authors would later join me at Roland.

We visited six subscribers who had contributed articles on their prototyping efforts, and saw how each of them had made impressive electronic organs. I remember being surprised at how a number of them would play the organ themselves to demo it for us. Susumu Shirashoji, one of these contributors, would later help me out with semiconductors. I am very happy to say that we are still good friends.

At the time, few people in Osaka were involved in electronic musical instruments, so I very much looked forward to my information-gathering trips to Tokyo. I would have heated discussions on rhythm instruments into the wee hours of the night with Tsutomu Katoh, who was then president of Keio Electronic Laboratories (presently Korg). And each time we met, he would remind me how he had a hard time hanging out with me because I did not drink.

Even fifty years later, I'm still connected, in interesting ways, with many of the people I've met through my involvement with electronic musical instruments.

It would take the field of electronic musical instruments in Japan over ten years to grow from its amateur prototyping stage to the point where it began to take form as a legitimate area of research, and we were able to hold an electronic musical instrument concert as part of the Audio Fair in 1965.

America, the Motherland of Electronic Musical Instruments

The foundations of modern music are based on the improvements made over many years on pianos, violins, wind instruments, pipe organs, and other instruments that originated in Europe. However, the passion of composers who were not satisfied with existing music prompted them to set their sights on novel raw materials—that is, electronics. You could even say their approach was philosophical. Early electronic musical instruments that used sound generators consisting of vacuum tube oscillators were all being developed in Europe, so Europe was a step ahead in this area as well. Judging from the fact that mechanical metronomes, which were invented when Beethoven was alive, were heavily criticized at the time, one can imagine that the misunderstanding of and resistance to novel musical instruments whose only visible source of sound was a vacuum tube must have also been quite intense. In particular, it must have been the rare performer who leaped at the opportunity to play a novel instrument that in some cases nullified all previous practice that performers had accumulated and sometimes required them to learn completely new performing skills. The composers who were searching for different ways to expand the potential of music and the philosophers who provided them with ideological support were vastly outnumbered by those with a distrust for technology who could not accept the new sounds. They were also subjected to criticism by musical purists, so it was still essentially impossible for electronic musical instruments, which had just come on the scene, to compete against pianos and orchestras, which had reached their pinnacles of perfection. The ondes martenot, one of the instruments developed in those days, is still in existence, but it did not become mainstream primarily because it was monophonic and technically difficult to maintain. However, in France, where the instrument was developed, the Conservatoire de Paris opened a class that taught ondes martenot in 1947. It was also used at prominent venues including the Paris Opera, the Comédie-Française, and the Opéra-Comique.

If we were to associate, by way of impression, each European country with a single musical instrument, it might go something like this: violins from Italy, pianos from Germany, bagpipes from the UK, guitars from Spain, and the ondes martenot from France. The ondes martenot is more strongly associated with France than the accordion used in French chanson.

Although the United States lagged behind Europe in the area of producing acoustic instruments, it had organs, so it began the production of pipe organs, which came into use at churches as well as in the area of entertainment—a characteristically American course of development. This led to research on electrical technologies for organs for home use, which made it possible for people to purchase organs for their homes as the technology became stable and cost effective, leading to affordable pricing. Thus, a breed of electrical organs derived from watchmaking technology, the Hammond organ, grew as an industry in the United States.

Thomas Edison, who attained great success after founding the Edison Speaking Phonograph Company in 1878, did not think much of radios that emerged in the mid-1910s and took no steps to develop them. Then in 1919, the Radio Corporation of America (RCA) was founded, a company that set its sights on making the radio a practical home product like the piano and phonograph. Working on phonographs, the polar opposite of pianos, Edison focused on faithfully reproducing live performances.

Boosted by dance music, which gained popularity in the 1920s, phonographs increasingly began to come with built-in electrical amplifiers. The transition of sound amplification methods on phonographs, from bell-shaped horns to combinations of vacuum tube amplifiers and speakers, naturally accelerated the development of electrical methods for amplifying sound. This formed the basis on which electronic musical instruments could be developed. It was the United States, which led the way in forming businesses around radios and electrical phonographs, that also paved the way for the industrial success of electronic musical instruments. Even Edison missed this wave of change.

In addition to radios, electric guitars were another development that spurred the evolution of electronic musical instruments. Electronic instruments cannot exist without amplifiers and speakers, which are the outlets of their sound. In this respect, the role that electric guitars played, in that they required amplifiers, was extremely important. Since they produced only small sound volumes compared to wind instruments, percussion instruments, and pianos, amplifiers became a must-have item. While acoustic guitars had a sound box that amplified the vibrations of their strings, the emergence of amplifiers enabled solid bodyguitars that had no sound box. These dry tones produced without resonance opened up new possibilities for guitars.

Leo Fender was one of the pioneers of electric guitars, and I had the chance to meet him just after he retired from Fender and started up Music Man. Based on what I knew of his history at Fender, I had imagined a person who was burning with excitement about his new company, and remember being pleasantly surprised to meet a warm, unpretentious, and cheerful engineer.

While we refer to instruments that electrically capture and amplify the vibration of strings and reeds as *electrical* musical instruments, and distinguish these from *electronic* musical instruments, when we look back at the innovation during the time we started to use vacuum tubes, which were essentially electron tubes, there seems to be little meaning to this distinction. Guitar amplifiers, with their limited range of reproduction and speakers that produced peculiar tones, later evolved into instrument amplifiers that intentionally exploited these peculiarities, which had become defining characteristics. The Leslie speaker also became a way for keyboard instruments to produce vibrant tones.

The first time I took part in the NAMM Show in 1964, when Japan was abuzz with the excitement of the Tokyo Olympics, coincided with the beginning of the growth phase of the electronic musical instrument industry. Vacuum tubes were still the main element in amplifiers and sound generators. I was blessed with many chances that allowed me to catch opportunities that came my way. While I still cringe in regret at the opportunities that I passed over, there were some that I did well to avoid. One could say that by giving birth to the electronic organ and solid-body guitar, the United States established itself as the motherland of electronic musical instruments.

Hammond Organ

I believe the most important contribution to the world of electronic musical instruments in the twentieth century was the Hammond Organ developed

Here we are showing our guitar synth ▶ GR-500 to Mike Rutherford, original member and guitarist of Genesis.

by Laurens Hammond. Indeed, it was a truly great invention, the first product that proved that electronic organs could be made for the home market. The other pillar of the organ industry was Lowrey Organ, started up by Frederick Lowrey. These Lowrey organs fell into the sound category typically referred to as "bright wave." Hammond organs belonged to the group that added sine waves to the sound. Companies that made organs in the sine wave category included Hammond, Conn, and Gulbransen, among others. Lowrey, Wurlitzer, Baldwin, and Kimball were some of the prominent names that made organs that produced the bright wave category of sounds. Japanese organs also belonged to the latter group, although the Ace Tone GT-7, launched in 1970, belonged in the sine wave category. I designed the sound-generating circuitry on this organ, which was able to produce a stable sine wave.

In Japan, Hammond organs are very well-known while other American organ manufacturers are hardly known at all, and there is a reason for this. In 1967, Ace Electronic Industries, the company I was running, launched an exclusive agent for importing Hammond products, replacing their previous agent, the Omi Brotherhood Ltd., which otherwise mainly sold Mentholatum skin care products. What we noticed at that point was that there were problems with the materials used in the electrical contacts of many keyboards as well as with the types of contacts used.

Owing to the climate and atmosphere in the United States—perhaps the air in America contained less sulfurous acid or humidity, or perhaps their climate was not as hot and humid—sulfurization and oxidization of these contacts rarely became a problem there. Meanwhile, these issues were quite serious in Japan, and most contacts suffered contact failures unless they were made of precious metals such as platinum, gold, or palladium. Electrical contacts were often made of alloys of silver, and these types of contacts were nearly useless in organs. (At the time, Hammond fortunately used precious metals in their contacts and this resulted in fewer failures.) As a result, although a broad range of American organs were imported to Japan, most of them would fail due to contact failures caused by contact oxidization, and this hurt their reputations. The concerns voiced by Japanese importers must have been incomprehensible to the American manufacturers as these problems almost never occurred in the United States.

In May 1979, a national musical instruments conference was held at Tsumagoi in Shizuoka, and the guests included Bob Campbell, then of CBS Musical Instruments, John McLaren, then of the Yamaha Corporation of America, and several others. On one occasion during this conference, I explained to our guests why organs other than Hammond organs were not taking root in Japan, and I believe this helped to dispel quite a bit of bias toward Japan. While I get cold sweats just to think of my English conversational abilities at the time, I think my effort was well taken. One of the reasons that Japanese organ exports were earning a good reputation was the reliability of their contacts.

Hammond was the leader in the electronic organ market in the United States, partly because they had entered the market early, but the share of bright wave organs grew rapidly and eventually exceeded Hammond in sales. While it is theoretically true that one could synthesize any tone using sine waves, it was practically impossible to create musical notes with more than ten harmonics using tone wheels. Bright wave organs used sawtooth and asymmetrical pulse waves, each of which contained tens of harmonics, and were able to produce sounds that were far superior to what sine wave organs could produce, particularly in the area of orchestral sounds such as strings and reed instruments. However, these organs were not able to garner a huge following for certain types of music, and only managed to survive in the home market and as alternatives to pipe organs. Ultimately, they became the primary players by finding their main market in the area of home organs, and Hammond also eventually began selling bright wave organs with their Everett series.

Meanwhile, Hammond had established itself as an important instrument in jazz, rhythm and blues, and gospel, thanks to its distinctive sound. The combination of the Hammond B-3 organ and Leslie speaker in particular was unrivaled. However, the fact that their organs were not able to produce bright waves was a source of great frustration at Hammond, and the organ's inability to produce decaying sounds such as those produced

▲ Tone wheel generators in a Hammond organ.

by pianos and guitars was considered to be a major drawback as well. The only way to overcome this issue was to take the electronic route, so Hammond developers began their efforts to transition from the tone wheel to electronics.

At the time, we were running a joint company with Hammond called Hammond International Japan, so I was deeply involved in this process. A peculiarity of Japan is that the Kanto area in the east operates on a fifty-cycle current whereas the Kansai area in the west runs on a sixty-cycle current, so with tone wheel organs, we had to carry inventories of two variations of each model, and you could not transport these organs out of Kanto and expect to use them in Kansai. The fact that you could not take your organ to a sixty-cycle region was a huge handicap.

This being the case, I had to develop a tone wheel sound based on electronics. What we developed to fulfill this need was a full electronic sine wave generator. This unit was not accepted by Hammond headquarters in Chicago, where they were exploring metal-oxide semiconductor integrated circuit (MOS IC) technology, which they eventually incorporated into their new model, the Concorde.

Instead, we ended up using the rejected sine wave generator in our Ace Tone GT-7, which became a huge hit as its low price and portability suited the trends of the time. Meanwhile, Hammond's Concorde was plagued with IC failures because its circuitry to protect against static sparks was not complete, and the company's efforts to make a major change in their design ultimately ended in failure. Consequently, visions for loading these tone wheel sounds on ICs had to be put on hold until the arrival of large-scale integration (LSI).

Years before we started up Ace Electronic Industries, I had the opportunity to purchase nine used Hammond organs put on sale by the American occupying forces who had been using these organs in their chapels on base. I gathered all the usable parts and put together three refurbished organs. These were all sixty-cycle models so this suited me well as I lived in Osaka.

The Three Suns toured Japan in 1959, performing their hit songs on a trio of instruments consisting of Hammond organ, accordion, and guitar. While it was no problem to rent a Hammond organ in Tokyo, you could not transport it to Kansai because of the frequency issue. So I ended up renting out the Hammond organ that I had and touring with the band to Tokushima on Shikoku Island. The guitarist of the band was Del Casher, and I was amazed at his ingenious use of his tape echo

▲ GT-7 combo organ by Ace Tone.

machine. The opening act at their Tokushima concert was the Mahina Stars. In 1977, Del Casher demoed our guitar synthesizer at its announcement event. We would not have met were it not for the peculiarity that Kansai runs on a sixty-cycle current.

Pipe Organs and Electronic Organs

Organs were a type of instrument into which new technologies could be incorporated relatively easily, and which tolerated the incorporation of these technologies. The history of the use of technology to improve organs—even before the emergence of electrical and electronic technologies—is quite remarkable. Furthermore, as organs, which originally developed in churches, were increasingly finding their way into concert halls as independent musical instruments, there came a need for new applications and technologies. In a church, the best conditions for an organ are essentially the worst conditions for a priest to make his sermon. In other words, there would be too much reverberation, which would reduce the clarity of the spoken word and make it very difficult to listen to. While these conflicting conditions have now been resolved for the most part thanks to the development of acoustic technologies, there still are many cases where a compromise is reached at levels of reverberation that are short of ideal for organs.

I believe the changes in the size of churches and the materials used to build them have added to the problem. While organ construction and development have proceeded with no direct correlation with the changes in church architecture, in the case of pipe organs, where the building itself is part of the musical instrument, there is no way of correcting the situation if there is not enough reverberation in the building. Electronic organs are able to handle these situations with more flexibility, and they often provide the most effective means, taking into account the overall balance. That is to say, the intrinsic characteristic of electronic organs, that their sounds are produced through a speaker and not through pipes, can be a big positive in these situations. Although various attempts have been made to create tones that mimic those heard in cathedrals with the use of spring reverb units and echo chambers that give the sound pleasant reverberation, the issue here is not only reverberation time. Methods are being developed whereby multiple speakers are arranged in a distributed fashion so that the volume of sounds from these speakers can be balanced to produce natural sound, and at the same time improve the clarity of the priest's sermon.

In any case, however, whether it be electronic or pipe organs, nothing comes close to the sound of an organ in a cathedral constructed of stone. I've listened to many pipe organs over the years, but there were few that were truly moving in an acoustical sense. Sometimes I would be disappointed to see the offhand way in which organs were positioned in place. However, since there are three elements that can dramatically alter the appeal of an organ—the hall, the organist, and the audience—it would not be reasonable to level criticism against any particular arrangement based on just one of these aspects. You certainly could not judge an organ by the number of pipes it had or the size of the hall.

In the case of electronic organs, because they are almost always installed in existing halls, there are limitations to where the speakers can be placed. Sounds coming from a limited number of speakers that are tasked to cover an organ's entire range are no competition against sounds that come from pipes arranged in a planar layout. That said, we are coming into an age where this shortcoming of electronic organs—that their sounds are produced by speakers—is actually becoming a positive attribute. We are now able to experiment with new acoustic characteristics that are not constrained by the acoustics and sound space of halls, which are an indispensable element of pipe organs.

An aspect that is completely left out of the picture when comparing electronic organs and pipe organs is the total cost of building them. It is highly problematic to compare pipe organs on the same playing field as electronic organs, whose developers strive to achieve the best results at costs ranging from one-tenth to as low as one-thirtieth of that of pipe organs. Needless to say, however, those who listen to and appreciate these organs should judge their sounds

◀ The organ hall at Alan Kay's home. Pictured here from left to right are Alan, Don Lewis, and myself. We later had the opportunity to perform experiments on RSS's 3-D sound-processing system with this organ.

based solely on the music created on them, and cost should not be a concern. With this in mind, I believe it is necessary to invest in the amplifier and speakers—the outlets of the sound—and the 3-D sound-processing system as much as one invests in the sound-producing components of electronic organs and their console, which encloses large portions of the system. This is because speakers are to electronic organs what pipes are to pipe organs. The latest technologies have reached a point where, with an investment of 10 to 15 percent of the total cost of the organ in these components, sound spaces can be created that are difficult to imagine as coming from the same organ.

In 2000, we set up an electronic organ with a 3-D sound-processing system in a concert hall where there was already an installed pipe organ to conduct a comparative experiment. The electronic organ did not pale one bit compared to the pipe organ. What was more, we found aspects where the electronic organ was more advantageous in that the performer could change the reverberation characteristics to suit his or her tastes. These comparisons are only possible when done side by side in concert halls with preinstalled pipe organs, and it is a time-consuming process to set up an opportunity for organists to experience such comparisons. Regardless, my belief is that our development and production should focus on how much an organ and its sound are able to move the audience's heart, without making any excuses based on cost or conditions. Instead of expecting quick results from our assessments, we need to accumulate numerous real examples for all different situations.

The history of electronic musical instruments has also been the history of cost reductions. One of the most important characteristics of Hammond organs, which are made with the same technologies used for making electrical watches, is that their sound is pleasant to hear, as their tones are made from combinations of different sine waves, and the other is that the proportional relationship between the different tones that make up a harmony is always guaranteed. It was not possible to create stable and low-cost sound-generating oscillators from vacuum tubes in the 1940s and '50s. It was thanks to the invention of their low-cost tone wheel method, which used different combinations of gears to cover the entire sound range, that Hammond organs were able to maintain their top market position for thirty years. However, because it was not able to produce harmonics in the way that pipe organs were able to, and because the cost of its sound generators—which consisted of complex gear mechanisms—could not be reduced, Hammond eventually conceded its top position to organs that used sound generators based on electronic oscillation.

The history of improvements made to sound generators is the history of electronic organs. The electronic organ started out as an instrument designed for home use, and misconceptions created in its early years when it was compared with pipe organs still linger on to this day. This vision of reducing the cost of these organs and marketing them to the general household was shared by Laurens Hammond and Frederick Lowrey as well as all executives and engineers at electronic organ manufacturers. My goal also is to create wonderful instruments that would be available to as many people as possible. Thanks to developments made in the area of circuitry elements and basic components, which have taken us from vacuum tubes to transistors, ICs, and LSIs, we have been able to simplify our circuitry, reduce failure rates, and dramatically expand our latitude for design. It is important that we leverage this latitude as much as possible in the performance of these electronic musical instruments.

In this respect, things are vastly different for makers of pipe organs who never have to think of how they might increase their popularity among the general consuming public. Since pipe organs are custom-made in configurations that meet the budget requirements of the customer, cost is not as much a concern as it is with electronic musical instruments. The goals that makers of electronic organs have set for themselves are to reduce cost and provide aspects of performance that could not be achieved by pipe organs, goals which have made possible things that would have been unthinkable in the past.

Efforts to reduce cost began with making the sound-producing elements smaller and simpler, and then enabling waveforms with sufficient amounts of harmonics to reduce the number of elements used in the circuitry. In the midst of such developments, Hammond's tone wheel generators, which provided excellent performance in terms of reliability, could not compete in the area of cost, and were discontinued around 1972. This coincided with the time that we started up Roland. In 1971, the year that was to be my last with Ace and Hammond, we received a proposal from Hammond VP Lawrence Zinder that although there were plans within the company to discontinue the production of the Hammond B-3, the company was open to the possibility of relocating all facilities to Japan if we were willing to manufacture the organs there. The organs were highly regarded in Japan but they were not big sellers owing to their price, which meant that whatever opinions we had had little chance of being reflected. This proposal was based on the idea that the company might be able to continue production of this organ in Japan as labor costs were still competitive in Japan at the time.

So we decided to take a look at Hammond factories with this idea in mind. We carried out an extensive and detailed tour of the factory that assembled the tone generators, and the facilities used there to make the different parts. As a result, we concluded that production would not be possible even if we were to relocate these facilities to Japan. This was not a matter of labor cost. The primary reason was that the total production volume was very small, and the manufacturing process involved a large number of machines. Additionally, the level of machining precision required was at the level of making table clocks, which required the work of master mechanics. Potential unit sales projections were also vastly lower than the level required to sustain the production line, so we very reluctantly had to decline this proposal. It would be true to say that this memory was not totally unrelated to our subsequent decisions to manufacture the VK-9 and VK-6 combo organs equipped with draw bars that allowed users to add harmonics, as well as the VK-7, VK-77, VK-8, and VK-88.

At the time, Hammond was in the process of designing the Concorde, which was kept highly secret from all outsiders. This was a turning point where the company was transitioning from mechanical generators to ICs. At the time, when we were given a tour of the factory, Mr. Bergslin, who was the person in charge of technology, pointed to an indentation in the brick wall by the staircase and joked in a somewhat melancholic tone, "ICs are stronger than gangsters." Although I did not immediately understand what he was saying, he explained that the indentation in the wall was made during a shootout between rival gangs during the Al Capone years. Although I did eventually get the joke, I was not in the mood to laugh.

In some instances, we hear people say, somewhat regretfully, that what they really want is a pipe organ but they have had to settle for electronic as their budget would not allow it. As makers of organs, there is nothing we can say to such statements. If one is going to install an organ with the budget that remains after building a hall, anyone can understand that an electronic organ would be the best choice, and this would also be a sign of a well-balanced decision. Thanks to the development of sound space correction technologies, all the conditions are in place for enjoying excellent organ sounds.

However, pipe organ "supremacists" show no interest in how the organs are equipped with new features and are able to produce tones that rival those of pipe organs. These people may actually harden their resistance to electronics in response to such explanations. We understand that sound is the top priority for organists, and no compromise should be made. This applies to both pipe and electronic organs. I have no qualms against a beautiful instrument that is capable of producing organ music even if it does not have pipes. All I can do is work toward enabling as many people as possible to enjoy organ sounds.

The Second Round

People who worked on electronic musical instruments in Japan then were invariably influenced by what was happening in the United States. In the early days, when it felt like we had caught up and were running alongside our American counterparts, we would often realize that we were actually a whole lap behind. By the time we were close to catching up with the top group, the tide of electronic organs was beginning to recede and we had entered the age of synthesizers and combo organs. At Roland, we were able to compete with the top players in the area of rhythm instruments as we had focused our development on rhythm instruments since our Ace Electronic Industry years. In the area of electronic organs in the United States, Hammond and Lowrey were competing neck and neck in the market. Over the years I became deeply involved with both of these companies. My first relationship with a foreign company was with Hammond. A lot went on until 1972, when I left my position at Ace and Hammond International Japan to form Roland.

Ace formed a joint company with Hammond in 1968, and our negotiation counterpart at first was the Hammond Organ Company. However, the company spun off their overseas business and export operations to Hammond International, with the Hammond Organ Company remaining responsible for American manufacturing and sales. As a result, while the organs we sold in Japan were made by Hammond Organ Company, our contact was now Hammond International.

Final negotiations for forming this joint company took place at the Hilton Hawaiian Village over a period of three days. Kazuo Sakata, president of Sakata Shokai, and I spoke with the top management of Hammond, Don Hayes, the president, and Bob Olsen, the vice president. For the first two days, we discussed the price range and naming of organs sold overseas, and had hardly any discussions on the core topic of the agreement. The only topic that remained for the third day had to do with the conditions of forming the joint company. To my surprise, however, Mr. Sakata had to leave on urgent business on a 9 a.m. flight, and I was left alone for our 10:30 meeting with the Hammond executives. Mr. Sakata left saying, "I'm sure things will work out one way or another" in the Osaka dialect, to which I halfheartedly replied, also in the Osaka dialect, "Okay then, one way or another." However, my feeling was that leaving before we got into the crux of the meeting was, to use a military analogy, tantamount to desertion. Since I had relied on Mr. Sakata, who was fluent in English, my heart sank thinking about the agreements that had to be reached that day as I had little confidence in my English ability. That being the case, I set out for the third day of our meetings resolved that the only course of action I could take was to set my final conditions and not budge from there, in order to minimize the need to converse in English.

Ultimately, our talks boiled down to our capital ratio. I surmised that the first hurdle in these talks would be that Hammond was altogether in a different league from us as a company, and the second would be that the holding of equal shares would hinder us from reaching resolutions to disagreements. As for the first hurdle, their proposal was fairer than what we had in mind and the difference in company scale that we thought might be a concern ended up not being an issue. It was clear that they had fairly assessed our success with the rhythm unit. So we were able to clear these apparent hurdles surprisingly smoothly, and prepare a level playing field for our negotiations. What I realized here was that we both needed each other. The next issue was how we were going to convince Hammond's legal counsel. At this point I proposed that our 50 percent would consist of 30 percent from Sakata Shokai and 20 percent from Ace Electronic Industries, making the ratio 50/50 between the US and Japanese sides. I also added that they had nothing to worry about in the event of a disagreement, as I would side with the Americans to bring the ratio to 30/70. This for them settled the potential issue of not being able to resolve disagreements. I made these decisions without consulting Mr. Sakata, who had left for Japan, and in any case, we would have run out of time if I had waited to consult him. Having reached a conclusion much more smoothly than I had anticipated, I felt a wave of relief and tiredness. In conclusion, our capital ratio was set at 50/50.

▼ Shiro Murai, presently representative director, chairman, and CEO of SIIX Corporation.

While it was unfortunate that Mr. Sakata had to return to Japan, it was very fortunate for us that we were able to have Ace Electronic Industries as a shareholder. The success of this meeting would not have been possible were it not for the groundwork laid ahead of time by Shiro Murai, manager of overseas sales at Sakata Shokai.

The fact that we acquired the rights to sell Hammond organs in Japan from Omi Brotherhood of Mentholatum fame in 1967 to become the exclusive agent for Hammond in Japan is another point that we cannot overlook as having enabled me to take part in this meeting and ultimately form the joint company. Mr. Murai is currently the representative director, chairman and CEO of SIIX Corporation, a global provider of unique electronics manufacturing services (EMS).

At the time, there was still a large technological gap with foreign companies so there were very few examples of joint companies forming at an equal capital ratio. This idea of running our business as equal partners became one of our basic principles in forming joint companies. One time, Mr. Olsen, whom I have since gotten to know better, recalled this meeting, remarking that I had actually spoken quite a bit. I wasn't sure if he was complimenting me or not when he told me that I was the first Japanese he had met who could make jokes without knowing more than fifty English words.

As Hammond's overseas business began to grow, relations between the two Hammond companies became increasingly convoluted. While we did not have access to detailed information in Japan, an outrageous thing happened one time.

The Hammond Organ Company decided to launch the Hammond Cadette in the US market. This was a product made by Hammond International Japan (i.e., Ace Electronic's Hamamatsu factory) and was selling well overseas. We welcomed this decision wholeheartedly as we could increase our production volume and have our facilities run at full capacity. However, a decision was reached to order organs for the American market from, of all companies, Nippon Gakki Seizo (presently Yamaha). This decision, which defied belief from our perspective, was the result of infighting between the two Hammond companies. If this became widely known in Japan, Hammond as well as Ace Electronic Industries would be adversely affected. So I immediately decided to invite Mr. Hayes, the president of Hammond International, to Japan, and held a reception with participation from dealers and suppliers in Japan. Nippon Gakki Seizo also immediately invited David Kutner, president of Hammond Organ Company, and held a party for press representatives. To the press who were not aware of events that transpired in the United States, it would not make sense unless one of these presidents was bogus. The more we explained, the uglier the picture would appear, and this also diminished our image. Of course, both Hammond presidents were real.

Very soon after I left Ace Electronic Industries in 1972, I received a proposal from Hammond about forming a separate joint company aside from Hammond International Japan. I unfortunately declined this proposal because the proposed capital ratio was 60 percent held by Hammond and 40 percent by the Japanese company. This ratio not only had to do with the distribution of profits, but also represented a very clear relationship of control. So although I appreciated their effort in making this proposal, I could not accept it based on my experience with Hammond International Japan.

By declining this proposal, I was able to deepen my relationship with the people at Lowrey, with whom I'd had exchanges during my Hammond and Ace years, and my involvement with the company deepened even further when Bob Olsen, former VP at Hammond International, moved to Lowrey. Dennis Houlihan, who was doing amazing work in sales at Lowrey and also as a demonstrator, would later become president of Roland US.

On the technical side of things, we formed Roland R&D Chicago with Alberto Kniepkamp, who had been chief engineer at Lowrey, and launched an operation geared toward development.

I became familiar with the background of both organ companies through these events, but it is unfortunate that companies other than Hammond are not well known in Japan. The Japanese market had been monopolized by Yamaha and Kawai, with Technics starting up later. And finally in 1994, Roland took its first steps in the area of organs. When we announced our prototype at the time, we were often asked why Roland was entering the organ market then at the tail end of the organ generation. Realizing that this was how we were being perceived, we had to recommit to our resolution. For me personally, the domain of pianos and organs was not something that was in decline, but important markets that were poised to grow from that point. If they were to decline, this would be due to the lack of effort on the part of manufacturers, and we would be taking away opportunities from people who cherished organ music and enjoyed performing it.

Just as various categories of instruments have seen the emergence of subsequent generations, I am engaged in this work with a vision to become the top runner in the second generation of electronic organs. In fact, what delighted us upon announcing the Roland Music Atelier organ was that it gave us a real-world feel of the large number of people who support organ music. Although their numbers are still small compared to supporters of piano music, this segment is steadily and surely growing. During the 1998 NAMM Show, I learned that not a single concert organized by an organ manufacturer had been held at the show for about twenty years. If that was the case, we wanted to be the first in a long while to hold an organ concert at the NAMM Show, and this aspiration was realized in January 1999 in the "Organ Power" concert organized by Dennis Houlihan, president of Roland US.

The first concert, which was held at the Los Angeles Marriott, featured Hector Olivera [see interview on page 272], Rosemary Bailey, Don Lewis, the Joey DeFrancesco Trio, Seth Rye, and Rob Richards. This concert turned out to be an exciting one and we were all very happy at the response because many of us were initially concerned that it might not draw much of an audience. The audience was very satisfied with the show as well and this led us to hold the second "Organ Power" concert during the 2000 NAMM Show, on February 4.

That concert was to be held at the Wilshire Ebell Theatre in Los Angeles, which had a seating capacity of 1,100 people, or four times the size of our first concert. Thanks to the efforts of our local dealers, the seats sold out at quite an early stage and we actually had to make contingency plans for overcapacity. Thanks to the staff at Roland US, the concert was a wonderful, moving experience for all who were present. The fact that we were able to draw a crowd of this size to an organ-only concert was a great confidence booster for us. Present at the show that evening were Don Leslie and his wife, former president of Hammond Mr. Kutner and his wife, and former VP of Hammond International Mr. Olsen and his wife, making this a truly enjoyable evening for me. The evening's stunning performances were delivered by a star-studded roster of musicians including Hector Olivera, Rosemary Bailey, and Don Lewis, who had played in the previous year's concert, as well as Dan Miller, Steve Fisher on V-Drums, and Yuri Tachibana from Japan [see interview on page 242].

▼ Roland's Atelier AT-900 organ opened up a new world of rich expressivity.

The *William Tell* overture, which all performers played together at the end of the program, was fit for the climax of the evening. The audience was delighted by the video shown on the large screen beside the stage during the theme song for the *Lone Ranger* TV series. Dennis, who captivated the crowd with his excellent MCing, was the only person fit for this job, as he was very knowledgeable about organs. After the show, we were delighted that many people came up to us saying, "We're looking forward to the third 'Organ Power' concert." This was also the first time we used the Roland RSS 3-D sound-processing system in a public venue and the results were amazing. This was an evening that gave us a real feeling that the second round of organs had begun.

In February 2013, thirteen years after the second "Organ Power" concert, I was given the Technical Grammy Award for my contribution to the development of MIDI at the same Ebell Theatre in Los Angeles. I felt a fascinating sense of connection. The crowd that packed the theater for the "Organ Power" concert largely belonged to completely different walks of life from those present at the Grammy Awards. And in terms of the people involved, the industry represented by the former was vastly outnumbered by that represented by the latter. I continue to believe that organs have a bright future ahead.

8

The Birth of MIDI

Real Time Is for Performers; Non-Real Time Is for Composers

THE NUMBER OF PEOPLE WHO ENJOY COMPUTER MUSIC INCREASED dramatically as personal computers came into widespread use. We now encounter electronic music in places we would never have expected, such as karaoke. Given the popularity of music created on electronic instruments, it helps to categorize musical expressions into "real time" and "non-real time" to understand the bigger picture.

In 1988, I was interviewed by the London-based magazine *Making Music*. Computer music had been born only a decade earlier, so I offered my personal views on the then current state of affairs and what we might expect for the future. This was the first time I used the "real time" and "non-real time" categories for the purpose of explanation, and I have made it a point to do so ever since. This was at a time when MIDI had just been born and not many manufacturers were well prepared for it.

It is a given that performances on acoustic instruments would be in real time; that is, music is created at the moment the player performs it and the audience enjoys that music right there and then. Meanwhile, with computer music, musicians record information such as pitch, duration (length of the note), and accent onto the computer's storage device. This information can then be used to play music by triggering synthesizers equipped with the sounds of various instruments. Thus, in the same way a performer works in real time, a composer works in non-real time.

The work of a composer traditionally involved conceptualizing the musical piece, trying out various melodies and harmonies on the piano, and finally writing these down on a chart. With the advent of computer music, musicians gained the ability to enter the information directly into a computer, replay the music, and make corrections as they listened to it, instead of trying various passages one after the other on the keyboard and writing the notation on a chart. In the sense that the composer in either case makes corrections to the piece until they are satisfied, the process is exactly the same. In recent years, an increasing number of people have begun making music through this computer-based non-real-time method.

The reason I began thinking of musical expressions in terms of these categories was that this non-real time concept became very important in many aspects of musical activities. This method of expression does not make musicians who perform in real time obsolete; I think the correct way to view it is not only as a way of composing music but as a mode of performance as well. It certainly was difficult to describe this idea thirty years ago. An American friend of mine remarked on the terms *real time* and *non-real time*, saying that the *non-* in the term *non-real time* gave it a negative connotation. But since he had no answer when I asked him what a good alternative would be, I have continued to use these terms, so much so that by now it makes no sense to change them.

Time is a critical element of music performance. You could refer to music as an art of time. I actually think that the non-real-time method of composing—in which the composer can evaluate pitch and the lengths of notes and try out all possibilities by carefully examining and changing all aspects of the music until he is satisfied—is making very large contributions to the creation and performance of music. In the creation and live performance of music, people tend to view the sound that comes out of speakers simply as something that is played back, but this is not true. Given that the process of composing a musical piece is in fact a non-real-time process, I believe we should be actively pursuing its possibilities.

Because of the limits of human imagination, I believe the number of people who are able to grasp and appreciate a musical piece, its motifs, the effects of its sonic images, and its impressions, upon being shown a score by its composer—"Here, this is my new symphony"—would be very few. The number of people who could comprehend the music if the score were accompanied by a tape or CD would be much larger. And almost everyone would be able to understand the same music if it were entered into a computer and digitally reproduced. You can make changes to nuances and other details later and also save the music in its best state.

Thanks to the emergence of movie soundtracks, and the opportunities they have created for composers who had been writing music for musicals and operas, we have been blessed with a large amount of great music. However, it appears that classical music composition is declining and this saddens me. Meanwhile, new work is being created at a rapid pace in the field of popular music, owing to the popularity of rock music and DJs. Setting aside the question of how much of it will be remembered years from now, the number of new pieces being created is staggering. By comparison, there are few opportunities to release new classical pieces (although the expression itself is an oxymoron). And yet if more opportunities were made available to introduce such pieces through the use of computer-based non-real-time methods, then I believe we would see an increase in the number of new classical pieces. And I believe that once these pieces were appreciated, orchestras would begin to perform them.

Regardless of the method used to produce music—real time or non-real time— there is no difference when one listens to it on media such as CD, MD, or tape. In recent years, programming technologies have made huge advancements that give us opportunities to listen to wonderful music. In the early stages of this development, the demand was high for those who had the skills to arrange songs for karaoke. Now, people are increasingly creating unique and original music on their computers. These people gradually expanded their scope into other areas, some even creating opera scores with desktop media production (DTMP) methods. Said another way, I believe we are seeing the potential for DTMP to revive classical music and bring it into the mainstream.

The association of real time with performers and non-real time with composers is just a simplification, and the real possibilities are much more expansive. In the non-real-time method of music production, the temporal vector, a critical element in music, can be freely manipulated, and composers are able to infuse it with their unfettered imagination to give their creations the best feel, performance, tone, and concept. And this certainly requires a different sort of musical sensibility. When transferring music from a score onto a computer, even if you were to enter the information on the score correctly onto your computer, that does not necessarily mean you would have rendered it accurately as music. In contrast to the routine stenographic work of writing notes on paper, the music will change depending on how you read the score and convert it to data. This is essentially the same as reading a score and coming up with a way of playing it on the piano that feels the best for you. We now have highly advanced methods of notation that can denote subtle nuances on the score just as the performer played it, so musicians and producers are able to use a combination of these two methods.

It takes a great deal of practice to perform music well in real time. Although you may be able to play a given piece, unless you have trained rigorously from a very young age so that the musical sensibilities have become automatic to the point that you are able to move your fingers perfectly to express the concept of the piece, musical expression will be a challenge for you. The level of perfection required to realize a complete performance is extremely high, and not everyone is able to fulfill the requirements of both technique and musicality.

As for non-real-time performance, songs can be inputted with one hand, to use an extreme example, so it appears at first glance that anyone can make music regardless of whether or not they can play a musical instrument. The assertion that "anyone can make music," however, is actually a slightly exaggerated marketing catchphrase. It does not mean that someone who knows nothing about music can create music. To be correct, you would have to say, "Anyone who listens to and enjoys music can create music." Although physically training to play music is important, this type of music making starts with assembling your music in your head, expanding your imagination, and transplanting the data you have created through your sensibilities onto your computer. It is easiest to begin with melodies, the element of music that we are most familiar with. You can listen to the sound coming from the speaker and make changes to it until you are satisfied. This process is exactly the same as practicing the piano over and over until you are happy with your performance.

Whether it be physical training to instill the correct sensibility into your muscles, or the emotional training of your composer's mind, we all need the exact same capabilities, or sensibilities, at the final stage of our music making. The intermediate processes may be different, but the results will be the same. I rather believe that non-real-time methods offer the possibility of opening up new areas of music as we are liberated from our restrictions such as the physical inability to move our fingers. This is a wonderful doorway to music for someone whose interest in music was piqued only after they reached adulthood. Once this aspect of the method is understood, we will be able to enjoy real-time performances twice as much as we have, and will come to understand the joy of music much more quickly.

To compare real-time and non-real-time methods, consider wonderful live theatrical and musical performances given in theaters and concert halls as compared with the expressive capabilities of film. The dynamic nature of a live symphonic performance is sublime, and represents the pinnacle of real-time performances. These art forms give us soul-moving experiences, and the feeling created between the stage and audience—although of course there is no direct conversation between the two—as well as the tension of knowing that all of this will be no more once the show is over, causes the impression of the performance to be retained clearly in the audience's heart. Movies, which are a form of non-real-time expression, are created by directors, cinematographers, and actors working on shooting locations, using a variety of methods to get the shots just right, and working through an editing process in order to tell a story. Movies can create a broad range of heart-moving experiences by portraying a time period that may be centuries in the past, or by enacting scenes out of someone's memory, or through the use of techniques such as flashback. As such, film has blossomed as an important field of art that is distinct from theater.

While I don't think anyone will disagree with the notion that both theater and film are wonderful forms of art, we should know that film was very poorly received in its nascent years. To be fair, it is true that much of the content of early films deserved such criticism. This was at a time when films had no sound and were short, so no real story could be told through the medium. Nevertheless, it would be unfair to assess the artistic value of film based only on early films made with a limited range of equipment. People in those days had no way of imagining the expressive capabilities of current films, or the amazing effects produced through the use of CGI in films such as *Titanic*.

Meanwhile, although live performances of symphony, opera, and other forms of classical music remain popular, it is increasingly becoming financially difficult to maintain orchestras. This is a sad fact, and we must come up with ways to continue these cultural activities. Having said that, one cannot help but be pessimistic when viewing things from a purely economic standpoint. This is because the size of an audience at any given performance is limited by the venue's capacity, which leads to higher ticket prices, which in turn naturally leads to diminished audience-drawing power. The audience must be at the theater at a certain time, so this adds another layer of difficulty. But it is a fact that the dynamic nature of a live performance in a theater or concert hall cannot be fully experienced on video. Are we then better off not viewing at all, if all we are getting is video? Not so. Videos can create an amazing effect when enhanced by great acoustics.

TV broadcasts show us images captured from a variety of angles on multiple cameras. We all know that video gives us opportunities to focus on aspects of the performance that we would never pick up on in a live setting. Screens set up behind or beside the stage dramatically enhance the enjoyment of concerts. Artists now use live performance (real time) and elements that have been produced beforehand (non–real time) at the same time. This is another phenomenon that illustrates how there is no meaning to an either/or debate about real time and non-real time. I believe the best approach is to integrate the two in whatever area of endeavor the artist is engaged in, or come up with novel styles of expression that incorporate the two as mutually valid modes of expression.

While I can agree, to some extent, with statements such as "music is art" and "we don't need bothersome technical contraptions to express our emotions," we cannot look away from the fact that technological development has gifted us with amazing ways for communicating our ideas. While film has proven this over a period of a century, I would like to hope that we will not repeat the mistakes made in the nascent years of film. New technologies are waiting for artists to make use of them. New technologies and methods occasionally have a way of transcending the proficiencies that we have accumulated up to that point. And then there are technologies that pass us by even before we understand whether they will be useful or detrimental. The same things are happening in the world of technological and stylistic design. This is a great time to be an artist. The makers of non-real-time equipment must increase their communication with leaders in the film industry.

The Birth of Synthesizers

I believe the first wave of non-real-time music began in 1968, when Walter Carlos released his album *Switched-On Bach*, produced using a Moog synthesizer. This started a huge wave of similar music created by a variety of composers. However, while the first generation of synthesizers was suited for producing the sounds found in baroque music, hardware constraints made them unsuitable for producing the smoothly flowing lines such as we hear in French romantic music.

The second wave originated in Japan. Isao Tomita's 1974 rendition of Debussy's "Clair de Lune" on his album *Snowflakes Are Dancing* transcended the limits of the hardware. On this album, the Debussy piece was performed with dramatically more expressivity compared to *Switched-On Bach*. Yet the hardware Mr. Tomita used was the same Moog synthesizer. As a researcher of synthesizer circuitry at the time, I remember being astonished at the difference in musicality and expressivity that could be achieved using the same hardware.

I was told that Mr. Tomita had visited record companies all over Japan with a tape recording of this work, but although the companies all showed interest, they would not sign him because they had no idea of how to handle this new type of music. RCA eventually released his album in the United States, and this synthesized version of "Clair de Lune" became an instant worldwide hit. Mr. Tomita became the first Japanese musician to be nominated for four Grammy Awards in 1974, and the album was chosen as the best classical album of the year by the Recording Industry Association of America. Thanks to this, Tomita became a familiar name, not only among my friends in the electronic musical instrument industry but among everyone who was interested in music. While I felt it unfortunate personally that the synthesizer Mr. Tomita used on his album was a Moog and not a Roland System 700, this was only natural as Roland at the time was four years behind Moog in synthesizer development. A quick study of album credits shows that six System 700s were used in the recording of Gustav Holst's *The Planets*, released in 1976.

Amid fierce competition, my goal at the time was to figure out how to create a synthesizer that was easy to operate, whose pitch remained consistent regardless of operating time and temperature changes, and that composers wanted to use. I also thought that synthesizers with a ¥2.4 million price tag, the price of System 700, would not become big sellers. So I was working to develop a smaller, low-cost synthesizer that was half the size of System 700, and that anyone could use. This smaller synthesizer was eventually launched as System 100. In the 1970s, in order to record music played on a synthesizer, you had to use a four- or eight-track analog tape recorder and record each track one by one. This limited the length of music that you could record in a single session. So the moment I played Isao Tomita's record, I could tell that it had taken a great deal of patience to create his signature "Tomita sound," which was so thick and rich. I had the opportunity to ask him how many overdubs he made to finish his pieces and I was simply in awe at his perseverance and passion to achieve perfection. He went on to release albums such as *Pictures at an Exhibition*, his 1975 interpretation of Mussorgsky, and *The Firebird*, his take on Stravinsky, in succession, all of which became best-sellers.

▼ Roland's synthesizer studio in the 1970s.

▼ I was awarded the fifty-fifth Technical Grammy Award.

▲ My second son, Ikuo (right), at the awards ceremony on my behalf, with co-awardee Dave Smith (February 9, 2013, at the Ebell Theatre, Los Angeles).

▼ With my synthesizer friends at a dinner in 1992. From left to right: Dave Smith (founder of Sequential Circuits), Robert Moog, myself, and Tom Oberheim.

▲ Graduation photo for the Mechanical Engineering Department of Nishinoda Technical High School. I am the fourth one from the left in the front row, wearing a geta (wooden clog) that I made myself (1946).

▲ Shown here with the first delivery scooter I purchased when I was running the Kakehashi Musen electrical appliance store (circa 1955).

▲ Photo with my fiancée, Masako, upon leaving the Sengokuso sanatorium (circa 1953).

▲ Our team when we started up Ace Electronic Industries (1962).

▼ A shot at our new company building two years after seven of us started up Roland (1973).

▼ Oscar Peterson (left) and Sakyo Komatsu (right) in the dressing room at the Third Conference for Osaka Prefectural Residents on Osaka's Economic Development (1982).

▲ With Stevie Wonder at the 1996 Winter NAMM Show where we announced VS-880, the world's first portable digital recorder.

▲ At Oscar Peterson's home studio in Toronto, Canada (circa 1979).

▲ Mr. Peterson at the Praemium Imperiale awards ceremony party with other jazz musicians. From right to left: Sadao Watanabe, George Kawaguchi, and Toshiko Akiyoshi (1999).

▼ At the same awards ceremony party. From left to right: Mr. Peterson's daughter, Celine Peterson, his wife, Kelly Peterson, and my wife, Masako. The three women got along very well and Mrs. Peterson picked up quite a bit of Japanese.

◀ With Don Lewis at his home in San Francisco where we discussed rhythm machine designs (circa 1968).

▼ Don Lewis and his wife Julie at a gospel event held in San Francisco (circa 2003).

▲ At the Nethercutt Museum, Los Angeles. From left to right: Katsuyoshi Dan (former president of Roland Corporation), Tony Fenelon, myself, and Hector Olivera (circa 2003).

◄ At the Musikmesse International Press Award ceremony where I received the second Lifetime Achievement Award for an individual. I am shown here receiving the trophy from the presenter, Robert Moog. This was truly a happy surprise (2002).

A scene from a TV ► appearance in Tokyo with Eric Burdon (left), vocalist of the Animals, the world-renowned British rock band (circa 1970).

▲ On a visit to Ray Charles's studio in California with keyboardist Scott Tibbs (Roland US, circa 1990, photographed by myself).

◄ Members of American rock band Toto visit Roland's Hamamatsu factory. Keyboardists Steve Porcaro (left) and David Paich (right) are wearing Roland sweatshirts of the era (circa 1981).

With Isao Tomita in front of a PC that I made myself by ▶
modifying an Apple II clone. Taking a cue from Apple,
I named this PC Uri II or Uri Futatsu ("two squashes").
This ended up being very useful for studying MIDI,
which we announced three years later. (1980).

▼ With Robert Moog at the NAMM Show (circa 1974).

▼ I made a PC based on an S-100 system
at around the same time I made the Uri II
and named it Data Rame 38 (word play on
detarame, Japanese for "nonsensical"). I
expanded the RAM area to sixteen mega-
bytes (not gigabytes) for the first time.

◀ I built a modified office computer into the Data Rame 38.

▲ Roland became the main sponsor
for the "Domu" team that raced in
the Twenty-Four Hours of Le Mans.

◀ The team raced in Le Mans three times but
the finish line remained ever elusive. (1982).

With Don Leslie and ▶ his wife at their home (1997). Mr. Leslie has created a wonderful lifestyle as an engineer, and is someone I consider a great mentor. This visit became the inspiration for Mr. Leslie to later produce an autobiographical video, *The Don Leslie Story*, completed two years later.

▼ At the grave of Laurens Hammond, an inventor, pioneer, and outstanding businessman whose impact on the development of electronic musical instruments is unequaled (Cornwall, Connecticut, 1997).

On my first visit to Italy in 1967, I visited long-established accordion manufacturers Paolo Soprani Menghini and Crucianelli in search of parts to use in electronic accordions. Unfortunately, neither company sold parts so I purchased two acoustic accordions, of which one is still with us (photo left). Shown here is Luigi Bruti (left) with a MIDI accordion.

▼ Alberto Kniepkamp, former chief engineer at Lowrey Organs, is shown here with a prototype of a Lowrey MX-1 organ (circa 1970).

Seen here with Itsuji Miyake, ▶
former Roland senior executive
director, who has taken over
operations at our head offices.

◀ From left to right: Dennis
Houlihan, former president
of Roland US; Bob Dove,
former director of Steinway;
Tatsuya Suzuki, former president of Steinway Japan;
myself; and Tadao Kikumoto,
former Roland senior man-
aging director (circa 1970).

Seen here with Takuji Tomita, ▶
who designed the Roland logo
(circa 1970).

▲ From left to right: Dennis Houlihan, Larry Morton, president of Hal Leonard, and myself at Roland's Hamamatsu Research Center (2005).

▼ Seen here with directors of overseas joint companies. Back row, from left to right: Cheng Jiantong, Alfredo Maroni, and Luigi Bruti. Front row, from left to right: Vic Keersmaekers, Paulo Caius, and myself (2013).

In Hawaii with Mr. Laurie Gillespie, former president of Roland Canada, and his wife. I received from them a special attaché case made with elephant skin as a commemorative gift (circa 2000).

Seen here with Harold Rhodes ▶ (left) and Henry Steinway (right) (circa 2000).

◀ Seen here at NAMM head offices with Dr. John Chowning, inventor of the FM method of synthesis (circa 1998).

Mike Rutherford (guitarist), one of the original ▶ members of British rock band Genesis, is seen here with (from left to right) Kozo Hama; my second son, Ikuo, and Takuhaku Nakajo (circa 1978, photographed by myself).

◀ Seen here with the drummer Tommy Snyder, consultant and demonstrator of Roland rhythm instruments. We have been friends since his days playing in Japanese rock band Godiego (1996).

▲ Seen here with composer Akira Senju and organist Hector Olivera. Mr. Olivera played Mr. Senju's "Furinkazan" (2008).

With film writer and director Nobuhiko ▶ Obayashi. Mr. Obayashi is a great colleague whom I respect as an innovator in the world of visual arts. He is a longtime jurist in the Roland Video Contest (2012).

▼ This was taken when we invited Yuri Tachibana (right) and her mother (left) to our home. My wife Masako is shown at center (2007).

◀ Roland formed an alliance with major guitar manufacturer Fender to expand the guitar synthesizer market. Shown at center is Bill Schultz, former Fender CEO (1992).

Seen here in Spain with ▶ Amalia Ramírez, president of the José Ramirez guitar company (2001).

◀ During a visit with virtuoso organist George Wright (bottom right) (1997).

◀ My handprints on the Guitar Center's Hollywood RockWalk. This was an unexpected birthday present on February 7, 2000. Adjacent to my handprints (clockwise from top left) were those of Jan and Dean, Brian Wilson of the Beach Boys, Buddy Guy, Smokey Robinson, Stevie Wonder, Robert Moog, and guitar maker C. F. Martin III. Closer to the camera can also be seen the names EL&P (Emerson, Lake and Palmer) and Johnny Winter.

At the honorary professorship ▶ conferment ceremony at Berklee College of Music in Boston. From left to right: Roy Haynes (drummer), Joe Zawinul (keyboardist), Lee Eliot Berk (president of the college), and myself (1991).

Eventually, Mr. Tomita began experimenting with how he could create three-dimensional sound space expressions with synthesizers. One of these attempts was a passage that featured a rocket launch. He tried a variety of things to express the sound of the rocket's initial ignition and the blast of its thrust, followed by the sound of the rocket gradually climbing up into the sky. His thinking was that these experiments gave him the inspiration to create different types of music, and his attempts represented huge challenges given the state of the art of electronic music at the time.

In the 1970s, because synthesizers could still produce only one note at a time on the keyboard, a big challenge for us was to find a way to make them produce as many sounds as possible simultaneously. While we were not hoping to replicate an orchestra, it was clear that impressive pieces of music could be created if a synthesizer could produce the same sounds as five to eight musicians playing simultaneously. While analog sequencers—machines that would produce the same musical information as someone playing a keyboard—were already available, these were complex pieces of equipment. They used potentiometers to create differences in voltage, which in turn changed the pitch of a tone or the spacing between them. Mr. Tomita used these early sequencers to make his music so the mind boggles at the hours that he must have put into his projects.

When I was in Vancouver in the mid-1970s, keyboard player Ralph Dyck showed me how he had been making an unprecedented polyphonic sequencer based on integrated circuit (IC) logic. Digital calculators in those days were big contraptions, and he had modified the interior of one of them, combining it with a large number of ICs to make a sequencer that he was actually using to produce music. The moment I saw this, I thought that this whole arrangement should be replaced with a central processing unit. By using a CPU instead, we would be able to dramatically improve all areas of its performance including programming, reading, and writing. So right there and then, I decided to begin developing such a sequencer with Ralph Dyck.

Development was done entirely in Japan, and programming was headed by Yukio Tamada, an engineer at Roland. In those days, programs were written using an NEC computer called PDA-80, a telex machine, and a very quiet-operating machined called a Typuter, or what we would call an ink-jet printer today. Data editing and programming were done by connecting the punch tapes that we had recorded. Since we could not waste a single byte in order to pack the program onto limited memory space, we printed our data out on rolls of toilet paper to check how we were doing, and we would make our punch tapes only after we had thoroughly verified and completed the data. We did not use A4 paper until the data was finished. This was a far cry from the programming

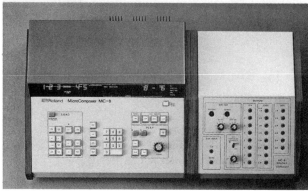

MC-8

MICROCOMPOSER ¥1,200,000 ●本体＋インターフェース

シンセサイザー音楽に無限の可能性をインプットするマイクロコンポーザー。

▲ The world's first MicroComposer, MC-8.

equipment and methods that we use today. This was around the time that sixteen-track analog tape recorders came into use.

What resulted from this development process in 1977 was the MC-8 MicroComposer. Because it was equipped with a microchip and memory, this sequencer enabled users to replay pro-grammed data as many times as they wanted. Additionally, the finished data could be stored on tape and played back and reproduced as many times as they liked. The only floppy disks available at the time were the large eight-inch ones, so it was customary to store data on audiocassette tapes. This was the birth of the first CPU-based musical instrument. The MC-8 was at the heart of the music of Yellow Magic Orchestra, a Japanese band that unleashed a huge wave of techno music.

▼ Isao Tomita's *Bermuda Triangle* (1978).

When Mr. Tomita, an MC-8 user, built a studio in Higashi Izu, I visited him there along with my son Ikuo. This was an amazing studio that overlooked the Pacific Ocean, and at the time we were there, people were still carrying in new equip-ment. During our visit, he said that he wanted to include digital signals in his upcoming album, but since it would only sound like grinding, which on its own would not be very interesting, he asked me if I would do the recording, as he wanted the digital signals to mean something.

As I was very enthusiastic about the S-100 bus computer at the time, I wasted no time in recording this using the Tarbell system on a cassette tape and sent it to him. The contents of the code on side A was: THIS IS THE BERMUDA TRIANGLE, OVER. SLOW DOWN. TARGET FIFTY MILES OFF SOUTH FLORIDA, A GIANT PYRAMID AT OCEAN BOTTOM, and on side B was: THIS IS THE BERMUDA TRIANGLE, OVER. LOOK OUT! A CYLINDRICAL OBJECT JUST LIKE THE ONE THAT EXPLODED OVER SIBERIA AND CRASHED INTO TUNGUSKA IN 1908 HAS JUST COME INTO THE SOLAR SYSTEM.

These codes, each of which sounded like digital noise and lasted about a second, were inserted into the music on the *Bermuda Triangle* album released from Victor Company of Japan (JVC). This album contained a medley of pieces by Prokofiev, Sibelius, and John Williams, all rendered in the "Tomita sound." The MC-8 was credited as one of the pieces of equipment used.

By using the MC-8, musicians could easily switch the instrument playing a particular melody simply by changing the tone settings on the synthesizer from, say, flute to trumpet, or from trumpet to trombone. Not only that, sequencers enabled the development of completely new musical expressions and ways of composing music.

By 1980, American synthesizer manufacturers were moving toward large-scale systems. Roland was also developing large-scale synthesizers, but we realized that we were at a huge disadvantage competing against American manufacturers who already had contacts with universities and various research labs. So I decided to focus on smaller synthesizers that rock musicians, bands, and musicians in general could use as their melody instrument. Accordingly, I terminated our production of all large analog models such as System 700. It was a major decision at the time to put an end to this entire product line, which included sequencers we had put a great deal of work into developing. But had

▼ Jupiter-8, a polyphonic synthesizer masterpiece, is still being used at the forefront of music today.

we not made this decision, Roland would have probably seen the same fate as the majority of companies who went the large-scale system route and eventually gone out of business. This was a struggle of my egos: between myself as an engineer and myself as president of the company.

Although it is natural for an engineer to aspire to creating something that no one else has ever made, it is the president's job to make these tough decisions if there are concerns about the direction the company is heading, even if everyone else in the company is against you. The frustration and chagrin of the engineers was written all over their faces. This was a difficult decision to make, as there were quite a few people whose reason for joining the company in the first place had been that they would be able to work on the System 700.

In order to overcome the limitations of early synthesizers that could produce only one note at a time, we continued to work on increasing the number of notes a synthesizer could produce simultaneously from two to four, and then from four to eight. This was also what the market had been demanding. It also happened that around this time, the waves of transition from analog to digital, and from monophonic to polyphonic, arrived simultaneously. At the time, we were making models for the organ market, such as SH-1000, and SH-2000, as well as analog synthesizers such as SH-1, SH-2, and SH3 that students could buy, and our goal was to expand these markets.

We saw that there was a market for synthesizers because they were capable of producing unique solo orchestral voices that organs could not produce. This eventually led to the development of Jupiter-4, a synthesizer capable of producing four notes at a time (four-voice polyphony), in 1978, and Jupiter-8, an eight-voice polyphonic synthesizer, in 1981. The latter was capable of producing a rich array of tones and many musicians used it despite its price tag of ¥980,000. Price-wise, this was not something that many people could buy, but it was received very well in the market and helped build our name in the world.

The Digital Tidal Wave

The transition from analog to digital brought a great deal of confusion not only to engineers but to musicians as well. Sequencers—devices that produce the same musical information as when you play a keyboard and are used in combination with synthesizers—also make up an important area. The MC-8 that we launched in 1977 was a computer-based sequencer, but the eight output voltages that the unit produced were analog. You could connect this to an analog synthesizer to drive eight oscillators, producing tones at eight different pitches. Needless to say, you could produce music in a dramatically shorter amount of time compared to when you had to enter everything manually. In that sense, the MC-8 brought about major progress in the process of music production, but as engineers involved in the designing of this unit, we were aware of the limitations of a system that converted its signals to analog and triggered oscillators based on incrementing or decrementing analog voltages. If we could take all processes into the digital realm, the system could be made considerably simpler, and we thought that we might even be able to eliminate the cables that connected the various units in the system. To do this, we needed to create a new standard for the digital age that would supersede the one volt/one octave standard of analog synthesizers.

The questions of whether we should take the analog or the digital route and, if we were to go digital, how we should define a new standard to replace the one volt/one octave standard, were both critical. What was more, the size of the synthesizer and its presumed modes of usage would also have an impact on the standard that would be required. For example, in order to digitalize a large system, given the speeds of CPUs available then, it was clear that we could not satisfy speed requirements unless all the various information was provided in parallel fashion. Meanwhile, parallel connections would be too much of a hassle for portable synthesizers used by bands, private individuals, and musicians, and we did not think that such a system could be expanded beyond a one-to-one synth-to-sequencer configuration. Serial connections would not fare much better because although they were easy to connect, they were limited in terms of information transmission speed. The standard clock speed of CPUs circa 1980 was one to two megahertz. And over the years this surpassed one hundred megahertz, reaching two hundred, three hundred, four hundred, and five hundred megahertz. A simple comparison of clock speeds then and now gives us a good picture of how fast CPUs have become. Clock speeds now exceed three gigahertz.

One of the breakthroughs for synthesizer digitalization was the hybrid approach of using digital oscillators—the mode of oscillation that synthesizers are known for—and analog controls. By doing so, we were able to lower the price of synthesizers that were capable of six or eight polyphony to levels that some have called revolutionary. In fact, these synthesizers that were sized conveniently and priced reasonably were very popular, and became big sellers. Similar products were being sold by a number of our competitors and the market was soon dominated by relatively small polyphonic synthesizers. The larger ones continued to be used in labs and testing rooms.

It was during this time, in 1983, that Yamaha launched a digital synthesizer that used FM oscillation. This FM sound-generating system was developed by John Chowning of Stanford University, and was revolutionary in that it was able to produce new tones in a very flexible manner. Since I was aware of these developments from the literature that was available at the time, I visited Dr. Chowning at Stanford before Yamaha launched its new product. Unfortunately, he had already entered an agreement with Yamaha six months earlier, and was excluded from entering a license agreement with other companies.

It was only natural that Yamaha became Dr. Chowning's partner as they had the in-house capability to develop LSIs that were needed to commercialize this system. However, because we had taken the time to visit him, he was kind enough to show us some of the other research he was engaged in at the time, and this was very inspirational for us. This was also the moment that we got clear confirmation that the transition from analog to digital was well on its way.

Roland was also involved in the development of digital devices, but the state of the art was far more advanced. No matter how revolutionary a new system or sound might be, there has never been a time that the market, in particular the music market, upon the introduction of a new system or sound, embraced that innovation in one fell swoop. The emergence of digital synthesizers with FM sound generators had a major impact on a technological level, but my greatest interest at the time was how much longer the current types of analog devices would continue to sell and when they would be replaced.

This was a question that nobody had the answer to, and there was no point in agonizing over it or consulting with others. So the only path for Roland was to develop our own digital products, but the big question was what types of methods were available to realize this objective. At the time, several ideas were being put forward for digitalizing synthesizers in their entirety, but the problem was where we could find the semiconductors that would make this possible, and the costs involved. These problems took some more time to sort out, so as a result, our products that consisted of a combination of digital oscillation and analog control actually sold for a longer period of time than we had imagined.

However, it was quite difficult to have our flagship products be analog synthesizers and still direct the company with confidence. In particular, there was no way we could avoid the decline in morale among our sales force. We later learned that the total numbers of Roland analog synthesizers and Yamaha DX7s sold during that period of time when analog and digital were competing against each other were not that far apart. Still, we had to wait until 1987, when we released the D-50, a digital synthesizer based on our proprietary linear arithmetic system, for sales morale to recover.

The Grammy Awards

In 1981, Roland developed a standard for electronic musical instruments called Musical Instrument Digital Interface, or MIDI. This was a standard for unifying the signal that connected the keyboard and sound generator. By unifying all the different types of signals that manufacturers had been using into the MIDI standard, we were able to give electronic musical instruments from different manufacturers the ability to communicate with each other.

While this may seem to be no wonder, the true aim of MIDI was to enable connectivity between computers and electronic musical instruments. The year 1981, when the MIDI standard was born, may also be seen as the inauguration year of personal computers, with

▲ Technical Grammy Awards trophy.

IBM launching their first computer that ran a Microsoft operating system, and NEC launching the PC-8801 in Japan. We had been forecasting that computers would come into the world of music in the near future. So we began developing MIDI as we felt that a uniform global standard would be needed for electronic musical instruments.

It was a great surprise and joy that in 2013, thirty years later, I was awarded the Technical Grammy for establishing the MIDI standard. It was deeply moving that the musician and engineer Dave Smith was awarded alongside me because he was the first person to evaluate and advocate the MIDI standard that I had presented.

A great deal of research and debate went on between 1980 and 1982 with regard to the standardization of methods for exchanging digital performance information. But most of the debate among competing companies did not go beyond discussions on the trade show floor, and none of these discussions really reached the point of someone calling a conference. The great majority of American manufacturers, who focused on large system synthesizers, leaned toward parallel systems because of their emphasis on speed. And it was only Roland and Dave Smith, founder of the California-based company Sequential Circuits, both of whom were primarily developing portable synthesizers, who were advocating the serial method, which offered easier connectivity. While it was preferable that all devices adopted a single unified standard, we thought that those supporting serial and parallel could each go their own ways to create their own standards, and decided that Sequential Circuits and Roland would go ahead with developing our own. This is how our efforts to enable electronic musical instruments of different makes to connect with each other began.

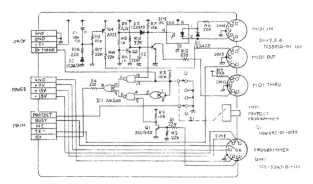

▲ Diagram of the MIDI circuit on the Roland JX-3P, one of the early models to be fitted with MIDI. The photocoupler (enclosed in the dotted line) was indispensable for commercializing this standard.

By 1981, Roland had already developed a proprietary serial interface called the Digital Communication Bus (DCB), and incorporated the DCB, which used a fourteen-pin connector, in the Jupiter-8 (DCB was optional in the earlier models) and Juno-60 in 1982. So our discussions with Dave Smith were based on this standard. Mr. Smith's suggestion was a method that used a regular two-core phone cable and he had already proposed this method to the Audio Engineering Society. According to our tests, this phone cable method would work reasonably well for connecting a single sequencer with a single synthesizer, but in instances where both devices had an analog output, or when two synthesizers or sequencers were connected in a more complex configuration, it was likely to produce ground hum (noise caused by phase differences in the power supply), which would be a problem for practical applications. To counter this issue, we were developing a system that used a photocoupler—a device that connects only optical signals—to send only digital signals and cut off the earth line.

By mid-1982, we decided that the new interface would be called MIDI, and in October of that year, we announced the MIDI 1.0 specifications. This was the birth of a global standard. At the 1983 NAMM Show, we were able to present a historic public experiment of digital communication between Sequential Circuit's Prophet-600 and Roland's Jupiter-6 synthesizers. No press invitations were sent out for this low-key event and there were no more than twenty people—a group consisting of representatives and developers from both companies—who applauded the success of this test, but this was a revolutionary moment in the history of electronic musical instruments. This was the moment that a global standard for exchanging digital data between electronic musical instruments became a reality. This series of events is covered in the book *Electric Sound* by Joel Chadabe. It was Tadao Kikumoto, manager of engineering at Roland, who was directing the development of MIDI at the time, and MIDI is one on a list of important contributions that he made in a variety of R&D projects.

This was how MIDI came about as a world standard, and today, you would not be able to find an electronic musical instrument that is not affected by MIDI in one way or another. With the adoption of MIDI, electronic musical instruments for the first time gained the capability to communicate with other devices. MIDI brought many benefits, including the improvement of sound and functionality through digital control, but I personally feel this capability of an instrument to communicate with something other than itself is the largest benefit to electronic instruments. The emergence of this functionality brought an end to an era in which musical instruments were limited to the world of music, and ushered in an era in which we have the freedom to think in terms of the fusion of video and music. I have no doubt that a variety of other interfaces will be developed moving forward, but I believe that MIDI's current functions will surely be incorporated into these new standards as well.

One area transformed by MIDI is karaoke. In the early 1980s, the majority of karaoke tracks were recorded on eight-track tapes, and by the late eighties, laser disks became the most popular medium. When karaoke using data transmission came on the scene in 1992, almost all karaoke rooms in Japan made the transition to this system. All of the features of this mode of karaoke—including the rich catalogue of songs, the quick access to new songs, and the way it enables users to control the tempo and pitch to their preferences—became possible thanks to MIDI. In recent years, it has become commonplace to use songs as ringtones on our cell phones, and this again is an application of MIDI where the MIDI data is used to play music on the sound chip built into cell phones. It is also thanks to MIDI that we are able to download data for the latest songs and enjoy them immediately.

MIDI, which handles performance information by digitalizing it, is capable of controlling pitch, tone, and timing, or synchronization. This functionality revolutionized the music-recording process and brought about huge changes to recording equipment. If you wanted to overdub multiple parts over others back when tape was the only available way of recording music, in addition to ensuring the quality of the performance, you would have to go through great pains to match the timing and make the already recorded performance sync with the new performance you were recording. But with MIDI, the tempo of the performance can be controlled at will. It also makes it easier to re-record your

performance, and you can do so as many times as necessary. Also, by prepro-
gramming your data, you can send a variety of control signals to other electronic
musical instruments and recording devices at predefined timings. In this way,
MIDI has expanded the musical instrument industry's scope of business to the
realm of recording.

While musical instruments and recording equipment are both closely related to
music, in the beginning they were manufactured in completely different industries. While musicians were responsible for performing on their instruments,
the recording process was an area that was separate from what the musicians
did. Such being the state of affairs, musical instrument manufacturers made
only instruments, and recorders and mixers were predominantly made by
audio manufacturers. Subsequently, at around the time when more and more
singer-songwriters came on the scene, some musical instrument manufacturers
began developing recording equipment. As a result, microphones, which in the
1960s were produced mainly by companies in the electrical devices industry,
were increasingly made by musical instrument manufacturers. In the 1990s,
when digital became the norm for recording, digital recording equipment made
by musical instrument manufacturers became the mainstream. Today, a broad
range of manufacturers market a variety of software-based recording systems
that run on computers.

With the development of digital technology, digital recording equipment and
computer software have become easy enough for musicians themselves to
operate, and their prices have come down to levels that are affordable to private
users. Twenty years ago, it would have been fantasy to think of creating a CD
in your bedroom, but now, anyone can easily create his or her own CD with less
than a hundred dollars.

Thirty years has passed since the establishment of the MIDI standard, but this
is just the beginning when we look at the long history of musical instruments.
Progress in digital technology is expanding the possibilities of MIDI even further,
and we have yet to see applications that fully utilize all of its features.

A Unified Standard and the Future of MIDI

My inspiration for MIDI was the Esperanto language, which I learned of when
I was sixteen years old. Esperanto was an artificial language developed by
Polish linguist Ludwik Zamenhof in the nineteenth century. He envisioned the
entire global population using this language as their second tongue. I studied
it for about a year but ended up quitting. While the concept was wonderful, you
needed some proficiency in Latin to learn the language, which made it difficult

for me, a Japanese, and I felt that it was more advantageous for me to learn English given the university entrance exams I expected to take. Esperanto associations still exist but there are only about a thousand people who are fluent in the language. And we all know that, in a development driven largely by business needs, English has now become the standard global language instead.

To draw an analogy with electronic musical instruments, the lack of a global language would be a state in which the signals that connect company A's keyboards and sound modules cannot be used on keyboards and sound modules made by company B. This is because their signals are based on different standards, which in human terms means that they speak different languages. By unifying this language we could use keyboards made by company A to play sound modules made by company A as well as those made by company B. You could also use a computer instead of a keyboard to trigger these sound modules.

Having said that, no one had attempted to create a unified standard for electronic musical instruments in 1981 so this was a situation where we had "no samples." Where were we to start?

Our first question was, "What signals do we need to send?" The three must-have elements of music are the pitch, the note length, and the strength of the sound. Our idea was to pare down the elements in the main signal that would be sent to the sound module to these three elements of information, and assign tone, portamento and other elements to other parts of different signals.

The next thing we had to decide was the type of jack to use. As I mentioned earlier, although the phone jacks that Dave Smith proposed were inexpensive and readily available, our tests showed that this method could not be used for MIDI as it was not able to carry enough information. However, the RS-232C connectors used in computers, although they supported our specifications, used jacks and circuitry that were too expensive to build into a $1,000 synthesizer. They also had too many pins which made connection difficult and were not suited for electronic musical instruments where we expected the users would be connecting and disconnecting these jacks frequently.

In the end, the method that caught our attention was the five-pin Deutsches Institut für Normung (DIN) jacks. DIN is a German industrial standard that corresponds to the JIS standard of Japan. The jacks were inexpensive, easy to connect, and very robust. Having five pins meant that we could use one for the ground, and use the remaining four to send four different types of signals in parallel. These specs were more than enough for MIDI. In MIDI, we use three of these pins—one for the ground and another pair for sending signals—with the remaining two reserved for future expandability.

Another important point was that, in addition to "MIDI out" and "MIDI in," we designated a "MIDI thru" jack. This was a jack that would send the incoming MIDI signal directly through to the next device, drastically improving the potential for system expandability. In a configuration where multiple devices are connected via MIDI, if the process of receiving signals at the "MIDI in" jack, followed by signal processing, and then transmission from the "MIDI out" jack is repeated over and over, a time lag will eventually result between the time the devices receive and send their signals. This obviously would be detrimental to musical performance. With the "MIDI thru" jack, the signal-processing time can be eliminated, which means we can minimize the time lag even if multiple devices are connected.

One of the factors that accelerated the widespread adoption of the MIDI standard was that we provided it free. At the time, some people at Roland thought that because we went through the trouble of developing it, we should patent it and license it to other companies. But I did not budge on my decision to keep it free because our intent was to establish this as a unified global standard.

One of my convictions is, "Industries with no standards do not prosper." It was imperative that we make MIDI free for it to become a world standard. If we had patented it and licensed it, our company might have made some money from royalties for the first few years, but I don't think that MIDI would have become the world standard that it is today.

I believe MIDI will continue to evolve. In 2008, we announced a proprietary standard called V-Link. This is an advanced iteration of MIDI for connecting the video market with keyboards. I believe this will be the key to connect music with video. In January 2011, MIDI Visual Control, which provided even more generic usability, was officially adopted by the Association of Musical Electronics Industry and MIDI Manufacturers Association Incorporated. Based on our vision for the future, Roland has already announced the V-Link and Video Synthesizer CG-8. The CG-8 allows users to create video from still images, making it the world's first video synthesizer.

In recent years, video editing has become much easier, and V-Link will have many areas of application for synchronizing music with video.

Just as W PRO has taken on half of the expression, I believe it is only natural that video take on the remaining half. However, we have yet to see products that are capable of creating video with the flexibility of W PRO. The world is waiting for MIDI to connect expressions with video.

9

From Silk to Automobiles

Vantage Location

SHIZUOKA PREFECTURE IS SITUATED BETWEEN TWO MAJOR CITIES, Tokyo and Osaka, in an area known for its warm climate. As can be seen from the number of Shinkansen stations in the prefecture (Atami, Mishima, Shin Fuji, Shizuoka, Kakegawa, and Hamamatsu), it is a long stretch of land on the Pacific coast. It is also home to various tourist destinations including the hot springs that center around Hakone and Izu, as well as the beautiful Suruga Bay area with Mount Fuji looming in the background. Shizuoka City, with Suruga castle located at its center, still retains its history as a castle town, and Hamamatsu is known for its manufacturing industry. As such, Shizuoka Prefecture is a unique mix of a variety of aspects and history not found in other prefectures.

In terms of electric power, homes to the east of the Fuji River receive fifty hertz, whereas those to the west receive sixty. As far as I know, although there are countries that use a mixture of DC and AC, I don't think there are many countries that use two different cycles of AC. These two different cycles coexist in Shizuoka. It would be a massive undertaking to modify existing facilities so it is too late for consolidation. This fifty/sixty cycle predicament is the reason the eastern and western regions of Japan are not able to freely share the power from their respective nuclear power plants. Even Ieyasu Tokugawa, who forbade the construction of bridges over the Oi River to prevent attacks from the west, would not have been able to imagine that the Fuji River that flows nearby would eventually become the delineation between these power cycles.

The eastern Kanto region imported all of their facilities for everything from power generation to distribution from Britain so it naturally came to run on fifty cycles. The western Kansai region, however, imported their facilities from the United States so they ended up running on sixty cycles. The voltage was fortunately unified at one hundred volts, but the hundred-volt standard used in Japan represents a minority in the world. Many countries use 220 or 240 volts because there is less transmission loss at higher voltages. While urban legends abound on the topic of why Japan settled on one hundred volts, one of the most interesting is that the various regions of Europe at the time all had their own standards for light bulbs, and it so happened that Germany had a large surplus inventory of hundred-volt bulbs, so Japan decided to adopt this voltage to take advantage of the low-priced bulbs. Others say that it was for the very simple reason that the one hundred volt standard was the most readily acceptable because Japan had been on the decimal system. Although no definitive information remains today, these are good stories, whatever the case.

It was only natural for industry to boom in the Shizuoka region, and many Shizuoka-made products enjoy top market share in Japan. For example, the city of Fuji, with its many paper mills, manufactures the largest share of paper products. In the Hamamatsu area we have musical instrument manufacturers who produce pianos, as well as manufacturers of air conditioners and plastic models. Motorcycle manufacturers Honda, Suzuki, and Yamaha have their key manufacturing facilities in Hamamatsu. Electronics makers, who initially came to Shizuoka to make their instrument and amplifier cabinets here, eventually expanded their factories. The structure of various industries has changed over the past fifteen years, however, and the types of products that command top share are very different now.

The tea industry grew based on large-scale developments carried out following the Meiji Restoration, and Shizuoka Prefecture holds the top spot in Japan's tea industry for both name value and quality. The transition to electronics has changed the face of the musical instruments business and has attracted the electronics industry to this same prefecture. The Faculty of Engineering at Shizuoka University, which carries on the heritage of the Hamamatsu Technical College, has graduated many unique talents. Hamamatsu is also the place where Kenjiro Takayanagi, known as the father of Japanese television, developed his invention. Hamamatsu Photonics, a company that develops unique products primarily in the realms of optical and electronic engineering, is also well-known throughout the world. Hamamatsu became globally known when electron multipliers made by the company were used in Nobel Prize–winning research carried out by Dr. Masatoshi Koshiba. Teibow, which specializes in felt-processing technologies and holds the top global share in tips for marking pens, is also located in Hamamatsu.

Thus, Hamamatsu is unique in some ways even among the other cities in Shizuoka. Since the Edo period, the region was known for its silk and cotton textile production, as well as the processing of lumber that was transported down the Tenryu River. These two basic industries combined in a variety of ways as they developed over the years. Hamamatsu is also known for its inhabitants' fondness for festivals, possibly linked to their proximity to Hamanako Lake and Sea of Enshu. Even people who have lived in Hamamatsu for only a short time can get involved without feeling like outsiders. As far as I know, the two biggest festivals in Japan, in which the entire city is engulfed in festivities, are the Awa Odori of Tokushima and the Hamamatsu Matsuri. In 2011, the Hamamatsu Matsuri was canceled because it was too soon after the Great East Japan Earthquake. The cancelation gave us a feel for the impact of this festival on the local economy and vibrancy of the city. This was a sobering experience that made me ponder the significance of traditional cultures and arts, including the festivals of various other regions in the country.

Local Industries

Local industries are industries that are founded on centuries of history. These industries have developed by making gradual transformations to meet the needs of the times, creating new products, and providing fertile ground for the interplay of various skill sets and technologies. One can clearly see these traits in the industrial structure of Hamamatsu.

In the 1600s, Ieyasu Tokugawa called upon a variety of trades, primarily those related to woodworking, to build the Asama Shrine. Many of these craftspeople and technicians settled in the area, which led to the rich tradition of woodworking in Enshu region. The region's textile and silk industry was founded upon the practice of silkworm growing, which then led to the development of different dyeing techniques, and eventually to the development of automatic looms for weaving fibers into fabric. The technology that went into the automatic loom was developed by Sakichi Toyoda and this enterprise eventually formed the basis for the machine industries that make up our current automobile industry. At one point, possibly more than 90 percent of Japan's motorcycle manufacturers operated out of Hamamatsu. I believe that this level of concentration was unique even in the world. Unfortunately, however, most of the motorcycle production has now moved overseas. Meanwhile, dyeing and automatic loom technologies have continued to develop, and Hamamatsu is the top producer of *yukata*—light, casual kimonos—in Japan.

The mechanical industry sparked by Toyoda's automatic loom expanded into Toyota, a city near Nagoya, and continues to develop as Toyota Motor Corporation. Meanwhile, Hamamatsu is home to Suzuki Motor Corporation, which also started out making automatic looms before moving on to motorcycles and automobiles. Suzuki, currently the largest company in the Hamamatsu region, developed a motored two-wheeler as one of its efforts to expand beyond the realm of automatic looms in 1951, and developed a motorcycle in 1954.

The motorcycle industry began to take off in 1946 when Soichiro Honda launched the Cub, a bicycle fitted with a small engine. Mr. Honda, who founded Honda Motor Co. Ltd. in 1948, was from Tenryu, a city in the northern part of Hamamatsu. It is no coincidence that key manufacturers Yamaha, Suzuki, and Honda are located in Hamamatsu.

Meanwhile, Hamamatsu is also known as a center of furniture making, and its woodworking industry is known throughout the country through furniture trade shows. The musical instrument industry in the region was formed through a marriage of these mechanical and woodworking technologies. Torakusu Yamaha, after repairing an organ in 1887, founded the Yamaha Fukin Seizosho (Yamaha Organ Manufacturers) in 1888 and began manufacturing organs.

With this basis of foundational industries, the city of Hamamatsu has a large population, counted at 810,000 people in 2013. More people live here than in the city of Shizuoka (700,000 people), the capital of Shizuoka Prefecture, and because Shizuoka is surrounded by mountains, the number of industrial companies headquartered in Hamamatsu is significantly greater. Hamamatsu is known for its industrial capabilities, and the city has the top production output in Shizuoka Prefecture.

Together, transportation machines (including automobiles, motorcycles, and outboard motors) and musical instruments (such as pianos, organs, and electronic musical instruments) make up 50 percent of this output. When people visit Hamamatsu from overseas, we tell them, "Hamamatsu has two major industries: motorcycles and musical instruments. These two products have something major in common: they both make noise!" I think people involved in rock music will get this joke.

If asked, "What is your image of Shizuoka?" I believe most Japanese people would reply, "Tea and Hamamatsu eels." Some might even say, "Unagi Pie"—a type of cookie flavored with eel. Shizuoka makes 39 percent of all the tea in Japan, making it the top tea-producing prefecture.

As for exports, the export of tea produced in Shizuoka to the United States and other countries began after the Meiji Restoration. Shimizu Port was developed for this purpose and grew through the tea trade. Tea exports from Shimizu Port peaked at fifteen thousand tons in 1918, which represented 70 percent of all tea exports. This is undoubtedly a unique city even by international standards. Hamamatsu is only an hour-and-twenty-minute drive away from Nagoya, so people making business trips to Europe, the Americas, Australia, and other parts of Asia can conveniently catch flights from Nagoya Airport. Business travelers to Seoul, Shanghai, and Taipei can fly from the Fujisan Shizuoka Airport.

Roland has consolidated most of its factories in Hamamatsu. We built factories in five or six locations after we founded Roland in Osaka, but over time, we have relocated most of them to Hamamatsu. One incentive for this was the warm temperament of the people of Hamamatsu. Their culture of welcoming outsiders was a very big plus and we had no qualms about relocating our factories here.

In addition to Hamamatsu, we run our Roland Matsumoto factory in Matsumoto, which is in the Shinshu region. The history behind this is that we established Fuji Roland as a joint company with FujiGen, the guitar experts, to launch our guitar synthesizer products. Founded in 1977, Fuji Roland was the producer of the world's first guitar synthesizer, GR-500. Shinshu is renowned throughout the world for its precision machines and guitars, which indeed represent the local industries of this region. Shinshu is sometimes referred to as the Switzerland of Asia, in part because it is home to a large number of companies that specialize in watches, cameras, and precision components, which are competitive in the world market. The region also underwent a major influx of electronic technologies over the years, and is now known for its computer peripherals and digital cameras. Currently, Roland's Matsumoto factory produces professional audio equipment and digital video editing equipment, both of which leverage the region's local infrastructure. We were right on the mark to choose Matsumoto with its hard-working people, and Hamamatsu with its open and innovative culture, as our bases of operation.

Our Move to Hamamatsu

There was a time after the war that urban planning became a huge topic as Japan's economy grew. This was also a sign that industries were transitioning from "hard" to "soft" manufacturing. Many argued that factories should be relocated to the suburbs and cities should be redeveloped and redesigned to improve their urban functions. In the moves that followed, the companies that left Osaka first tended to be the larger companies and not the small to medium-sized ones. These companies relocated not just to locales in the proximity of Osaka, but to other prefectures altogether throughout the country such as Kyushu, Shikoku, Chugoku, Sanin, and Tohoku. While small to medium-sized companies lacked the resources to move out immediately, the medium-sized companies also eventually left the city, leaving only the small companies. And of these small companies, those that were not able to compete with the labor costs of Southeast Asia went out of business, and only those companies that had unique proprietary technologies were able to remain in the city and survive.

While the diminishing economic base in Osaka has been a topic of debate for many years, my belief is that the root cause of this issue is that the city's urban planning was wrongheaded from the outset. On top of that, the coasts that line the southern part of Osaka are now occupied by plants operated by major steelmakers and petrochemical companies, completely destroying the beautiful coastlines that these areas were known for. The areas near Osaka Bay are off-limits to swimmers, and the scenic beaches and shorelines are long gone. These are examples of what can come out of bungled political decisions.

We started up Roland in Osaka, where I was born and where I retuned to live until I was fifty years old. However, the rising land prices in large urban centers such as Osaka and Tokyo made it very difficult to secure industrial land, so we had to relocate from Osaka. Under these circumstances, it was quite a feat to find a good location that had future potential. Even for private individuals, relocating one's home is a major undertaking. More so for a company seeking to relocate its head offices and production facilities. There has to be a compelling reason to do so. At the time, we scouted for land in Okayama, Hiroshima, the countryside of Hyogo, and industrial parks in and around Shiga, as well as Tohoku and Kumamoto. In the end, we concluded that Hamamatsu, which was located between Tokyo and Osaka and provided access to export-related

▼ We acquired the land for the Roland Hosoe factory (presently Head Factories) in 1985.

infrastructure including the ports of Shimizu and Nagoya, was the best location. So we decided to relocate our primary production facilities to Hamamatsu. Our small factory in Hamamatsu, which we started up at the time we started up Roland, continued to expand as we relocated all of our factories, until that process was complete. This entire relocation process took about eight years.

This was a major undertaking because in addition to relocating our factory, we also had to solve the issue of relocating our employees and their families. Although some unfortunately had to leave the company as family circumstances prevented them from leaving Osaka, we were very fortunate that almost all of our employees agreed to move. So overall, this major relocation went very well. The culture of Hamamatsu is very open and relaxed, and the people of Hamamatsu are open to new and different ideas.

The first time I visited Hamamatsu was around 1956, when I was searching for organ keyboards. I took a night train from Osaka, which arrived at Hamamatsu after 3 a.m. Obviously accustomed to these late arrivals, the ryokan near the station had left their doors open, awaiting my arrival. This meant that I could have a short sleep of about four hours, start my day early in the morning, and take the train back to Osaka at the end of the day. This was what amounted to "business express" in those days.

In 1968, we acquired a piano factory and began producing Hammond organs and Ace Electronic organs. It was a challenge to teach the production of electronic musical instruments to piano craftspeople. They all had their own huge toolboxes and would not let go of them. These toolboxes were traditionally indispensable to piano craftspeople, who worked with their hands. At the time, although major piano manufacturers had already made the transition to mass production and their production lines no longer required the skills of experienced craftspeople, many small to medium-sized manufacturers still retained their archaic production methods. As for our factory, our modifications had to start with repairing the floors, and we threw all of the equipment in the factory out in the yard to install our production lines. After we did so, we prohibited people from bringing any personal items or toolboxes to the factory. We were able to avoid any problems by allowing our employees to take their toolboxes home, although technically they were company property.

I spent about three days out of the week in Hamamatsu, and continued traveling back and forth between Osaka and Hamamatsu for about two years. Based on this experience, my conviction that Hamamatsu was a very suitable location for production grew stronger. When we started up Roland, we leased a small factory in Hamamatsu in addition to our factory in Osaka. In 1980, my family sold our home in Osaka and moved to our current residence in Hosoe-cho. I have been

▲ We started up our factory in March 1986.

a resident of Hamamatsu for thirty-three years—forty-four if I include the early days when I rented a small house in Hamamatsu when we started up our factory. Although it may smack somewhat of favoritism on my part, I have lived in Hamamatsu longer than I have in Osaka, my birthplace, and I think that this was only a natural turn of events. I have moved a total of seventeen times since 1945, and I have already lived at my current address for longer than at any other location.

Hamamatsu is home to a larger number of venture companies than other regions. Even on a national basis, the ratio is quite high. One major reason for this is that the city and surrounding municipalities are well versed in these matters. Neither Roland's relocation nor my personal move would have been possible were it not for our inclusion as part of the Hamamatsu Region Technopolis program that was being promoted by the Ministry of International Trade and Industry and the helpful cooperation of Mr. Hayado, then mayor of Hosoe-cho. We waited for Hosoe-cho to be annexed into Hamamatsu when the city's status was amended, and we relocated Roland's head offices to Hamamatsu in July 2005. This worked out well for us as it allowed us to complete the necessary address-change procedures in a single step. So one could say that the threads spun by the silkworms are now connected to automobiles as well as to electronic musical instruments.

The Hamamatsu Museum of Musical Instruments

The history of musical instrument production in Hamamatsu goes back to the Meiji period, and the region is still the bustling center of Japan's musical instrument industry. This history can be traced back to 1888, when Torakusu Yamaha started up Yamaha Fukin Seizosho, an organ manufacturing and repair company. In 1897, he embarked on manufacturing pianos, and completed the first piano made in Japan in 1900. In 1927, Kawai Musical Instruments Manufacturing was also founded here. After this, many technicians from both companies struck out on their own and musical instrument manufacturing became one of Hamamatsu's major industries. According to 1995 statistics, Hamamatsu was home to fifteen manufacturers of pianos, electronic organs, and other musical instruments. In Japan, Hamamatsu manufacturers commanded a 100 percent share in piano production, 80 percent in electronic organ production, and 50 percent in electronic piano production. However, a large portion of piano production has moved abroad since then. Although sales of Japan-made pianos have declined as the popularity of pianos made in China has grown, public perceptions persist that piano manufacturing is Hamamatsu's major industry. We at Roland make a point of manufacturing our pianos in Hamamatsu.

If we regard these musical instruments as the hardware, then music education and concerts can be regarded as the software. Industries with no software have no future. The residents of Hamamatsu expressed their wish to build a good concert hall in Hamamatsu. After the hall was built, Japan's first public musical instrument museum opened its doors in July 1995.

With the Robert Rosenbaum Collection as its centerpiece, the museum exhibits a wide range of musical instruments from around the world. Permanent

▼ A piano with five pedals (Hamamatsu Museum of Musical Instruments).

exhibits include instruments from Japan, other parts of Asia, Africa, Oceania, the Americas, and Europe, as well as parts for keyboard instruments from Europe, Western instruments made in Japan, and of course electronic musical instruments, all of which are laid out by time period in a very visitor-friendly way. Visitors can also listen to sample performances of representative instruments on headphones. The museum is very extensive; in particular, its collection of pianos and other keyboard instruments is quite large, ranging from early harpsichords to modern pianos. There is an exhibit of cut-away samples of keyboards, which shows in sequence how keyboards have changed over the ages and why these changes were necessary. In the last section of this exhibit is shown a replica of a piano made by Bartolomeo Cristofori (1655–1731) said to be the prototype of the modern piano, of which only three remain in the world today. A 1720 model is held by the Metropolitan Museum in New York, a 1722 model by the Museo Nazionale degli Strumenti Musicali in Rome, and a 1726 model by the Museum für Musikinstrumente of Leipzig University. The replica at the Hamamatsu Museum of Musical Instruments was made by Kawai Musical Instruments Manufacturing.

In the early 1800s, pianos were being made with four to six pedals, which were used to alter the tone of their sound. I was surprised to learn that so many pedals were being used then. While I do not know whether they were the result of requests made by musicians or inventions conjured by the fabricators, they remain very interesting nonetheless. An explanatory plaque lists nine different types of pedals and their effects.

- Damper (also called the loud, sustain, or open pedal in modern pianos): This is used to release the damper (a device that otherwise stops the strings from vibrating) to sustain a note.

- Sostenuto: This moves the hammer laterally to sustain selected notes.

- Una corda (called the soft pedal in modern pianos): This reduces the distance from the hammer to the string to produce a gentler tone.

- Piano (celesta): This inserts a piece of felt between the string and hammer to produce a muted tone.

- Sordino (lute stop): A rod wrapped with leather is made to contact the string to reduce its sustain.

- Harp stop: A rod wrapped with wool or silk is made to contact the string to reduce its sustain.

- Bassoon stop: A piece of paper is made to contact the string to produce a bassoon-like tone.

- Swell: This is used to open and close the piano cover to adjust the volume.

- Drum: This is used to hit the soundboard to produce a drum-like sound. There are pianos with bells as well.

Only three of these pedal types are still in use in modern pianos.

While many two-pedal pianos were made in the 1870s, it appears pianos with a variety of pedal mechanisms, equipped with one to six pedals, were common in those days. For example, a six-pedal type had one pedal had that created the damper function, which was initially developed as one way to alter the tone, but performers and composers were interested in its function of allowing the sound to sustain for as long as possible and gradually moved away from looking at it as a device for altering tone. Notations for this pedal gradually disappeared from scores, and pianos settled on the two- or three-pedal configuration of damper, sostenuto, and soft pedal that we are familiar with today. My guess is that keyboard actions underwent dramatic improvements over the years, which increased the expressivity of pianissimo and fortissimo. As performers were given the ability to infuse their emotions into subtle touches that played a crucial role in expressivity, the need for these complex tone-altering mechanisms must have lessened, and with that the need for a large number of pedals.

The piano keyboards on exhibit have very light touches compared to modern pianos. Their fortes are weak and pianissimos are difficult to play as well. In other words, they have a narrow dynamic range. This exhibit makes clear that modern piano actions came to be what they are today over a period of two hundred years. Pianos made for about one hundred years after Cristofori are categorized as fortepianos. In other words, the fortepiano category preceded the development of what we currently refer to as grand pianos.

The load on a pianist's fingers is quite intense, but because this touch is something that pianists become accustomed to from childhood, piano actions have not changed very much over the past hundred years. In the 1800s, there were a variety of pianos in different European countries with a wide range of touch, and pianists in those days must have come across pianos that were quite different from what they were accustomed to. I have heard stories of people placing weights on their keyboards to train their fingers. I think it would be possible to come up with different types of keyboard touch if we could come up with ways to expand the dynamic range, which plays a major role in expressivity. In fact, I think it is the responsibility of manufacturers to come up with such innovations. Based on our experience with developing digital pianos, what we call key touch refers not only to the weight of the keys but also to the depth of the key strokes, the point in the stroke at which the sound is produced, and the differences in the initial sound. Of course, definitions of touch will be different from one piano maker to another, but this is how I see it.

In September 2000, I had the chance to attend *Piano 300*, an exhibition at the Smithsonian Museum in Washington, D.C., which I viewed during the quiet pre-open hours, personally guided by the curator, Patrick Rucker. This exhibit was very in-depth, offering an amazing overview of everything to do with the history of pianos. Of particular note was a piano made by Cristofori, on loan from Italy, and a six-pedal piano used during the time of Beethoven. Stepping on the rightmost pedal produced a drum tone. I was told that this had been used to perform the "Turkish March," and our guide gave us a personal performance to show how this was done. By Beethoven's time, pianos had undergone various improvements, and these improvements had a major impact on the work of composers. An example of this type of piano with six pedals can also be seen in a piano exhibited at the Hamamatsu Museum of Musical Instruments. These aspects of the history of pianos are explained in more detail in the book *Ongaku Kikai Gekijo* (*Musical Machinery Theater*) in the chapter titled "The Hard and Soft of Pedals: Beethoven and the Piano." As a designer of musical instruments, I found this a very interesting book.

Many historical records attest to the extensive dialogue between performers, composers, and piano makers. I suspect that the makers were able to accommodate requests as they were craftspeople who made their pianos by hand, and I believe that modern manufacturers will eventually be required to do the same. Although pianos may not change in just one or two decades, judging from the history of pianos, if someone is able to make a piano that does not make excessive demands on the pianist, allows the pianist to channel his or her energy into artistic expression, and allows the pianist to concentrate on his or her performance, then I believe such a piano will eventually be accepted over a period of time.

I have had many opportunities to visit the museum

▼ This piano exhibited in *Piano 300* at the Smithsonian Museum was made in the late eighteenth century and is the same model used by Mozart.

in Hamamatsu with my friends, and these are very enjoyable occasions because I make new discoveries every time I visit. Archaeologists study items dug up at ancient sites and are able to reconstruct the past based primarily on the surrounding conditions and the latest analysis technologies. This is because they have no reference literature. Fortunately for designers of modern keyboard instruments, we have access to reference literature and artifacts that still exist in complete form. It was very fortunate and a source of pride for residents of Hamamatsu that such a museum, a portal into different ages, was built here.

I had the opportunity to visit the Bösendorfer factory in Vienna in the spring of 1990. I was accompanying Michael Heuser, the president of Roland (Switzerland) AG, who was visiting the company to inspect a grand piano that he had special-ordered. Coincidentally, the first name of the president of Bösendorfer at the time was Roland and, whether for that reason or not, we were given a tour of their factory as well. Bösendorfer has since been acquired by Yamaha and continues to manufacture pianos. I have had the chance to visit four other piano factories. Three of these factories—Steinway's New York factory, Bösendorfer's Austria factory, and Beijing Hsing Hai of China—allowed me access to every nook and cranny.

Since I was in Vienna, I was not about to miss a visit to the Collection of Early Musical Instruments and arrived at the museum with Mr. Heuser only to find out that they were closed that day. This was around the time that we started building harpsichords and I was very much looking forward to visiting the museum, so I still regret that I did not stay another night. It has been twenty years since that time and I still have not had the chance to visit. The saying, "You must grasp the opportunity when it presents itself" is always true.

The clavichord, which is a precursor of the harpsichord, is an instrument that I would like to reproduce one day. Although the instrument made a revival in the heyday of rock music, it has since gone out of favor because not much attention was paid to the ever-important issue of producing a stable pitch.

Automatic Instruments

Instruments capable of automatic performance were invented early on in the history of improvements and developments made to musical instruments. Devices were developed that could deliver performances to large audiences; others could be integrated into pianos used in homes. Amazing performances by a variety of performers are still with us in the form of piano roll tapes. Piano rolls have holes punched into them where notes are supposed to sound, and these holes control the flow of air as they pass over a detection unit that then hits the keys.

An article in the July 1995 issue of *The Music Trades*, an American musical instrument trade newspaper, mentions that of the 2.3 million pianos sold between 1920 and 1929, 1.4 million were automatic pianos, or player pianos. The magnitude of their popularity is difficult for us to imagine and suggests just how many people were enjoying these pianos that played automatically. The idea of entertainment was completely different from what it was in Japan at the time.

▲ Tony Fenelon and a theater organ exhibited at the Nethercutt Collection.

This automatic playing feature went beyond pianos to a variety of other instruments such as organs, violins, banjos, and percussive instruments. There were sets made up of a combination of banjo and percussion instruments that mimicked Dixieland jazz bands, as well as those that played orchestral pieces. Many of these were shown and played in amusement parks and theaters. This coincided with the time period when theater organs were used as accompaniments to movies. Later, in the 1950s through the 1980s, jukeboxes became popular and inserting coins into these machines to play records even became fashionable. I believe that record-playing jukeboxes were well received because of the public's familiarity with piano roll tapes.

These automatic instruments have become collectors' items and many are still around, a number of them in good condition, fortunately. I had the chance to visit the Mechanical Musical Instruments Museum, which opened its doors in the outskirts of Copenhagen around 1980. I was amazed at the breadth of exhibits, which ranged from large music box–type instruments to those that could fit on a tabletop. Many of these instruments were made in the United States. Instruments from this time period are described in detail in the *Encyclopedia of Automatic Musical Instruments*. (The museum in Copenhagen has since closed down.)

The best of such collections from the perspective of the scope and condition of the exhibits would be the Nethercutt Collection, located in the outskirts of Los Angeles. I was able to view the piano roll tapes stored in their archives and was stunned at the sheer number of these rolls. The Nethercutt Collection also featured an exhibit of an almost brand-new Wurlitzer theater organ where visitors could enter the pipe room and experience the full splendor of this theater organ. In addition to musical instruments, the collection is also famous for its collection of classic cars, which are all maintained in operating condition, just as the musical instruments are. Standing among these items, I could only be amazed by their grandeur. I was told that this collection had been affected by the earthquake in Los Angeles in 1994 and that the museum had been closed for a period of time. I had the privilege of taking a tour of the collection, which had been restored to its previous glory, guided personally by Gordon Belt, assistant director of the museum at the time. This was a place that gave you a sense of opulence.

Even while manufacturers were working to improve the quality of their instruments and address the needs of performers, they were also mass-producing automatic musical instruments that were a combination of mechanical "hardware," such as pianos, and "software," such as piano rolls. Not only were the mechanisms of these automatic performance machines fun to watch, they also produced music, and that is why I think it was quite natural that a large number of these curious instruments found their way into restaurants and bars at a time when many people and children might not have had easy access to theaters. In any case, one is never bored by the sight of these mechanisms working in perfect coordination.

The connection between clock making, which represented the pinnacle of mechanical technology at the time, and music begins with music boxes. While these machines are called *orugoru* in Japanese, possibly from *orgel*, the German word for organ, no one overseas would understand what you were saying as they are typically called music boxes. As a matter of course, these mechanisms became highly developed in Switzerland, which was the center for clock-making technologies at the time. Many marvelous products were developed that combined a variety of elements, such as little dolls that were made in neighboring France. There is a music box museum in Utrecht, Holland. I remember visiting this museum over twenty years ago with Mr. Takada, who was in charge of technology at Roland. The museum featured an amazing collection that started off with early music boxes and progressed to large automatic playing machines. This was truly a first-class museum in terms of both the quality and quantity of its exhibits.

In October 1999, the Hamanako Music Box Museum opened at the summit of Okusayama, which visitors can access by cable car from the Palpal amusement park in Kanzanji Onsen in Hamamatsu. While it pales compared to the museum in Utrecht in terms of scale, it features amazing exhibits of representative machines for each category. Several times a day, the museum stages musical performances orchestrated to play with mechanical dolls, making this a very fun museum to visit. The souvenir shop next door sells a variety of music boxes and mechanical units without their enclosures. They also have a section where you can build your own music box to suit your tastes. I owned a music box that I purchased in Sorrento, Italy, and I took it apart one time because the music would not start even if I opened the lid. What I found inside was a marking on the mechanical unit that read "SANKYO." The mechanism had been made in Japan. The outer box was a wonderful sound box made by local Sorrento craftspeople. Combined with Japan-made units, these music boxes had become one of the most popular souvenirs purchased by visitors. It was heartwarming to know that these boxes were producing melodies for people all over the world.

Most of the music boxes that we are familiar with today have a metal cylinder with protrusions that "pluck" the sound pieces (tuned teeth) of a steel comb. In the early days, music boxes had steel disks on which a different type of protrusion would "hit" the sound pieces. I believe this was more popular as disks were easier to replace than cylinders, and some of the disks were up to fifty centimeters in diameter. I particularly enjoy the large ones with glass windows that show the internal mechanism and are designed to play rhythm instruments as well as harmony. There were also devices that would start only when you dropped a coin into them.

As automatic playing devices became smaller, the majority began to consolidate into either the disk or cylinder format. The cylinder configuration was passed down to Edison's wax-coated cylinder type records and small music boxes. The disk format became the ancestor of vinyl records, SPs, LPs, CDs, MDs, and DVDs. And while many efforts were made in both categories to enable users to easily play a variety of tunes, the disk format eventually prevailed as they were easier to organize in libraries, easier to store, and more suitable to mass production through the pressing process. Phonographs, invented by Edison, which were based on a cylindrical medium, competed against new systems developed by competitors, but over time transitioned to using disks as well. This story is told in detail in *Edison and the Business of Innovation*, which gives a clear account of Edison's struggle. I highly recommend this book.

The history of music box development becomes especially interesting when this process of shifting technologies is considered from a business perspective.

Driven by a precision mechanism that glistens with the sheen of brass and turns a regulator fan to control its speed as it plays music, music boxes have a different feel to them from other automatic playing devices. Although the actions of music boxes would be defined as automatic playing, they are a very special breed whose focus is on compactness, low cost, and sound box design. As such, I believe these devices opened up a whole new world outside the realm of automatic playing devices. The sounds of music boxes do not have to be loud; rather, it is better that their sounds are gentle. I've played them on amplifiers to see what they would sound like, but it just broke the mood and did not sound interesting at all. Even if the sound is small, the resonation it makes in the sound box gives it a tone that is very delicate and rich at the same time. Slits are sawed into a piece of steel, creating a comb-like structure that produces the different pitches. The vibrations of the tuned teeth of the steel comb are transmitted to the sound box and dramatically transformed. I have only great respect for the many people who have contributed to perfecting this device into such a simple mechanism.

Clocks use chimes that announce the time. There are a variety of types of these: some simply strike the number of hours while others play melodies on the chime. Of these melodies, the Westminster chime is the most popular. Chime systems found in table clocks and floor clocks in many people's homes will play a melody when they hit the top of the hour, and some even have cuckoos that pop out and sing. There was a time when clock shop windows were decorated with such clocks.

When I was running my clock repair business immediately after the war, I had the chance to do an overhaul repair of a stately German-made floor clock with a Westminster chime. The bars that produced the sound were made not of iron but of some metal that had a glister similar to that of phosphor bronze and were shaped slightly narrower at the bottom. These were attached to a massive cast iron platform. The pins that made the melody were embedded in a cylinder. These pins would lift up the part near the base of the hammers and when they released, the hammers would gently hit the bar to produce a tone. This sound resonated in the sound box, which was the outer enclosure of the clock, and even though this was a small space, it made an amazing sound. The hammer head was embedded with a piece of hardened tanned deer hide, and the hardness of this piece had a subtle effect on the tone. When I did the overhaul, I accidentally let the hammer dip into some cleaning oil, which resulted in the clock making a completely different tone after I reassembled it. I remember having to replace the leather on the hammer, changing its hardness many times, and having a very difficult time reproducing its original tone.

▲ The serinette is a music box that uses pipes to produce its music. This was made around 1820.

Clocks with high-end Westminster chimes often used a melody that went *do re mi so, do re mi do, mi do re so, so re mi do*. This was a pentatonic scale that the Japanese people were familiar with, so together with the beautiful tones, this melody became popular among many people. I have recently learned that there are many types of Westminster melodies and many different variations.

One evening after dinner during my visit to the Roland Europe factory in Italy in 1997, I had the chance to visit a musical instrument shop that was run by an older brother of Francesco Rauchi, the company's director in charge of technology. Though it was already late at night, his brother, who had closed his shop for the day, was repairing a small old box at his desk. A variety of parts had been removed from the box and laid on the desk, and I noticed that some of them were small pipes. This was actually an automatic playing device that used ten pipes. This was a serinette, which was estimated to have been made around 1820, and it measured twenty-seven by twenty-two by sixteen centimeters. It was capable of playing eight different tunes. The tunes would be played by manually cranking a cylinder on which a paper roll was attached. It was a very unusual device that used a bellows to blow air through the pipes. This idea of using pipes in a music box was something that I had not imagined before. I look forward to hearing this "pipe music box" played during my next visit.

Even in various places in Japan, there are a number of exhibit venues that call themselves music box museums. For example there are the ones in Kanzanji, Hamamatsu, and Kawaguchiko, Yamanashi. In the summer of 2013, I visited a museum called the Kawaguchiko Orugoru no Mori (Lake Kawaguchi Music Box Forest), which had a very extensive collection of large items. There I saw a pipe music box that was much larger than the serinette I had seen earlier, something that I was not expecting to see in Japan. I was stunned to know that there were people who actually made these devices whose size defied my imagination. The museum also featured an item that had been scheduled to be loaded onto the *Titanic*.

Viva Italia!

Why Accordions Now?

THE FIRST MUSICAL INSTRUMENT TRADE SHOW THAT I ATTENDED OVER-seas was the 1964 NAMM Show in Chicago during my Ace Electronic Industries days, before I started up Roland. I had the idea that an American trade show would be dominated by electronic musical instruments, but I was surprised to see that accordions were all over the place. Our exhibition booths were hotel rooms with the beds still in place, and it was quite a sight to see these rooms filled to the brim with accordions.

Distribution for musical instruments in those days was divided into three categories: pianos, organs, and electronic musical instruments, which were in their experimental stage. And distribution for all other instruments was done by the wholesalers. Products that were not a particularly prominent brand were exhibited under whatever brand the wholesaler used, and there was an almost uncountable number of accordions on exhibit and competing against each other as flagship products of major wholesalers. The accordions were designed with loud colors, which made them seem even more prominent in the show. Most of them were made in Germany, Italy, or France, but there was no way of telling how many manufacturers were actually being represented there. Since all manufacturers exported their products to multiple wholesalers, one could imagine that the competition must have been intense. When American soldiers were in Europe during World War II, many of them encountered accordion music, which perhaps reminded them of their grandparents, and they brought this culture home to create what eventually became a huge market for accordions.

At around the same time, more than ten electronic organ manufacturers were competing against Hammond and vying to establish new markets. In the area of keyboard instruments for home use, organs had become an important item for musical instrument stores in addition to pianos. Electronic musical instruments were also important products, ranking second after radios along with TVs. Although TVs were already being mass-produced and were therefore in a different league from electronic musical instruments, almost all electronics manufacturers were involved directly or indirectly with making organs. The situation was the same in Japan as well, with manufacturers such as Matsushita Electric, Victor Company of Japan, Toshiba, Hitachi, Sanyo, and Brother making organs and other keyboard instruments. In Europe, Philips of Holland had launched an organ. If we were to define the production of the theremin by RCA in 1920 as the first wave of electrical manufacturers' foray into the electronic musical instrument industry, then this move to produce electronic organs can be said to be the second wave.

Accordion players were called upon to teach organ classes and conduct trade show demonstrations. Accordion players switched to organs en masse because of the similarities in the ways these instruments were played, and this created a boom in the American musical instrument industry. In Japan, the number of accordion players was limited, so we had to train organ players from scratch. The history of the Japanese people studying and mastering Western music since the Meiji era paid off and a large number of players were born. In the United States, the popularity of accordions began to wane, unfortunately, when a prominent accordion player fled from the army and was jailed as a draft dodger, accelerating the shift to electronic organs. The launch of organs with only one row of keys and touted as "easy play" dramatically changed the public perception of keyboard instruments for the home. This was ironic because the fun of "easy play" was what accordions were originally all about.

The NAMM Show was replete with glamorous accordion exhibits and the aura of novelty surrounding electronic organs, and there was no way of getting a full picture of the industry by simply setting up a booth there. I still remember how I felt so very distant from the action, a nobody exhibiting a small instrument called the Rhythm Ace and a small monophonic keyboard instrument called the Canary amid this massive display of musical instruments that I had never seen before in my life. In addition to this, the accordions I saw at this show made a vivid impression on me. Since I was so overwhelmed at the difference in the technological capabilities between myself, who had just managed to finish a prototype of a classical organ, and the American companies that I saw, I was not able to come up with any specific counter ideas for some time. I thought, however, that I might have a chance with accordions as they were a manageable size.

Ironically, it was actually our organs that took off first. As for accordions, it would have been very difficult to make the parts for a prototype so I had to begin by searching for existing parts that I could use. While I had no time to think in Chicago, once I was back in Japan, I began searching for keyboards. I was thinking that I might be able to make an accordion using the keyboard on the Canary, but its shape was unusable on an accordion. It would have been easy to ask an accordion manufacturer but that meant that I would have to divulge my idea of making an electronic accordion.

I had heard before that there was a town in Italy where there were several accordion manufacturers who exported accordions under other brand names, so I decided to visit the town. I was able to follow through on this plan in 1967 after the Frankfurt Messe, when I visited Italy for the first time. My intention was to visit a town called Castelfidardo, a major production center for accordions located near Ancona, to find out more about the industry and search for parts that I could use for my electronic accordion. I boarded a twin prop plane from Milan and arrived at Ancona Airport via Bologna. At the time, the only notice-able feature at the airport was a windsock and there was no terminal building to speak of. It has now grown to a very convenient medium-sized airport with flights to major Italian cities such as Rome and Milan, and even cities outside of Italy such as Munich. But when I first visited, the plane's engines were left on while the passengers disembarked and embarked. Once we were off of the boarding ramp, it felt like we had landed in the middle of a farm field. That's how rustic the airport was.

At the time, I did not even imagine that we would be starting up Roland Europe in San Benedetto, about fifty miles south of Ancona, in 1989 and producing electronic accordions at the factory there. Roland Europe's current factory is located about an hour's drive south of Ancona by freeway along the Adriatic coast. Castelfidardo has subsequently grown into a production center for all electronic musical instruments, not just accordions. And while the number of manufacturers of electronic keyboard instruments has declined, makers of traditional accordions are still going strong, making this a town of musical instruments along with Cremona, which is known for its violins and other string instruments.

Back in 1967, my first two destinations in Castelfidardo were Paolo Soprani and Crucianelli. My first visit was to Paolo Soprani, where I tried to explain in faltering English how I was not there to import accordions but to search for parts to use in an electronic accordion. The company had previously employed nine hundred workers and made large numbers of accordions, but at the time they had only two hundred people in their employ. They explained that while they were always interested in novel ideas, the topic of electronic accordions had never come up. Paolo Soprani, the president of the company whom I met then, had a striking resemblance to Paolo Soprani I, the founder of the company who was depicted in a wall portrait. He was a short man with a warm demeanor, and was probably the second-generation owner of the company. As soon as we finished with our initial greetings, I was offered wine, which was quite a surprise, as I could not drink. It was in the morning and they were having wine during a business discussion. I supposed that wine was like tea for the Italians.

He gave me a tour of the factory and although they were equipped with large machinery, I noticed that their layout was quite haphazard and the company seemed to have no interest in production efficiency. Instead, what struck me was how experienced craftspeople had set up shop in whatever area of the factory they fancied and were all enjoying their work. The items they held in their hands were complex parts that could rightfully be called craftwork, and the interior of the accordions, which I saw for the first time, was very beautiful. While I had been lousy company for a glass of wine, I felt as if I were in an otherworldly amusement park during the factory tour. It so happened that Hiroo Sakata, an Akutagawa Prize–winning writer, accompanied me on that trip from Milan to Ancona, and our travails during our visit to Ancona were described in detail in his later book *International Complex Journey*. This was the first time I became the subject of a book, and specifically one written by an Akutagawa Prize winner.

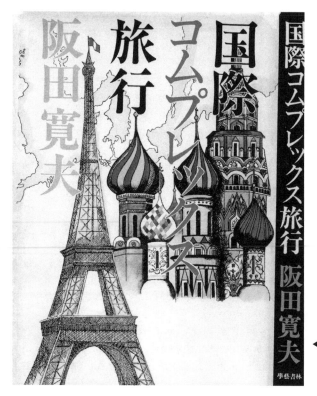

The same afternoon, I visited Crucianelli, which manufactured guitars and electronic musical instruments in addition to accordions. The factory was equipped with measuring instrumentation and their range of products was much larger than Soprani's as they had already shifted their primary focus from accordions to guitar amps and electronic keyboard instruments. It would have been extremely risky to mention the topic of electronic accordions here, akin

◀ *International Complex Journey* by Hiroo Sakata (Gakugei Shorin, 1968).

to lighting kindling in a place that already had the parts, the technology, and a factory. I knew that my idea was timely but I thought that the Italians would beat me to it.

It was clear that, at the time, the electronic musical instrument industry in Japan lagged far behind not only the Americans but also the Europeans. My hunch that someone would beat us to it became a reality when Farfisa of Italy exhibited their electronic accordion at the Frankfurt Messe. Crucianelli would also become a key player in the area of organs and portable keyboards, which they marketed under the Elka brand. Although I was not able to achieve my objective of sourcing parts for electronic accordions during my first visit to Europe and a couple of its factories, I believe my tour of the factories of two very different companies—remember, I had no interpreter with me—was very fruitful. Ultimately, I purchased two sample accordions from a different company and paid overweight fees to take them back to Japan. I took one apart for its parts but have kept the other one as a memento.

By the way, I made another very important connection in Italy. I was able to meet with Alfred Dronge, founder of Guild, a guitar company that was squarely competing against Martin and Gibson, the two major American acoustic guitar makers, which were doing very well in the folk music boom of the 1960s and 1970s. Mr. Dronge, who reminded me of Dwight Eisenhower, was on his way to Ancona after the Frankfurt Messe just as I was, and we were on the same plane from Milan. Although I do not know which factory he visited that day, we met again at our hotel in Ancona that evening and he treated me to dinner. At the time, Guild had its factory in Hoboken, New Jersey, just across the river from New York City. He cracked a joke, "The Statue of Liberty is my neighbor, so I'll introduce you," and invited me to tour his factory.

The Leader (front), an accordion made ▶ by Tombo Musical Instrument Company and exhibited at the accordion museum in Castelfidardo.

I met with Mr. Dronge several times after that at NAMM Shows and other events, and I remember being amazed when he told me that he commuted on his personal plane, which he piloted himself, to the company's new expanded factory. This was when I was traveling back and forth between our headquarters in Osaka and Hamamatsu, so what I learned from him about the thinking that guided American manufacturers was very helpful during this transitional time. When he came to a trade show in Osaka, I was able to treat him to a sushi dinner as I had promised in Ancona, but sadly, he died in 1972 when his private plane crashed and I never did get to tour the Guild factory. This was right after I had started up Roland and I still feel that I lost a great friend and colleague.

Was Tango Born in Italy?

Fast-forward to 1992, during my visit to Roland's factory in Italy, Roland Europe, after the Frankfurt Messe. Just as we were getting ready to head home, I learned that there was an accordion museum nearby, and I was very keen on visiting. So three of us—Carlo Lucarelli, president of Roland Europe, Mr. Takada, who was in charge of technology at Roland, and I—visited the museum. From the visit, I got a very good picture of the large number of countries around the world that accordions had been exported to in their heyday. Exhibits also included a variety of early accordions, making this a very extensive museum. The literature I was handed was very informative, describing in great detail the history of Castelfidardo through its booming as well as its waning years and how it came to be what it is now. I was surprised to see a Tombo accordion from Japan on exhibit, and I was also very happy because I personally knew Mr. Maya, the president of the company. Since many of the Italian names ended in vowels such as *i* and *o*, I remember feeling that the Tombo name blended in well.

Upon seeing these exhibits, as well as the figures describing the production and population of Castelfidardo, I surmised that perhaps the entire village had been involved in the manufacture of musical instruments. According to the information I received, this turned out to be true, and it illustrates how the majority of people in the village made their living making musical instruments. Accordion manufacturers ranged from large factories that hired several hundred people to cottage industries where the only employees were family members, and it struck me that this was reminiscent of what Hamamatsu had been like in the past. Under these conditions, the division of labor advanced to the point that expert craftspeople became specialized in making individual components such as the bellows for blowing air, the keyboard, the reeds that produced the sound, and mechanisms such as the bass buttons, and others specialized in tuning the instruments. The entire village worked together to produce accordions.

The museum also had an exhibit of a Chinese instrument called a *sheng*, with the explanation that this instrument shared a common feature with accordions in that reeds were used to produce the sound. Needless to say, the sheng is different as the player blows into the instrument whereas the airflow of accordions is produced by a bellows; still, it can be considered one of the possible origins of this method of producing sound.

If the sheng is the origin of accordions, then the history of accordions can be traced back three thousand years, but the production of accordions in Italy did not begin that long ago. Stories abound of how accordion production began here and the material that I was given describes one version that appears to be the most likely: "Loreto, a holy pil-

▲ Facade of the Holy House of Loreto.

grimage site near Castelfidardo, attracted a large number of pilgrims. And in one of the houses that sheltered these pilgrims, one pilgrim left a small, strange instrument as a token of gratitude, and this became the origin of accordions. Paolo Soprani took this instrument and improved upon it to create the basic construction of modern accordions and worked tirelessly to grow this into an industry."

Based on this story, it would be natural to think that this instrument most likely originated not in Italy but perhaps in one of the Eastern European countries or even in Germany or France. It is probably true that it was in Italy that this instrument was first mass-produced and grew into an industry, eventually spreading to Germany and France. In any case, it is indisputable that the entire town of Castelfidardo was involved in the production of accordions. The competition must have been quite intense, which means progress must have also been fast. Also, because there would have been no use for tuning or other final tests on the instruments if there was no music in which the accordion played an important role, it is natural to assume that music that featured accordions prominently must have existed in the area. It is not difficult to imagine that accordion manufacturing and the cheerful nature of the Italian people contributed to popularizing this type of music.

Instruments such as accordions and harmonicas that use the vibration of metal reeds to create sound are able to produce a rich range of high frequencies, which means their sound travels very well. Given this characteristic, accordions played a central role as accompaniment in folk dancing and other outdoor events at a time when microphones and amplifiers were not available.

The Holy House of Loreto, which was also described in the material I received, stands on a hill facing the Adriatic Sea. There is a freeway that passes between the Adriatic coast and the cathedral, so I get a chance to see this magnificent building to the right every time I visit the Roland Europe factory. To followers of the Catholic faith, it is also known as a place where special rosaries are made. With pilgrims visiting the site from many different regions, a market developed here. Records show that Italian musical instruments made their way to various parts of Europe in the hands of pilgrims. Additionally, early export records show that the two most popular destinations outside of Europe, by a wide margin, were New York and Buenos Aires, and also show how these instruments were exported in large volumes to the countries of Argentina and Brazil, both destinations of a large number of Italian immigrants. This is perhaps one of the reasons the bandoneon has become an indispensable instrument in tango.

There are various theories on the origins of tango, which became popular in Buenos Aires in the late nineteenth century. It is often said that it was based on a type of dance music called *milonga*, which blended African rhythms and Latin music from Cuba. It was around 1920 that bandoneons came to be used in tango accompaniment. Perhaps because of its melancholic tone, which was different from that of accordions, it eventually became the central instrument in tango ensembles.

When I first visited the NAMM Show in 1964, I was amazed at the number of accordions on exhibit. Almost all of those instruments had been made in Castelfidardo and exported. The museum wall featured a large poster of Hollywood star James Stewart playing an accordion. According to the director of the museum, he had been quite the player and was not featured in the poster just because he was a film star. You can see him playing the accordion in the 1957 film *Night Passage*.

Accordions were also made in volume in Japan, and even in 1943, before the end of the war, thirty-eight thousand were produced. After the war, the skills lived on and played a part in the reed organ boom when, in 1969, a whopping 560,000 organs were sold in a single year. I once mentioned these numbers to one of my American friends, but he would not take me seriously, insisting that there were one or two extra zeros in the numbers. The skills needed for playing reeds are directly related to those needed for playing the organ and harmonica so there is no reason for accordions not to sell well. Unfortunately however, I think accordions took on a negative image in the ten years after the war, when it was commonplace to see people on the streets in white robes and military caps, playing their accordions to ask for donations from passersby. Although it is true that there were a large number of injured veterans after the war who faced dire circumstances, it was disastrous for accordions that they were used for gathering donations. It would take many more years for accordion production and sales, which completely shut down for a while, to recover.

Currently, thanks to the amazing legacy of great players and instruments such as those from Castelfidardo, Italy, considered the global home of the accordion, and the use of accordions by younger bands, accordion performances are receiving more media exposure and the fan base is broadening.

Accordions also enjoyed a boom in the United States after World War II. And this became a turning point for their popularity, which had already been starting to wane at that point. Retailers and accordion players then began switching to electronic organs, which were starting to gain popularity, as I have mentioned earlier. While no one can tell what caused the tide of popularity turn, one thing that can be said with certainty is that these events sent seismic shocks through the town of Castelfidardo.

My tour of the museum gave me a good idea of why the accordion became the folk instrument of the Italian people. It is also true that accordion music is enjoyed by people all around the world. There must be a reason why the production and popularity of accordions declined despite this. If we can eliminate this reason, accordions should be able to make a revival. Accordions are rich in expressivity and suited to crowd-pleasing performances. Then why? There appear to be several reasons, and we have been missing the most fundamental of these. Although the alleged draft dodging by a star American accordion player may have played a role in the instrument's declining popularity, this certainly was not the only reason. Paolo Soprani was eventually forced to shut down its factories. Crucianelli, which had already made a successful shift to electronic musical instruments, did not go back to accordions, and its accordion production is now defunct. Looking at the trends in music, one notices that during the time when pop and rock became mainstream, keyboard instruments tended to take a supporting role to guitars and drums, which were usually the main features of a band. There was no role in this context for accordions either.

The reason seemed to lie in the accordions themselves. This was something that performers had also noticed, but it can often be difficult to observe your favorite instrument—an instrument that you love to play—with a critical objective eye. I felt that someone like myself, someone who was fond of accordions but able to look at them with a little distance, would be in the best position to study the potential causes of this instrument's lagging popularity. Since the accordion market was rarely featured in trade magazines I had to make a lot of guesses as to what was going on, but in order for us to engage in the manufacturing of accordions as a business, I had to convince the people at our company and reach a consensus. No project can succeed if the people in charge do not have their hearts in it, and things can get unnecessarily difficult if the people making the instruments do not understand the history of the instrument.

At the time, I was chairman of Roland Europe, which had its factory in San Benedetto. The technical staff included Luigi Bruti, an accordion contest champion, and Francesco Rauchi, the company's manager of technology who had no shortage of unique ideas. Given these favorable conditions, we certainly could start manufacturing accordions if we could only identify the reason for the instrument's decline.

Our process involved making a prototype and having a performer test it. If the performer was not happy with it, we would go back to the drawing board. We repeated this over and over until we were able to come up with a finished product that we could then market to our customers. This would not have been possible without the help of Sergio Scappini, an internationally renowned accordion player who offered his cooperation from the very start.

Actually, the reason for the accordion's declining popularity was quite simple. Over the years, manufacturers had increased the number of reed sets to expand the instrument's tonal variations, which led to the instrument becoming heavy and, consequently, increasingly expensive. This led to smaller production volumes, which then led to higher costs. It was a vicious cycle. Increasingly, performers played the accordion sitting in chairs as they could not support its weight standing up. In other words, all we had to do to solve the accordion's predicament was to make it lighter and slimmer. (In any case, hadn't she been a beauty to behold at one point?) At least, that was the theory. It would take

▼ The principal engineers involved in the development of the V-Accordion, Francesco Rauchi (left) and Luigi Bruti.

eight years from the time we began development to the launch of our first electronic accordion, which we called the V-Accordion. Midway through the development, Mr. Francesco passed away from lung cancer, and we had concerns as to whether we would be able to continue the development project, but thanks to the efforts of the rest of the development team, we were able to finish a lineup ranging from high-end instruments for professionals to smaller ones for beginners. The popularity of the V-Accordion has now reached a level where we are able to hold an international V-Accordion contest in Italy every year. Instruments in the V-Accordion series have model names such as FR-7 and FR-3. Although we had never used personal names on Roland instruments in the past, this "FR" is an exception in tribute to Francesco Rauchi, who passed away during the development process.

Yesterday's Foe Is Today's Friend

As I have mentioned earlier, after World War II, American importers sold a large number of accordions across the United States, and the accordion boom arrived before organs began selling in large numbers. Castelfidardo boomed as the supply center of these instruments, and as the market for electronic organs subsequently grew, manufacturers in Castelfidardo quickly began producing electronic musical instruments to take advantage of existing sales channels. And while research into electronic musical instruments had also started in Japan by that time, the Italians had a huge advantage in that they already had established distribution channels and a rich network of people in the trade through their accordion business.

Farfisa, a manufacturer of electronic organs that gained prominence in the 1960s and '70s because their instruments were popular with American and British pop artists, was also based in Castelfidardo. Needless to say, Farfisa also made accordions and even acoustic pianos. At one time, the company was one of the major manufacturers of electronic musical instruments in Europe, competing neck and neck with Hohner of Germany. In the United States, Farfisa allied with Chicago Musical Instruments and was hugely successful in selling their portable keyboards in the United States. As musical trends, influenced by the Beatles, began to shift and portable keyboards came into wider use, accordion exports began to dwindle, and the majority of production shifted to electronic musical instruments and electronic organs.

Farfisa was in a very strong position on its home turf in Europe, and its name was synonymous with portable keyboards in the United States as no American manufacturer was making portables. Carlo Lucarelli was manager of technology at the company at the time, and Francesco Rauchi was his assistant. These

▲ With Mr. Kniepkamp at the NAMM Show.

two individuals were to eventually become president and manager of technology, respectively, of Roland Europe and take charge of keyboard and electronic piano production.

Chicago Musical Instruments, which had been importing and selling Farfisa organs, was the parent company of Lowrey Organs, which was a major force in the world of organs along with Hammond. As a matter of course, the chief engineer at Lowrey worked alongside Carlo Lucarelli in the design of export products. This was Alberto Kniepkamp, who eventually came to work at Roland as patent consultant, and was one of the original members who designed Roland's electronic organ, the Music Atelier.

Jumping back in time for a moment, recall that Hammond had been the first company in the world to release a single-row keyboard instrument equipped with rhythm accompaniment. The development code name for this product, which was managed by Jim McLean, was Mustang. I was put in charge of developing the prototype of the Mustang, as we had been exporting rhythm units to Hammond at the time, and we sent three prototypes to Chicago. However, we were not informed of the official product name until it was announced at the Miami NAMM Show. The Mustang made its debut as the Piper in Miami, where the main campaign personality was the young Rosemary Bailey. In response to the Piper, Lowrey also launched an organ equipped with rhythm accompaniment called the Teenie Genie, and these developments brought a lot of excitement to the electronic organ market. The Teenie Genie was developed by Alberto Kniepkamp and its operating manual was written by a fifteen-year-old boy. This was Dennis Houlihan, who eventually became president of Roland US. Back around 1967, many Japanese companies—Ace Electronic Industries, Korg, Yamaha, and Kawai, among others—entered the electronic musical instrument market and competed against the Italians, and I remember the competition being very intense.

The late 1970s—more specifically, the period between 1976 and 1978—saw the development of instruments called string machines, which were a breed apart from existing portable keyboards. These instruments, with their ability to reproduce extremely realistic sounds of string ensembles, created another boom. At the time, Roland was exporting synthesizers to the United States, where our competition included companies such as Moog and ARP. ARP had an Italian-made string machine named Quartet that was selling very well, partially owing to the excellent demo performers the company hired.

This string machine was manufactured by SIEL, a company that was formed by three individuals who had left Farfisa, and the president of this company was Carlo Lucarelli. Although there was no way we would have known each other back then, we were indeed competing against each other in this fiercely competitive market. It is deeply moving to know that I am now able to work on electronic musical instruments with my former competitors. Indeed, "yesterday's foe is today's friend."

Come Back to Sorrento

I had always had the urge to travel to Italy without any premeditated plans, and in a sense this wish was granted in 1996 when Roland Europe (Roland Europe S.p.A., hereafter referred to as RES) was listed on the Milan Stock Exchange.

We launched RES in 1988 and the company was on a steady growth path by 1994. This coincided with the time when the Italian government was taking steps to increase the number of publicly traded companies to promote industrial growth and vitalize their stock market. Many of the Italian companies in the automotive, aviation, and telecommunications industries at the time were nationally owned. Expansion of the country's stock market, a symbol of the free market economy, was desired by many, and the government also introduced tax incentives. I think it was good judgment that RES decided to list its stocks on Milan's stock exchange at this time.

I believe that the perception that Italians often go on labor strikes is a result of the fact that so many of their companies were nationally owned. This is probably one of the reasons only a very few Japanese manufacturers have set up facilities in Italy. Although preparations for listing a company on the exchange was a lot of work in Italy, as it would be in any other country, it was not much of a mental burden for me, partially because Roland was already listed in the Second Section of the Osaka Securities Exchange in Japan. Having said that, it must have been a lot of work for Mr. Lucarelli, who had to travel between Ancona and Milan many times in preparation for the company's listing.

I visited Milan with my wife for the first time in a long while to attend the company's listing ceremony. We stayed at the Four Seasons Hotel near the exchange, a little ways in from the Via Montenapoleone, a street lined with fashionable boutiques. Bruno Barbini, president of Roland Italy, the company in charge of sales, was kind enough to book this hotel for us. It was Saturday afternoon when we checked into the hotel, so the shopping district was full of customers and the city was bursting with energy. We decided to rest at our hotel and begin our shopping in the late afternoon. By the time we left our hotel at a little past five, some of the shops were already getting ready to close and there were noticeably fewer people on the streets. I did not know that the stores closed early on Saturday afternoons. My wife seemed quite disappointed but we reasoned that we could shop the following day and decided to return to our hotel. However, we learned that all the stores closed on Sunday and this was another disappointment for my wife.

Still, Milan is replete with things to see. We decided to tour the Church of Santa Maria delle Grazie and the Leonardo da Vinci Museum of Science and Technology. My plan was to have a good look at the two aspects of Leonardo da Vinci: art and technology. By the time we arrived at the church, a long line of visitors waiting for the church to open had already formed. I was not studied enough to discern the differences between the several chapels in this Renaissance-style building, but the interior was much more interesting to view than the exterior.

The mural in the refectory of the convent adjacent to the church was the high-light for everyone: the timeless masterpiece *The Last Supper*. This mural was painted over a period of two years starting in 1495 and because it was painted in tempera, it had undergone considerable damage over the years. Restorers were busy at work removing those areas that were added later and restoring those areas that were damaged during World War II. A scaffold had been erected in front of the mural but we were able to see the entirety of the painting. We decided to get a photo of the both of us with the mural in the background but the mural was very large so we had to move away quite a bit for it to fit in the back-ground. Once we found a good spot, we asked another visitor to take the shot for us, but as soon as the flash came on, an attendant gave us a stern look saying, "No! No!" Now that I think about it, it was thoughtless of us and we deserved to be reprimanded. So we scurried out of the church. When we developed our film once we were back home, the photo showed the two perpetrators with *The Last Supper* in the background. I hope to visit this extraordinary masterpiece once again, this time without my camera.

The following day, Monday, the opening price of our listed stock was to be determined, and this was to be followed by a certification ceremony and an afternoon banquet. When we listed on the Second Section of the Osaka Securities Exchange, I remember the wild hand waving of the traders on the floor as we watched the price on the electronic ticker display change every moment and waited for the opening price to be determined. Once it was determined, we were greeted with a "Congratulations!" and a round of applause. I was hoping to see the same wild hand waving of the traders in Italy, but by then, trading had been computerized so we stared into a computer display to watch our opening price, which was somewhat anticlimactic. But still, when the opening price was determined, we all shook hands as if to congratulate each other on the birth of a baby, and a big round of applause arose. The opening price of our stock was 6.38 million liras. Soon after the afternoon banquet was over, it was decided that we would travel straight to San Benedetto, where RES headquarters was located. We had to hurry as this year also happened to be the twentieth anniversary of SIEL, the precursor to RES, and a party had been planned to commemorate this anniversary along with RES's listing on the stock exchange. As a result, our stroll on Via Montenapoleone would have to wait for our next visit.

The drive on Italy's autostrada (freeway) traveling from Milan to Bologna and then southward toward the Adriatic Sea is always enjoyable. A few years earlier, I had the chance to drive from Ancona along the Adriatic coast and on to Venice via Ravenna to attend the annual European musical instrument dealers meeting. At the time, we headed northward along the Adriatic coast so we must have crossed the historic Rubicon River, but this did not even occur to me at the time. In elementary school, during one of our writing classes, Mr. Tago, our teacher, read us Plutarch's *Parallel Lives* over a span of five or six classes. Of the people cited in *Parallel Lives*, I still remember Hannibal, Alexander the Great, and Julius Caesar, although they all lived in different time periods.

▼ Statue of Julius Caesar.

One of the illustrations in that book showed Julius Caesar, mounted on his horse, looking upon the Rubicon, and I had arbitrarily imagined that the Rubicon was a large river. This time, we would be traveling southward, in the same direction that Caesar had crossed the river, so I said to Mr. Lucarelli that I would definitely like to take a photo of the river. However, Mr. Lucarelli told us that the Rubicon should be there somewhere along the way but he had no idea where it was. So we decided not to use the freeway and take the local roads to look for the river. We searched areas where the river should be located according to our maps, but could not find it. We stopped by a convenience store along the road and the clerk told us that we had already passed it.

In the end, we traveled back the way we had come for about three hundred feet and found the Rubicon, which at only about forty feet wide was more like a brook. I was somewhat disappointed, thinking that the shape of the land must have changed in the two thousand years after Caesar. But thinking about it later, I realized that if it had been a larger river, it would have been difficult for Caesar to cross the river mounted on a horse, kicking up water as he went. Just as Caesar's words, "The die has been cast!" illustrate, "crossing the Rubicon" has come to represent the making of a huge decision, but this is not because the river was difficult to cross but because the crossing of that river represented a rebellious act against the senators of Rome.

If on many occasions you have had to make big decisions, that means you have come across opportunities just as many times. I am glad that I visited the place where Caesar actually stood. Looking back now, my personal crossing of the Rubicon came when I decided to quit Ace Electronic Industries. I had not thought up until then that I would end up leaving the very company that I had built up. Once back in Japan, I looked up the Rubicon on a map and noticed that it branches off into three rivers. I could not tell which of them we had seen that day, but my image of Julius Caesar has since returned to the original image I had of him looking down on the river from his horse, regardless of the width of the river.

After SIEL's twentieth anniversary party was over, we had the good fortune to take an impromptu three-day trip. The four of us—my wife and I, Mr. Lucarelli's wife Gabriella, and Mr. Lucarelli in the driver's seat of his car—set out on a road trip to southern Italy. We first went directly to Sorrento, which many must know from the famous song. We booked a hotel in Sorrento along the Mediterranean coast, where we had a view of Mount Vesuvius, and toured different destinations every day, including Pompeii, Positano, Amalfi, and Ravello. On our tour of Pompeii—which was preserved just as it had been two thousand years ago—we were able to hire a very good tour guide thanks to Mr. Lucarelli, and this became the highlight of our trip. We stayed in Sorrento for three nights, so we had three opportunities to "come back to Sorrento." As a souvenir, I bought a music box that featured the marquetry finish that the town was famous for, and the song it played was, naturally, "Come Back to Sorrento."

Organ Journey

St. Thomas Church, Leipzig

FOR SOMEONE WHO IS INTERESTED IN ORGANS, THERE IS NO DESTINA-
tion that is more enjoyable than Europe. In particular, Leipzig is one of the
most prominent of music-oriented cities. In Europe, you will come across trade
shows in a variety of locations that have been going on for over a century. The
Frankfurt Messe, which we take part in every year, is one such show, and Leipzig
also used to host an annual trade show that was well-known in Europe. The first
time I visited this trade show was in 1967.

At this time, Germany was still divided into West and East Germany, and it was
very inconvenient, to say the least, to visit Leipzig, which was located on the
eastern side of the border. Unless you had all the paperwork indicating that
you were taking part in the Leipzig Messe, you could not even purchase a plane
ticket. The nature of the human beast is that the more difficult it appears, the
more you feel you have to go. It was on my return from the Frankfurt Messe that
I was able to obtain an entry permit to attend the Leipzig Messe. In Frankfurt,
East Germany's state-owned musical instrument company, Demusa, exhibited
a large booth every year, exhibiting a broad range of musical instruments. While
they did not have any electronic instruments on display, they had almost all of
the traditional instruments, and because the quality was good, I needed to see
what kind of place East Germany was.

My translator and I flew into Leipzig from Frankfurt, which was such a short
flight that we arrived before we knew it. Still, though the two cities were close
together on the map, in another sense Leipzig seemed very far away. What
surprised me upon arrival was that the airport facilities were very different
from the facilities in Frankfurt, and also the fact that soldiers armed with
semiautomatic weapons stood guard about every fifteen feet along the path

from the boarding ramp to the terminal. I felt a wave of tension rush through me, followed by feelings of, "What have we gotten ourselves into?" and, "Will we be able to return home?" We left the airport but had no hotel reservation. It's a mystery now how we pulled off such a thing, but in any case we lined up at the counter in the city hall and waited our turn for the clerk to arrange a hotel for us.

The hotels were all full and we were booked into a bed and breakfast, but at this point, we felt lucky just to have a place to sleep. We were given the bed and breakfast's address but we did not know how to get there. There were no taxis in the city, so we hired a car that private citizens operated during the show. Since we spoke no German, we showed the driver the piece of paper with the address on it and headed for our lodge.

The private apartment to which we were assigned was very comfortable. It was equipped with a boiler, and the faucet had handles marked hot and cold. We got hot water when we turned the handle marked hot. At the time, most homes in Japan still did not have hot water, so to me—as someone who had been told that the standard of living in communist states was low—it was surprising to learn how well the people lived. In contrast to the negative impressions we got from the soldiers at the airport, the queue at the city hall, and the private taxi, this situation at the bed and breakfast was unexpected and gave us a sense of relief. Having said that, we still could not get over the feeling of, "What have we gotten ourselves into?"

The following morning, we left early for the show. The venue in which it was held was larger than we had imagined. I could not believe that such a show was possible in the communist bloc, where there was little freedom of exchange. On display were various kinds of items ranging from large construction machinery to musical instruments. The exhibit floor was also very large and my impression was that this seemed like a big show, based on my experience of other trade show floors such as Frankfurt Music Messe, NAMM, and Osaka. However, the musical instruments booth, which was what we had come to see, was small and underwhelmed our expectations. There was not much for us to gain from its small display of pianos, harpsichords, and accordions. But since we had gone through the trouble of visiting, we asked an attendant if we could visit a factory. With unexpectedly little fuss, he told us that we could visit an accordion factory if that interested us. While we did get an okay, we were not sure if we would be able to see anything useful there, and when we learned that it was five hours to the factory round-trip, we had to give it up. The biggest problem was that we would have no way of returning to our lodging.

However, when we brought up the topic of electronic musical instruments, the attendant's eyes gleamed and he said, "We don't make those types of instruments yet but we are making prototypes. Would you be interested in seeing those?" He also offered, "We would be interested in discussing the possibility of forming a technical alliance with you." So we changed our destination right there and then to the electronic musical instruments research lab. It was only two hours round-trip, and he said he would drop us off at our lodge after the visit.

Upon visiting the "lab," we found that it consisted of only two apartment rooms, and the instruments they were prototyping were a hodgepodge of parts that had been removed from Italian and Japanese products; nothing close to being market-worthy. Although we were somewhat disappointed, it was enough to learn that even in the communist bloc, there were people who were engaged in research in this field. It was as if we were looking at what we had been doing ourselves a decade earlier.

We were inundated with questions during our two-hour visit and, upon our departure, we promised the engineer that we would ship him some parts that he wanted. It was a memorable and enjoyable visit as we were able to communicate with each other using circuit diagrams and technical English. However, as heart-ening as it was to see this engineer engaging in his research so enthusiastically, my heart also sank when I thought of the future that likely awaited him. I left with the strong impression that electronic musical instruments would not be able to grow in the communist bloc. I recollected the worries I had when I first stepped off the plane at the airport, and although I felt that it had been worth the visit, I also realized that I would not be visiting here again for a long time. Indeed, my second visit to Leipzig was in 1988, twenty years later.

St. Thomas Church in Leipzig. ▶
(Photo courtesy of Haruaki Matsu-shita.)

The following day, as we had nothing more to see at the show, we decided to visit St. Thomas Church. The church was within walking distance so we visited in the morning. It was quite compact and not very large. For no particular reason, I had imagined it to be huge. Still, I was satisfied just to know that we were in the church where Johann Sebastian Bach had played the organ. I saw a plaque embedded in the floor commemorating Bach that shone with the light coming in through the stained glass window directly across from the entrance. A small bouquet of flowers was placed on the plaque. For some reason, I was transfixed by the plaque and stained glass window, and forgot to look at the organ. I saw the assembly of many pipes, but I left without actually looking at the organ's console. I was satisfied just to see Bach's epitaph.

The Berlin Wall had fallen by the time I made my second visit to Leipzig. This time again, the main purpose of my visit was to attend the shows in Frankfurt and Leipzig, but not much had changed in twenty years and there was not much to see. Time seemed completely at a standstill. During the show, I had the opportunity to meet and enjoy a dinner with Hirotaka Kawai, president of Kawai Musical Instruments Manufacturing, and Masako Koyama from *The Music Trades* magazine. Aside from that, I went to the same places I had gone on my previous visit, which was St. Thomas Church and a restaurant in a half-basement that served excellent soup. These were the only two places that I wanted to visit other than the shows, so I was able to fulfill my objectives.

My impression of St. Thomas Church was the same as it had been the first

time, and I remember being deeply moved. This time, I was not going to leave without seeing the organ. The organ console seemed relatively new and not something from Bach's era. But there was no one to ask and no brochure so I was not able to confirm my observation. The book *A New History of the Organ* introduces organs from a variety of regions in Europe. In it, there is a chapter titled "The Organ of J. S. Bach," which includes a stop

◀ Bach's epitaph in St. Thomas Church. (Photo courtesy of Haruaki Matsushita.)

list, and I was surprised to learn that the organs made in the seventeenth and eighteenth centuries were larger than I had thought. I realized I was not sufficiently versed in this area.

The first time I had visited the church was about the time we were making electronic organs at Ace Electronic Industries. At the time of my second visit, the manufacturing of synthesizers and electronic pianos at Roland was going well, but we were not sure when we would be able to begin developing organs. Since organ development was always on my mind, this visit was a moving experience for me. Of course, I was not expecting to find any concrete answers at St. Thomas Church. Still, this second visit was based on a rather misguided idea that there might be something that would provide inspiration.

While in Leipzig, I asked the representative from Demusa how their electronic musical instruments lab was going, but he seemed not to have any idea. Seeing how the state of affairs had retrograded in some ways from 250 years earlier when Bach was making music brought up mixed feelings in me. I felt a sense of dread toward this societal structure that could erase pipe organ manufacturing and electronic musical instruments even from Germany, traditionally known as the Mecca of organs, and sorrow at how the town had hardly changed in twenty years. I also felt a sadness at the fact that there was no way I was going to find out anything about the engineers I had met twenty years earlier; engineers whose eyes sparkled with enthusiasm as we engaged in lively discussion.

As I thought of what those engineers might be doing now, I felt very grateful that I was able to concentrate on making musical instruments in Japan. I told myself that things would turn out okay as long as I kept at it and picked myself up with my usual optimism.

A book of photographs titled *A Trip for the Soul: Churches of Europe and Their Pipe Organs* by Haruaki Matsushita features St. Thomas Church on its first page. I found a photo in this book of the statue of Bach at the front of the church and realized that I had missed this again on my last visit. My consolation is that I have another reason to go back.

Given the advancement of the Internet, it should be easy to track down those engineers, but I just don't know what keywords to enter. Europe is in the same situation as the rest of the world in that the organ market itself has not yet recovered, so one cannot even imagine how engineers in pre-PC years were even involved in the business. Perhaps even the almighty Net is powerless in such situations?

St. Peter's Basilica, Vatican

In the late spring of 1995, my wife and I had a chance to spend a full day in Rome as tourists. This was my wife's first visit to Rome, so this was truly our "Roman holiday." We started out early in the morning visiting various places in the city. While there were places that I had been to before, I did not get tired of revisiting any of them. We decided to travel between the main destinations by taking a series of taxi rides.

I thought that if we were to arrive at St. Peter's Basilica at the right time, there would be some kind of service and we might be able to hear an organ performance. So I paid attention to the time and we arrived at the cathedral at around 10 a.m. The circular plaza in front of the basilica was already bustling with people, and when we proceeded to enter, the Swiss Guards stopped us. I recalled that I had been able to enter the last time I visited but there was nothing we could do. I barely understood from what I was being told that this was a Sunday and that there was apparently going to be a mass attended by Pope John Paul II. Formally dressed couples were entering through the door, while tourists were being denied entry.

Just as I had given up and we were about to head back, one tourist told us to walk over to the back door of the building. This was a small door but people were getting in and out without being stopped. No guards were there either. Once inside the hall, we found ourselves about a hundred feet from the altar. The altar was huge and was an imposing fixture even among the large crowd. Soon, we saw monks entering from the right, solemnly walking in line and swinging incense burners in front of them like pendulums. The pope was in this line, and I got a good look at his face because we were standing quite close. I wondered if it was safe for him to enter this place where there was so little security. In any case, we decided to take part in the mass quietly with the rest of the crowd for the duration of the rituals. Once the pope was at the altar, we could only see his back.

All of a sudden, we heard an organ begin to play. An organist wearing a white gown was slowly playing the organ. The organ's console was a very large one with four rows of keyboards, a truly stately instrument whose cabinet including its side panels probably measured ten feet wide. The organist began playing nonchalantly, apparently not intimidated by the elaborate ceremony that was going on. While I don't know how he discerned the different sections in the proceeding, he would play for a while and rest, and play again and rest again for about an hour until the mass was over.

Regardless of the huge crowd, there was no babbling of voices and it was very quiet in the hall, so much so that I did not feel comfortable moving about to take a look at the organ console or its pipes. But I was happy to have had the chance to listen to this organ in the same hall that the pope was in. While I am not a Catholic, there was something special about being able to see the pope close by and in the flesh; someone who obviously had a huge influence around the world. I later saw a live TV broadcast of the Christmas mass held at St. Peter's Basilica in 1999, in which the presenter reported that there were more than seven thousand people at the mass and over fifty thousand in the plaza. On the TV screen, the altar, which is located at the far end of center, appeared to be even larger than I had remembered.

▲ Console of the pipe organ at St. Peter's Basilica.

In February 2013, Pope Benedict XVI voluntarily resigned from his position. The resignation of a living pope was very unusual; it was said that this was the first time it had happened in about six hundred years. That night, after he announced his resignation, St. Peter's Basilica was hit by a direct lightning strike. There was a great deal of buzz around this event, with photos of the bright flash of lightning hitting the basilica carried in newspapers and magazines, and videos uploaded on the Net. This event was also mentioned in a book by Nanami Shiono that I recently read. Although I am not a religious person—or perhaps, if I were pressed to make a choice, I'd be a follower of a religion with elaborate rites and rituals such as Catholicism or even Buddhism—even I did not feel that this was mere coincidence.

One of the businesses that Roland is involved in is classical organs. Sales in this area have recently begun to decline. One of the reasons is that many church congregations are now made up of younger generations and the styles of the services have changed where they are now using electronic musical instruments. While there are differences between denominations, some incorporate

▲ Lightning strikes St. Peter's Basilica (2013).

pop, rock, and jazz, and of course they use MIDI. Also, the number of churches made of stone is declining, and some churches have forgone the installation of and classical electronic style pipe organs that are designed to match the acoustics of stone structures. Hence, sales of classical electronic organs to churches is declining. As an opportunist, about the only hope I can have is that the lightning strike will spark a recovery in this market.

Typically, white smoke wafts out of the chimney of the chapel to signify that the conclave has chosen a pope. I hope that they will signal the improvement of sales of classical organs to churches with white smoke too.

Trinity Church, Boston

During a stay in Boston in 1997, I had the chance to visit Trinity Church just as they were holding services. According to a brochure I picked up there, this church was founded in October 1733 and rebuilt in its current location between 1874 and 1877. It is known as a masterpiece of church architecture in America. It is also known for housing one of the very few existing Æolian-Skinner organs, so I visited in hopes that I might be able to listen to the sound of this organ. Installed in 1926 and modified in 1963, it features 6,898 pipes, including one thirty-two feet long for ultra-low bass, and is played on a three-row keyboard console. The church's choir is also very famous. There is a circular indent at the front of the hall where the choir lined up. The voices of the choir reverberated throughout the church and produced a truly amazing effect.

After the services were over, the people at the church let me see the organ's console. When we acquired Rodgers Organ Company from Steinway and Sons in 1987, we learned that Rodgers had all the drawings for this Æolian-Skinner organ. At the time, electronic organ manufacturers were competing against makers of pipe organs, so design documents were very important as reference material. However, I had no intention of making a pipe organ per se; I was committed to advancing the electronic organ. So I decided to donate these drawings as I thought it would be better if they were carefully preserved by an appropriate organization. Of course, we have made copies of essential sections of the drawings. I never thought that I would encounter the actual organ that was the basis for the drawings we had accidentally acquired.

Trinity Church is a famous tourist destination, featured in all the guidebooks to Boston. It exudes an amazing presence amid the many modern high rises that surround it. I would recommend a visit to this church to anyone who is interested

▲ The Æolian-Skinner organ at Trinity Church in Boston.

in organs. I subsequently had another opportunity to visit Boston so I visited Trinity Church again. During that visit, I noticed another church with a gothic tower just next to the large plaza in front of Trinity Church; this was Old South Church. Although these two churches were of different denominations, I was surprised to see two large churches in such close proximity. The design of the interior of this church was wonderful, with wooden organ pipes flanking a stained glass window. The organ console was installed at the front, one tier lower than the floor. This organ was also an Æolian-Skinner. This was the first time I had seen an organ console that the congregation could look down at from floor height. I was not able to hear this organ being played, but I was blown away by the depth of American organ culture, such that there were two rare Æolian-Skinner organs not even a block away from each other.

Bamboo Organ, Manila

When the Philippines were still a colony of Spain, before they were occupied by the United States, Spanish missionaries who lived in the country built churches and installed organs in them. However, they did not bring pipes from Europe but used bamboo that was available locally, making bamboo pipe organs.

If memory serves me, it was in 1969 that I visited the Philippines for the first time. I had heard that there was a bamboo organ in the village of Las Piñas, in the outskirts of Manila, so I took a taxi there. I found the organ in a small church quite a distance away from city center, and while its keyboard was nearly

▲ Bamboo pipe organ in Las Pinas.

broken it was indeed a pipe organ with bamboo pipes. The organ had hardly been maintained so it was not capable of making proper music. Still, a nun summoned a shirtless little boy who, upon sitting on the bench, immediately began playing the organ. He was skipping all the broken keys so I could not tell what the piece of music was but the organ was producing sounds. All I can say about this visit was that I heard the sound of a bamboo pipe organ. I was deeply moved by the persistence and passion of the people who made this organ using bamboo four hundred years ago.

When I visited Manila again in 1994, twenty-five years later, I decided that I wanted to see the organ again so I asked the president of G. A. Yupangco & Co., our agent in the Philippines, to take me to the same church. The organ had undergone substantial repairs since I last saw it and it was capable of producing better sound, but the materials were very old so it was not in its best condition. An organist kindly explained the construction of the organ and even played it for us. He explained that after the bamboos were cut, they had to be soaked in mud for a long period of time to age them in order for them to produce a stable pitch. I mentioned my visit twenty-five years earlier and asked him if he might know the boy who played the organ for me then. To this he replied, "That would have been me." After this tour, we were taken to a separate room in which was installed a fine modern pipe organ. We were told that this organ was used to give organ classes.

When I first visited in 1969, I had little cash on me as there were still foreign exchange controls in place. Still, I made a small donation toward the rebuilding of this organ—making sure that I had enough cash remaining for the return taxi fare. It was deeply moving to ponder that numerous supporters subsequently came forward to aid in rebuilding this organ and providing organ education, to improve conditions at this church to this extent. Later, I read in Ikuma Dan's *Personal History of Japanese Music* that two pipe organs were brought to Japan in 1579, and several bamboo pipe organs were made in Amakusa in 1600. I was simply amazed at the passion and range of activities of these early missionaries.

▲ *Personal History of Japanese Music* by Ikuma Dan.

Bel Air Presbyterian Church, Los Angeles

During the 1994 NAMM Show in Los Angeles, I was staying on the fourteenth floor of the Marriott Hotel in Torrance where, early in the morning, I felt very strong shaking. It was an earthquake. But because I was on the fourteenth floor, and because the quake did not seem very serious, I stayed in bed with my eyes open to see how things would go. Soon the quake ended and I went back to sleep.

Perhaps because the hotel was some distance away from the epicenter, I did not get the impression that it was a large quake. What was more on my mind was the possibility that the number of visitors to the NAMM Show might decline as this was just before the show was to start. Some Japanese participants did decide to cancel their visits, as the extent of the damage was unknown and there were some news reports that the organizers might have to cancel the show. In fact, the earthquake caused extensive damage in some locations. It fragmented the freeway system, caused some buildings to collapse, and created a variety of chaotic situations somewhat unique to the automobile-centric nature of the region's infrastructure.

Exactly a year later, I was staying at the same hotel to take part in the NAMM Show when I saw the news of a major earthquake hitting the Kobe area in Japan. Detailed information on the seriousness of the quake and the extent of the damage was not available in initial news reports. Nevertheless, the news reports that came in by the minute reported that the damage from this quake was on a par with the Great Kanto Earthquake. I tried phoning Japan from Los Angeles but it was very difficult to get a connection, and when I finally did, the information that I got was not much more specific than what I could get on TV in America, which compounded my confusion. Japan is a quake-prone country and there had been various reports on the dangers of a major quake in the Tokai region, but nobody thought that a major one would hit Kobe.

The 1994 quake in Los Angeles has since been named the Northridge Earthquake. Because the West Coast sits on the San Fernando fault, this type of quake may have been known to be within the range of possibilities, but natural disasters have a way of hitting when they are least on our minds. It was also very unfortunate that some Roland US employees experienced damage to their homes. We completed the NAMM Show that year without knowing much more than what was reported in the newspapers.

When we took part in the 1997 NAMM Show three years later, I visited the showroom of Robert Tall & Associates, fulfilling a promise that I had made years earlier. Dr. Tall was one of the major dealers of Rodgers in the United States and was also very knowledgeable about organs. Back in 1976, we'd developed and launched a sound system called Revo-30 that created a rotating sound space and a chorus effect. This was a unit that users could attach to an electronic organ to improve its tonal qualities. I had heard that there was a dealership that was selling this unit, which was originally designed for home organs, to users of classical organs, and this was Dr. Tall's dealership. We did not personally know each other then, but we had worked together for over twenty years through the sales of our products. That day was all about organs: he had set up visits to three churches where he had delivered three- and four-row Rodgers organs. The day's plan also included a visit to the home of Don Leslie after the church visits.

Of the organs that we saw, the highlight of the day was the organ at Bel Air Presbyterian Church, which had long intrigued me. Fortunately, the organist Hector Olivera joined us for this visit, so we were able to hear an authentic per-formance of this organ. The church's organists and directors were kind enough to show us around, making this a very enjoyable visit. The view of Los Angeles from the church's window was also quite amazing. On our way to the church, we passed the spot where Bill Cosby's son had been killed a few days earlier. I remember how several bouquets of flowers had been placed by the road.

Bel Air Presbyterian Church installed a Casavant pipe organ in 1991. In the earthquake of 1994, 65 percent of the pipes toppled over and the console sustained major damage. Rebuilding this organ and its console promised to be a major undertaking both in terms of time and cost. The church had to decide between replacing it with an electronic organ, or rebuilding the entire organ. I believe the people must have found it difficult to decide one way or the other, because not all of its pipes were damaged—about a third of them were in usable condition—and also because there must have been a great deal of emotional attachment and aspiration for having a pipe organ. Ultimately, the church decided to use a Rodgers four-row console and

▲ With Hector Olivera in front of the Rodgers organ at Bel Air Presbyterian Church.

retain sixty rows of pipes. The decision was made to choose 151 rows of digital tones from Rodgers's custom digital sound library, and to replace the major parts consisting of 118 stops with electronic tones. This would result in the largest combination pipe and digital organ in the world. It was easy to imagine that the considerations that went into reaching this decision would have been intense. I believe that a variety of matters—not just having to do with installing a new organ—had to be discussed to address the extraordinary circumstances that arose from that natural disaster. It must have been a major undertaking just to identify all the technical issues and develop resolutions for them.

The church committee had to be comfortable with the technological capabilities and track record of whoever was going to carry out this feat. Just off the top of my head, the technical issues would include connecting the sounds made by the pipes and electronics, matching their tones, tuning, and designing an interface between the console and the remaining pipes, to name only a few. The external appearance of the pipes and moving parts were retained in their original state, but there must have been numerous other issues including where to position the speakers to ensure that the tones matched, and where to segregate these sections. The magnitude of this undertaking was clearly evident in how the speakers were arranged in the pipe room.

Electronic organs have been compared with pipe organs ever since electronic musical instruments first arrived on the scene. Over the past decade, the application of electronic technologies in music has made dramatic advances, but I think it will still take some time to convey the results of these efforts to all organists. It is quite difficult to give organists the opportunity to try out both types of organs in the same location. Also, because the stop tone series of electronic and pipe organs will naturally be different, it would be difficult to make a comparison even if the organist was well versed in the strengths and weaknesses of both types of organs. In the case of Bel Air Presbyterian Church, because the pipe and electronic organs both needed to be played on the same console, it would not have been possible to produce a good musical instrument if only one or the other was good. Since the pipes were not changeable, the electronic section had to match the pipes, and this is precisely the kind of thing that is possible with the flexibility of electronic organs. When considering such cases, the most critical issue is whether the instrument is capable of meeting musical needs, and there is no point in having either/or debates. Everyone can understand this once they hear the performance and that will leave no room for debate.

Pipe organs, which have undergone structural and mechanical improvements over centuries, are now coming to a point in their development where they will be undergoing changes in terms of the use of sound generators, as well. This integration brings changes not only in the sound generator itself but also in the organ's relationship to the size of the hall in which it is played, as organs by nature are played to a large audience. Also, from an acoustical standpoint, it is a fact that you will not get the desired sound from a pipe organ unless the locations of the organ console and pipes are determined at the time the building itself is designed. I believe electronic organs have a role to play in overcoming architectural impediments as well. The organ at Bel Air Presbyterian Church is an example of these possibilities and shows the way for pipe-electronic hybrid organs. I have great respect for Dr. Robert Tall who undertook the rebuilding of this organ and the managers of the church who made the decisions that needed to be made.

As part of our efforts to communicate the allure of organs to as many people as possible, we decided to record on HD video a service held at the church on January 30, 2000. As part of the recording, we interviewed a number of people involved in the process that led to the building of this new organ in the aftermath of the earthquake. Our participation in the two-part service was made possible by the kind understanding of the church's pastor, Dr. Michael H. Wenning. Hector Olivera's performance of "Joyful, Joyful" was the icing on the cake of this service. This was an amazing performance in which the sounds of the traditional pipe organ and the digital tones fully blended. As a memento, I received a book of hymns personalized with my name and signed by the directors of the church.

There will be no outcome in which organs, with their many musical assets, become extinct. Things that exist as part of history in an "age without samples" are things that actually transcend samples. I would like to think that history will repeat itself. I believe we will see white smoke at the conclusion of the conclave.

Professionals

In order to begin a project such as the development of organs, one must adhere to the intrinsic requirements of that particular musical instrument. For example, there are numerous requirements in the areas of structure and playing method that must not be changed. Above all else, we must make instruments that players can play comfortably. It is very difficult to create unique musical instruments within these constraints, and if we are to achieve it, knowledge, design, and ideas must become essential components of our undertaking.

At the time, it was no easy feat to create a new, third style of organ that belonged neither in the realm of classical organs nor in that of Hammond organs, which were widely popular then. This was precisely why I was so motivated.

In times such as these, the best way to discern how to proceed is to speak to and sometimes enter into heated debates with excellent organ artists, or ask them what they are having the most trouble with.

The transition from accordions to organs took place in 1964 and 1965. Electronic organs were becoming highly popular and the most prominent of these was the Hammond organ. It was Don Lewis who first played the Hammond organ with a rhythm machine made by Ace Electronic Industries attached to it. His style of performance—based on a combination of the Rhythm Ace, Ace Electronic Industries' representative product, and the Hammond organ, which was synonymous with organs—inspired me anew. He called this playing style "clazz"—a combination of classical and jazz. I still remember going to listen to him play at a restaurant called the Hungry Tiger every time I was on a business trip to the San Francisco Bay Area. This was the beginning of our friendship. Right after the NAMM Show in Miami, I asked him to demonstrate our product and decided to

▲ Yuri Tachibana.

▲ Don Lewis.

▲ Tony Fenelon.

invite him to Japan. It was Don Lewis who pioneered blending the rhythm machine with organ performance and who also provided the impetus to integrate the machine, which had been an accessory to organs up to that point, into organ design. He was the one who infused human feeling into what had previously been seen as a mechanical rhythm machine.

We worked with a broad range of organists in the process of developing the Music Atelier, the Roland organ that we have today. Hector Olivera played classical pipe organ pieces, music that was readily understandable for organ, but gave it the expressivity of an orchestra. Rosemary Bailey made liberal use of the harmonic bars and infused her performances with a jazz feeling. Yuri Tachibana blended the feeling of Japanese music with electronic organs in her approach to popular music. Tony Fenelon gave us extensive advice on tones and performing styles that would enable us to bring the feel of theater organs into home organs. And there was also Ryoki Yamaguchi, who had a wide repertoire ranging from authentic classics to popular music. We listened to input from a variety of other musicians as well. I would like to express my heartfelt gratitude to everyone who worked with us on this product. Needless to say, there are many musicians creating music in Europe, but the opportunities to speak with them were limited by geography so we gained inspiration from them by viewing and listening to recordings of their live performances.

I am convinced that the Music Atelier is an electronic organ that gives musicians the ability to express themselves in real time, in any way that they want. I actually believe that the development of electronic organs was all about developing specifications and structures that would stimulate the player's creativity and potential without infringing on the player's territory.

▲ Hector Olivera.

Indeed, since launching the Music Atelier development project, we have not changed the design or operability of the organ's switches, and the concept of the product has not changed either. The ideas that we adopted in the early stages continue to live on to the point that we have even incorporated some of these concepts into synthesizers. This has renewed my realization that the goal of our organ

▲ Ryoki Yamaguchi (left).

journey was always to establish a universal concept for our organs, and create a lineup through which this concept runs, from our entry models right up to our top model, without sacrificing functionality.

Music Paradise

Organs Are the "King of Musical Instruments"

COMPARED TO ORGANS, WHOSE ORIGINS CAN BE TRACED BACK TO before the current era, pianos have a history of development dating back about three hundred years to the harpsichord, from which the piano can be said to have originated. The piano's history is obviously shorter than that of the organ but the number of people who play it is overwhelmingly greater. Except for early organs, the positioning of pipes of organs that were built into buildings was also an important ornamental element, and these organs cannot be transported. Naturally, they are larger than pianos. They require mechanisms for blowing air as the instruments produce sounds by opening and closing airways with the movement of the keys on the keyboard, and this also takes up a lot of space. Meanwhile, pianos were designed with transportability in mind from the outset. And because they were designed to provide musical expressivity depending on how hard you played the keys, they have a very different key touch.

Based on the way it produces sound, the piano can be called a string instrument in that it transmits the vibrations of its strings to a soundboard. Pipe organs are nothing short of a horn instrument. However, in the realm of electronic musical instruments, the sounds of electronic pianos and electronic organs are both delivered through speakers. You cannot see their sound generators. I will not go into the details of the internal electronic circuits; their designs are such that they are very difficult to comprehend unless you are a circuit design engineer. It is true that this aspect of electronic musical instruments has been the source of a variety of misconceptions.

In the 1970s, when sound generators based on electronic circuitry became mainstream, electronic organ production increased. In the 1980s, electronic organ sales reached the same level as pianos and became a key product category for musical instrument dealers. It was around this time that Roland began using the slogan, "From jazz to classics." Notwithstanding, organ design gradually branched off into three categories for different musical genres. This was because the tones and touch that were required were different, and it was becoming impossible to cover all genres on a single organ. The three categories were as follows:

- Classical: For classical organ pieces and church music.

- Jazz: For jazz, rock, and popular music.

- Home: For a wide range of music genres.

As organs increasingly found their way into churches, chapels, and concert halls, the manufacturing requirements for these instruments also underwent major changes. The audience expects to hear cathedral-like reverberations in solo organ concerts, but this level of reverberation would be too much for other instruments playing alongside it in a performance. Still, the organ tone would not meet our expectations if there was not enough reverberation so it is difficult to satisfy both of these conditions. These are the types of problems organ manufacturers are faced with. Perhaps for this reason, concert halls with organs tend to have a relatively low level of reverb. When you consider the increasing demand for pipe tones that resemble the tones of orchestral and other types of instruments, it is easy to see that the basic design principles have dramatically changed from those of organs made in the seventeenth and eighteenth centuries.

Theater organs, which were originally used for musical accompaniment to silent movies in the late 1880s, developed into large instruments capable of producing sound effects and onomatopoeia, and became a major draw of theaters. "The largest in the world" is a measurement that is easy to understand in any country, and organs have been described this way as well. The 1904 St. Louis World's Fair featured the "largest organ in the world," a huge instrument with five rows of keys, 232 stops, and 18,000 pipes. This organ was relocated to a department store in Philadelphia in 1917 and was eventually expanded to about twice the original size.

The trend toward larger organs continued unabated until 1932, when a mammoth organ with seven rows of keyboards, 1,439 stops, 455 ranks, and 33,112 pipes was made in Atlantic City. This took place during the Great Depression. As pipe organs became bigger and bigger, the first mass-produced Hammond organ was launched in 1935 and the market welcomed this compact organ that people could place in their homes. One factor that contributed to its success was that people were already familiar with its sound from listening to church and theater organs. The first electric organ ever developed was based on pipe organs.

The list of people who purchased the Hammond organ when it was first launched in 1935 shows the magnitude of the impact that this instrument had. The list included people such as Leopold Stokowski, Sir Thomas Beecham, Lawrence Welk, Roger Wolfe Kahn, Hal Kemp, George Gershwin, and Henry Ford. Ford, who had a keen interest in music, had seen the organ's design when it was still in the development stage, and had placed an order over a year before its launch. Unfortunately, I was only five years old and living in Japan at the time, so I could not order one.

A patent that was filed by Hammond Organ in January 1934 was approved in April. This was exceptionally quick. The approval number was 1956350. Just by looking at the attached drawings, you could tell that the design had been perfected to exacting standards. One aspect of these drawings is especially interesting. The organ was fitted with a cranking handle to start the synchronous motor that would provide the motive force, running on the sixty-cycle power available in private residences. If I remember correctly, no models that were sold had a cranking handle as they had already been fitted with the same type of starter motor used in automobiles, but I have not confirmed this.

▼ Patent bulletin of Hammond's 1934 patent application. Note the cranking handle to the right.

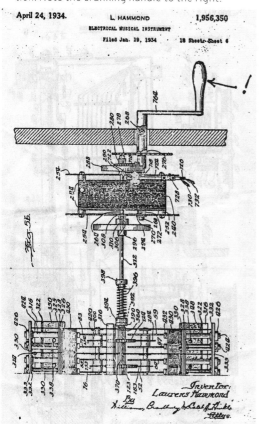

Looking at these drawings, I recalled how we used to use cranks to start engines after the war, and I wondered whether the technologies used in America—the automobile superpower—might have found their way into organs as well. In any case, Henry Ford sent two of his engineers to study the organ at Hammond during its prototyping stage and purchased the first organ off the line, so it would be no surprise if there were some kind of connection. It is a lot of fun just imagining these things.

The first Hammond organs sold for $1,250. Two years later, in 1937, the Federal Trade Commission filed a claim stating that Hammond must not call their products "organs." To this end, a test was conducted. A jury of thirty people—fifteen students and fifteen professional musicians—was assembled to compare a Hammond organ with a pipe organ. The results of the test? The people could not tell the difference between the two instruments. Their prices were not comparable, as the pipe organ was priced at $75,000 and the Hammond cost $2,600 at the time of the test, but one year later, the FTC approved Hammond's use of the term "organ" to refer to its instruments. Although Hammond's 1934 patent application was approved in just four months, this decision by the FTC, which now seems like a no-brainer, took a year. I would imagine that there must have been quite a bit of resistance from the academicians of the time as well.

With this decision, Hammond organs were recognized as musical instruments. I believe this event had the effect of empowering people who were eager to start up projects on electronic musical instruments and other new areas of endeavor, and had a major impact on the advancement of these areas.

In the early 1990s, Roland received complaints from some of our competitors calling for us to stop referring to our electronic pianos as "pianos." The rationale was that consumers might confuse them with "regular pianos," so we should not be using the name Roland Piano. This complaint confounded us because, although the principle by which the instrument produced sound was different, the tones that it made and the skills required to play it were

the same. So this gave me a real taste of how intense the resistance might have been to Hammond organs sixty years earlier. In the end, we agreed to call our electronic pianos Roland Piano Digital and we have not received complaints from any other party about the name since.

In the area of jazz organs, the Hammond B-3 received

The drawbars on the Roland ▶
VK-77.

exceptional acclaim. Both its unique tone and its reliability lived up to its reputation. I for one, having witnessed the discontinuation of the B-3, was especially fond of this organ.

In 1977, Roland launched our VK-9 combo organ with drawbars. We developed this model as an heir to the discontinued B-3 and were confident that its tones and playing functions were worthy of the role. However, we knew that there was not much value in making a copy. The VK-9 came built-in with a control voltage of one volt per octave so that a synthesizer could be connected to the upper keyboard. This was the only way to better the Hammond organ, which was limited in the harmonics that it could produce. However, just when we were beginning to receive great reviews, the yen rapidly appreciated against the dollar, which met a fatal blow to many high-priced products, and we were forced to discontinue our production of the VK-9, the VK-6, and the Revo sound system. In 1997, we released the VK-7, and reintroduced the drawbar system on the VK-77, which was released soon after. In addition to the standard nine-drawbar configuration that created the unique B-3 sound, the VK-77 was equipped with an extra drawbar for resolving the shortcoming of tone wheels, which was that they could produce relatively few harmonics. This drawbar was used to create tones such as jazz scat and brass. Without this drawbar, the organ would not have been able to produce the new sounds that Mr. Hammond had hoped to create.

Six years after the release of its first organs in 1934, the Hammond Company had already filed a patent for the Nova Chord, an organ capable of producing a large number of harmonics and decaying sounds, like a piano. While this was

▼ At Mr. Hammond's grave in Connecticut.

based on an ambitious design that aimed to create tones completely different from those made on tone wheels, it faced too many constraints as its sound generator relied on vacuum tubes. The Nova Chord failed to become a commercial success and remained in the shadows of the B-3, yet its highly refined circuit design was nothing short of amazing from an engineering standpoint. The feat of introducing decaying tones into the realm of sound generators alone was revolutionary. The Solo Box and the Chord Organ, both of which incorporated this technology, were released at about the same time and became a huge success. The Extra Voice, which did not sell well, was also revolutionary. As I mentioned in chapter seven on my relationship with the Hammond Company, I was keenly interested in Mr. Hammond's pragmatic approach to releasing new models into the market in succession and achieving commercial success with them. Some of his developments include:

* Tone wheel generators as epitomized in the B-3

* The development of the Nova Chord

* The development of spinet organs, which set the style for home organs

* The launch of the Chord Organ

▲ "Wonderful Rivals" Laurens Hammond (left) and Don Leslie.

One can see that most of what makes up modern electronic organs originated right here. But even with his genius, he continued to oppose the Leslie speaker, which had become indispensable for the success of the Hammond organ. I think this was because he wanted to complete everything up to the outlet of the sound of his organs with Hammond products. Perhaps the genius, though recognizing the true capabilities of the Leslie speaker, was simply not ready to acknowledge his fellow genius.

I received a Nova Chord as a birthday present from Roland US in 1998. I heard that they engaged the help of master theater organ player George Wright to acquire this hard-to-find model. I have yet to find a good place to put this organ.

In 1997, I was able to fulfill one of my long-held wishes, which was to visit the grave of Mr. Hammond in Connecticut. I expressed my gratitude to him in unspoken English.

Pianos Are the "Queen of Musical Instruments"

I wrote earlier that the history of pianos can be traced back about three centuries, but this refers strictly to the development of contemporary-style piano actions. In terms of comparing pianos with organs, we must go back to the fifteenth and sixteenth centuries when harpsichords became popular. Pianists can create gentle and strong sounds depending on how they hit the keys, but this was not possible with harpsichords because they produced sounds by plucking strings. Naturally, their modes of performance were different and they had certain constraints with regard to their expressivity. While their keyboards were also based on a scale of seven notes and octaves of twelve notes, the development of an instrument that allowed the player to change the loudness of the sound by key touch must have been a blessing for composers and performers. The transition from plucking to hitting the string did not occur overnight, however; it took over fifty years of improvement to create actions that would be playable even when the keys were hit in rapid succession.

While the piano, and the ability it gave players to modulate the loudness of the sound, must have been an invention long awaited by composers, the performers would have been required to master a new set of skills and it is difficult to imagine that all of them embraced this feature immediately. The quicker the rate of technological improvement, the harsher the opposition from musicians and critics tends to be. Of course, this is in part because not all "improvements" from the designer's perspective are always true improvements from the perspective of musicians. The designer must wait for the verdict of history, and this remains the same today.

The harpsichords sold today remain largely the same as the ones made in the eighteenth and nineteenth centuries. This is because the musicians wanted it that way. It is natural to want to reproduce musical pieces of a certain time period using the instruments of that period. Another reason for preserving the original construction of harpsichords is that the temperament used on those instruments is different from the equal temperament standard on other keyboard instruments today. If a harpsichord player plans to play music based on different temperaments in a concert, he or she will have to have two harpsichords on stage, because harpsichords, unlike violins, cannot be tuned by the player. It is impossible to tune three to four octaves of strings in a short amount of time. It is also convenient to have more than one harpsichord on stage since these instruments often require retuning during longer concerts. I suspect that players in an earlier era tuned these instruments themselves as they had only about three octaves on their keyboard. For this reason alone, pianos, with their robust construction and stability of pitch, must have been a huge blessing for players. Although it is true that certain constraints came into play, as one could not play different temperaments on a piano, this standardization into equal temperament was a major impetus for the development of pianos and organs.

Electronic harpsichords become a powerful tool in situations where a musician wants to play in an ensemble with classical instruments or a musical piece in a temperament other than equal temperament. First of all, by going the electronic route, the player can vary the sound volume to suit his or her preferences. But because harpsichords usually do not need to play at a high volume anyway, the most important points are that electronic harpsichords allow the player to select different temperaments and that they are able to maintain a consistent pitch. Another characteristic of electronic harpsichords is that they enable the player to play two strings at once to produce a richer tone or use the coupler function to play a string one octave above at the same time without relying on complex mechanisms.

In the eighteenth century, an instrument that was a combination of a harpsichord and an organ was built. This ended up being a large instrument and therefore did not become very popular, but I believe that designers built it in response to requests from musicians. The harpsichords that we currently make at Roland are able to produce the sounds of small organs, and the fact that this feature is well received by musicians tells us volumes about why this same combination had already been tried three centuries earlier.

Of the many musical instruments used today, pianos, organs, and guitars allow the player to play melody, accompaniment, and rhythm on a single instrument. They can also be used to play accompaniment for vocal or other melody instruments and enhance musical pieces with harmony. This was one of the reasons that the development of keyboard instruments was accompanied by the emergence of many amazing composers. I don't think modern music would have come this far had it not been for pianos and organs. The fact that organs and pianos are known as the king and queen of musical instruments, respectively, is testimony to how loved these instruments are by everyone.

You can play almost any type of music on the piano. It is able to produce enough volume, it has enough range, and many people know how to play it, so it is undeniably the queen of musical instruments. However, the piano is not without its shortcomings. For example, once a note is played, you cannot make changes to its sound or pitch. Its tone is also fixed. The fact that the instrument is capable of sufficiently delivering musical expressions given these constraints most likely has to do with its responsiveness to key touch and the two or three pedals it is equipped with.

Pianos, which evolved from harpsichords, have undergone a variety of modifications to compensate for their shortcomings. In the case of pipe organs, the entire building becomes part of the instrument; you can expand the range of tones by adding different types of pipes, and there is enough space to install these pipes. The piano's frame is limited in size, which limits its tonal options, so pedals were added and improvements were made to the keyboard touch to expand its dynamic range, which in turn contributed to its growth as a musical instrument.

The history of the evolution of the piano, which goes back three centuries to the piano invented by Cristofori, is enormously intriguing in the context of the development of musical instruments. While this is considerably shorter than the history of organs, when one considers the fact that the piano spurred the emergence of composers and performers who created the history of music from baroque to modern, the improvements made to the piano, especially in the first half of its three-hundred-year history, are stunning.

In terms of the size of the piano, the instrument underwent drastic transformations in the period between the eighteenth and early nineteenth centuries. I believe the final hundred years of this period were when the piano matured and was poised to undergo its next change. In terms of the instrument's appearance, we have the grand piano with its flat form factor, the upright piano, and the spinet piano. It is plausible that these models were designed to suit different lifestyles and improvements were made to accommodate players who sought to enjoy the instruments in their homes. I believe the general trends in American homes, with their open spaces, had a major impact in this regard. Although these different types of pianos employ the same system in that the strings are struck by a hammer, the actions—the mechanisms that come between the keyboard and hammers that strike the strings—in flat and upright pianos are different. Yet while there is a difference in how many rapid successive strikes one can play on a key between these two types of actions, it poses no problem for regular playing. Another factor in the changing shapes of pianos was the need to reduce costs to increase sales.

The piano, which was born in Europe, was nurtured by countless artists and gave birth to a magnificent age of music. It then migrated to America, bringing its craftsmen along. Mass production began in the factories of America, a huge, developing market. Though the term *mass production* may not give a good impression in the realm of musical instruments—even though I am not using it to strike a contrast with handcrafts—the consistent production of pianos required processes involving a large number of specialists in areas such as woodworking, metalworking, assembling, tuning, and factory operations.

Research into basic materials was also indispensable. So in this context, one could say that "mass production" was a fundamental requirement for producing excellent pianos. As division of labor and standardization became widespread, manufacturers were able to purchase keyboards, actions, and frames to make their pianos, and still manage to make excellent instruments. Just so long as you complied with the essential requirements of a piano, you could make one. In this regard, explanations given to customers at the point of purchase play a critical role.

Some might question how I can say these things without having experience in manufacturing acoustic pianos, but I believe I have gained enough experience, albeit in a short period of time, to understand the entire process. I had my first experience with acoustic pianos when we were looking for a site for our factory and I was shown a piece of property that had formerly been a piano factory. I think the person showing us the property might have thought that if we were going to be making organs, then maybe a former piano company might be the best choice. So I was looking at pianos and the piano production line from the standpoint of a person in the same industry and wondering whether there were any pieces of equipment that we could use—a different perspective from that of someone focused on piano manufacturing. This was at a time when there were over twenty companies in Hamamatsu that made finished pianos, something that is hard to imagine now. I think now that we would have been able to complete our manufacturing line quicker had we designed our factory from scratch, but we took the piano factory, and I think that this detour offered us some advantages. Specifically, it gave us some insight into pianos and we were able to hire experienced talent who worked in the piano factory process. I think our current unwavering focus on developing electronic pianos is attributable in part to this experience when we had to decide whether or not to discontinue the production of acoustic pianos in a very short period of time.

Quiet Are the Makers

Written histories regarding the processes of musical instrument development are very interesting and informative regardless of what perspective they are written from. From the viewpoint of an instrument manufacturer, why did Cristofori take on the challenge of making a new instrument from a harpsichord? If he had left his thoughts in his own writing, I would certainly like to read them. While there are many books written by performers, composers, critics, and historians of music, few have been written by those who make the instruments. I believe there are less than ten such books available in Japanese, and these are predominantly related to stringed instruments.

When one thinks back to the time when there were no patent systems and musical instruments were made by hand in a workshop, one realizes that there very well might have been books written by craftspeople that were forgotten over time and never saw the light of day. Still, considering the dimensions of pipe organs, it is difficult to imagine that these were built in small workshops. Perhaps the makers did not leave any documentation so as to prevent their manufacturing skills from leaking. Naturally, these skills were mostly transmitted from father to son. And because the makers of musical instruments played a background role behind the scenes in the music world, this aspect of the trade in combination with a certain craftsperson mentality may have made them more reserved.

Critics helped expand the popularity of music by explaining it in ways that were easy to understand, and their writings kept performers and directors, who could at times become quite self-indulgent, in check. At times, their criticism was also directed at musical instruments. The makers of these instruments had little opportunity or avenue to state their case, and had to take it all in without countering these criticisms. It was as if one were put on trial without a defense. In many cases, today's musical instrument manufacturers are not given the opportunity to refute criticisms, and particularly in the case of electronic musical instruments, it is critical that we prepare sufficient supporting information and set our goals ahead of time because these instruments are different from traditional instruments in terms of both form and sound. In the world of music, where there is constant tension between the conservative impulse—in the positive sense—to enhance the way traditional music is expressed, and the innovative impulse that is always in pursuit of new music, it is impossible to expect people to be satisfied with and understand everything that we do. For this reason alone, I am very curious as to what went on in the minds of innovators when they embarked on a new course.

A musical instrument that does not allow musicians to modulate the volume is incomplete as a means for expressing music. Organs, the most prominent keyboard instrument for centuries, did not provide the capability to play different volumes on individual keys, so this might have been one of the reasons that harpsichords, with their inability to express different volumes by touch, were also embraced. The clavichord, another keyboard instrument of the time, was small and easy to handle, but its volume was too low and its pitch was unstable. The harpsichord improved on these traits and was transportable, so it was embraced as a musical instrument that one could play without much worry, and many musical pieces were written for it.

Cristofori, who was in charge of maintaining and manufacturing musical instruments in the House of Medici, the ultra-rich family that ruled Tuscany, must have had many interactions with harpsichord players, and it would be natural to think that he attempted to make many improvements based on their feedback. However, the fortepiano—his new instrument that embodied his hard work and allowed musicians to express differences in volume by key touch—was not received well by Italian musicians, whereas it was embraced in Austria and Germany. Composers in these countries increasingly wrote musical pieces for this new instrument, and the piano gradually established a position in the world of music. Cristofori lived at a time of transition from the Renaissance into the Baroque period and his invention of the pianoforte was a major influence on the blossoming of Baroque music itself.

A large number of pieces were also written for harpsichord during this period. Of the famous composers of this era that I often hear mentioned, three were Italian, one was French, two were German, and one was British, whereas in the classic school period, most of the composers were either Austrian or German. I personally believe that this was because these composers embraced the piano. This would mean that it took eighty to one hundred years for the piano to replace the harpsichord as the primary instrument. The piano was invented in Italy, blossomed in Germany, improved upon in France and Britain, and developed into an industry in America. Japan held the record for the most pianos produced at one time but this record has now been overtaken by China, which continues to renew the record. This is the three-hundred-year history of the piano in a few lines.

In the late 1960s, the clavinet, or "clavi," was released in Europe. It used the same mechanism as the original clavichord to produce sounds, but it was fitted with pickups just as on electric guitars. It produced a unique tone and was embraced by rock musicians. While this instrument eventually disappeared from the scene as its pitch was unstable and it was expensive, its sound is still with us today. I think there are hardly any who know about this instrument's relationship to the original clavichord. My failed experiment in which I amplified the sound of a music box with a pickup notwithstanding, I believe the person who incorporated the clavichord into rock music was quite daring.

Based on this track record, one could say that the piano is fully qualified to be the king of musical instruments, but my personal hope is that it remain the queen. Organs, whether they be pipe organs or electronic classical organs, have a bigger feeling image-wise and are more masculine compared to pianos. I believe pianos have become too large so I hope the instrument retains its feminine feel. The likely reason that this instrument, originally called the piano-forte, is now called the piano is that the "forte" was simply dropped, leaving only "piano," which I think was a good thing. Attempts to increase the volume of acoustic pianos and produce fortes while retaining their current construction have resulted in numerous adverse side effects. There are also limits to how much the pianissimo can be controlled. Novel approaches would be needed to expand the piano's dynamic range, or the ratio between forte and piano. Instead of trying to design a piano that has sufficient volume to perform to a large audience with an orchestra yet is also capable of expressing delicate pianissimos, I believe it is much more wonderful to have a piano that is able to speak to an audience of five or six hundred people. Pianos are wonderful on a more intimate scale.

The Future of the Piano

In 2000, to mark the tercentennial of the birth of the piano, the Smithsonian Institute in Washington, D.C., held a special exhibit titled *Piano 300*, sponsored by the National Museum of American History. This exhibit was supported by concerts by top-rated pianists as well as a documentary program on the history of pianos, in which I was one of the people interviewed on the topic of digital technology and the evolution of pianos.

The special exhibit was quite spectacular, showcasing a total of about 250 instruments ranging from an early piano made by Cristofori (in 1722), of which only three exist today, to digital pianos. Since its invention, the piano has undergone a variety of changes affecting everything from the number, length, and thickness of its strings to the materials used to make its frame. It more or less settled into the instrument we know today about two hundred years into its history. The grand pianos we have today are beautifully balanced musical instruments and true masterpieces of human ingenuity.

Many feel that the acoustic piano, an instrument that produces sounds with strings that are hit by hammers, has reached the pinnacle of perfection, a point at which there appears to be no more room for improvement. Personally, I believe the violin is a perfect instrument. It has been perfected and there is no more room for improvement. I believe the piano, however, as nearly perfect as it may be, will continue to evolve as we move forward.

For example, the subtle touch with which the performer hits the key is an indispensable element in creating music on the piano. For those involved in the manufacture and development of digital musical instruments, the piano is a very attractive target; our efforts involve preserving the keyboard touch of pianos, which performers use to breathe life into their music, as well as developing elements not found in traditional pianos.

At the Hamamatsu Electronic Arts Awards ceremony in May 2007, Isao Tomita, one of the award recipients, remarked, "Painters can create unique expressions using colors that they make by mixing a variety of paints on their palettes, but the situation is different with orchestra conductors. This is because the sonic characters of the sounds made by different instruments such as violins and oboes are all predetermined." He said that he had encountered synthesizers while searching for sounds with which to create his own music.

While Mr. Tomita is the first name in synthesized music, he considers everything to be a musical instrument and sees no division between acoustic and electronic instruments. He says he would use a synthesized sound without hesitation if it happened to be the one most suited for expressing his music. My impression is that the potential for musical expression can be expanded considerably simply by removing the division between acoustic and electronic instruments.

During a dialog I had with the conductor Hiroyuki Iwaki and the composer Toshiro Mayuzumi, Mr. Mayuzumi remarked, "Why can't we make pianos that can play portamento or vibrato?" A very lively conversation ensued, during which he also remarked, "I would like to compose songs using such an instrument." This was a refreshing surprise that left me thinking, "It's amazing that there are composers who think this way."

Just as the electric guitar was derived from the acoustic guitar and eventually established its own place in music, I believe electronic pianos have reached a similar stage in their evolution. I have been involved in the development of electronic pianos for forty years but I remember how difficult it was to have them accepted back then. It was Laurie Gillespie, president of Roland Canada, who shared my belief in the future of electronic pianos and offered his support and help from the very beginning. And look where we are today. More electronic pianos are being made than acoustic ones. Electronic pianos have become popular thanks to technological innovations that enable us to produce high-performance musical instruments. Another possible reason for their popularity is that more and more performers and composers are seeking to liberate their musical expressions from the constraints of fixed concepts.

Going forward, I believe that, in addition to sound alone, the synthesis of sound and video will begin to gain major attention. At the "New Style Concert 2007" hosted by Akira Senju, jazz pianist Shinji Akita used V-Link in his performance. Images were shown on an onstage screen that synched in real time with the music being performed. The performer himself was able to control the video.

At present, we frequently take in concerts on TV and the Internet, and I believe that we will be able do interesting things by combining music and video. The age of the electronic piano—which is positioned as a "new" musical instrument based on an acoustic instrument—has already begun.

It was in 2007 that we launched the V-Piano, which used a new sound engine. Development had been ongoing, and was a major project that took ten years under the leadership of Tadao Kikumoto, our research lab director. We decided to take a fresh look at the modern piano and use this as our starting point for creating digital piano sounds. We called the sounds of acoustic pianos currently in widespread use "vintage," and sounds of pianos that had not existed heretofore "vanguard." Both words start with *v* so they were a perfect match for the name of the piano.

Because we had a clear image of what we were aiming for, the creation of sounds became easier. The sounds of electronic pianos improved dramatically with the development of sampling technology, called pulse-code modulation (PCM). Well-taken photographs often appear better than real life. The same applies to sound; we are now able to store the sounds of excellent instruments on memory, combine them to suit different performances, and create sounds that are dramatically better. These instruments, the product of years of work and ingenuity on the part of manufacturers, have now come to be regarded as sufficient for use by beginners and are actually used in piano education. They are now smaller and lighter, and also offer a solution to the problem of noise pollution caused by traditional instruments. The fact that they are easier to transport when moving is also a benefit from the user's perspective. As someone who makes musical instruments, my ultimate joy would be that people purchase these instruments for their superb sound, but we can't complain at this point because our first order of the day is for these instruments to be accepted by the market. It was thanks to sampling technology that digital pianos began to approach the quality of acoustic pianos and renewed the piano market. I believe improvements will be ongoing and out of this process will come excellent musical instruments.

Back when rock music became popular in the 1960s, at about the time the Beatles came on the scene, bands that included keyboard instruments became somewhat of a problem as their gear would be too heavy and difficult to transport. Thus I believe that the decline in the use of keyboard instruments came about not so much for musical reasons. The increasing presence of portable pianos on stage in recent years has to do with the fact that they have become easier to transport and offer a broad range of usable sounds. No one is telling us now that they are using their keyboards for their tuning reference tool. This is because tuning stability is widely available in various digital devices.

Nowadays, in most live performances, the sounds of all instruments are mixed and balanced on a mixer and delivered through a PA system. From the audience's point of view, the sounds of the instruments do not come from where they are being played but from within an expanded mix of all sounds. The sounds that the people on stage hear are different from what the audience hears. Another problem is that the performers are unable to hear the balance among the other performers. Concerts that sound great can happen only when all the performers are able to play comfortably. The development of audio equipment and electronic musical instruments has enabled people to put on large concerts, but this area is rife with new problems as well. In contrast, the piano is a mature instrument that has not undergone any change in the last century. What is being demanded are ways to create new possibilities and musical expressions without having to make major changes to playing style or techniques.

Why is the piano industry in decline in countries with an advanced piano culture? How can they preserve the skills that were accumulated over centuries? These and other issues apply to accordions as well. As I mentioned, concerts have grown from relatively intimate events to huge shows. It feels like things are going in a different direction from what musical instrument manufacturers like myself have in mind. Since I believe the joy of music comes from live performances, I want to forget for a moment my position as someone who works behind the scenes and get on a soapbox about this issue.

Keyboards represent the interface between performers and the music that they seek to express. If we can promise the performers that the keyboard touch that they have become accustomed to over many years will remain the same, and if they are able to get the results they seek even if the method by which the sound is produced is different, I believe there is a chance that these players will try the instrument out. However, it is often the case that the very same keyboard can seem to have a lighter or heavier touch if the sound is different, which is a common illusion. And because we are seeking different directions for creating new sounds based on input from musicians, we can easily end up in a futile loop of trial and error.

I remember how Engel's coefficient was often used to compare different countries during the postwar period of economic growth. This term was named after a theory forwarded by German economist Ernst Engel, who posited that the higher a household's income, the lower the percentage of that household's entire consumption expenditure that would go toward the purchase of food. This percentage was called Engel's coefficient, and the lower the percentage, the better off economically the household was. In recent years, we often see GDP per capita used as a measure of abundance, but Engel's law struck home for me at a time when the food situation was not as good as it is now. I have a feeling that there might be something to learn from a "music coefficient" that measures the percentage of money spent on music within a household's consumption expenditure.

Music Is a Venture

Typically, rationality, planning capability, and the ability to take action are cited as the primary attributes needed for running a business. However, people who are oriented toward venture businesses may not necessarily be those who excel in rational thinking. Additionally, these people often resist taking orders from others, oppose taking the same actions as others, and have a constant desire to take on the challenges of new ideas. Because they have this desire or goal, they are able to forge ahead with their business even if they are met with disappointment or setbacks.

When you review a venture business plan from a conventional perspective, you notice that desire makes up a disproportionately large part of most of these plans. The confidence in the ability to make a profit is overly strong and the rational underpinnings are weak in many cases. There will naturally be many setbacks, but because the pull of the person's desire or goal is stronger than the difficulties that lie in front of them, they do not hesitate to move closer to success through these setbacks and gain experience in the process. This being the case, I believe such people can dramatically improve their success rate simply by finding a way to compensate for the areas in which they lack.

While there is no across-the-board solution because the issues vary from case to case, there is a common way of thinking. Here again, I have seen examples where turning points came from meetings with other people. I myself believe that I have been able to continue my business so far thanks to the many people I have met over the years.

In Japan, the current wave of venture businesses is the third in history. The first wave came as far back as forty years ago. The impetus came in the early seventies at a time when the awareness of business leaders at medium-sized companies began to change, specifically with the research visit to Boston arranged by the Kyoto Association of Corporate Executives. At the time, Kyoto was home to a large number of postwar venture companies that were already running successful businesses. Hats off to their forward-looking vision and ability to take action.

Roland was founded in 1972 and I remember that the industrial world was vibrant with energy at the time. I was certainly very influenced by all of this too. The second wave came twelve years later, in 1984, when it became clear that computers were going to have an influence in a broad range of industries. Industries such as new material development and biotechnology were gaining attention and the booming economy provided a tailwind to all of this.

In Shizuoka, the International Venture Business Symposium was held at the Grand Hotel in Hamamatsu with participation by over a thousand individuals from various industries. Hamamatsu is a city that is very suited to this kind of atmosphere. Among the guest speakers was Zbigniew Brzezinski, aide to the US president. A panel discussion was held featuring the presidents from ten domestic and foreign companies and mediated by a member of academia. I was one of the panelists at the event. Of these ten panelists only three remained as panelists fifteen years later. A number of the remaining seven have started up new businesses since then so I have only respect for the unwavering fighting spirit of these venture business leaders. The event was filled with energy, possibly because there were more specific examples of venture businesses than in the 1970s and people could relate more directly to these matters.

Looking back, I'm not sure why Mr. Brzezinski, a specialist in politics and foreign relations, was chosen as the guest speaker, but I still remember the heady atmosphere of the event. At the time, there were still few women who took part in these meetings. Nowadays, more and more women business leaders are running successful business in all parts of the country. In Hamamatsu, the Hamamatsu Women Business Leaders' Association was formed, which is a very vibrant association that seeks to advance business from the unique perspective of women.

Currently, the government is implementing policies that support new businesses as part of its efforts to break out from the present economic stagnation. We are entering an age where a true venture spirit will be needed. To "start up a company" by definition means to "start up a venture business," so all the companies that have been formed to date were venture businesses at one point. While the risk involved in starting up a company has not changed over the years, the diversification in the ways that people can acquire capital has been a great advancement. In exchange for this, it is only natural that consolidations and mergers and acquisitions have become more commonplace. It is ironic, however, that these developments began in the financial sector, a sector that is characteristically the opposite of venture companies.

The current wave of interest in venture businesses is the third one after the war. In this trend, in which even the average person is interested in these things, there are great expectations for the new generation to become business leaders with the ability to reimagine business from completely new perspectives. I was recently interviewed by a magazine for a special feature article on Hamamatsu that they were planning as part of their report on the state of venture businesses in the region. I remember explaining that, as an individual who had relocated to Hamamatsu from another part of the country, I had heard many anecdotes about various local business leaders and the individuals they mentored, and I described the immense impact that these stories had on my outlook. In some cases, the anecdotes had been exaggerated for entertainment value, but even when one took this into account, the endearing way in which they were told spoke to the great influence of these leaders.

The process of starting up a business is a nonstop stream of unexpected events, so from this standpoint, I think that small businesses that can be started up without much overhead or do not require much purchasing are suited as venture startups. A good example of this is the software and network industries. In the area of music, I think it would be businesses related to music education.

Those engaged in venture businesses share many common traits with people involved in music. The main points are:

1. The goal that one sets for oneself takes first priority.

2. All decisions for moving forward are made by oneself.

3. One's ability is the greatest asset.

4. It is difficult to find a good advisor.

It is true that the fourth item applies to music because it is such a specialized field, which is all the more reason that one must work even harder. Although the first priority for someone who seeks to continue working independently toward a goal should be to have a good understanding of the business in which one is involved, I am sometimes surprised at the number of people who start out without doing much research. Doing your research on the fly can result in making more mistakes and taking longer than needed.

When we talk about music as an industry, we can cause much confusion unless we categorize the industry as follows:

1. Artists, performers, composers

2. Music publishers, record companies

3. Musical instrument manufacturers

4. Music educators

People in areas other than the music industry tend to see musical instrument manufacturing, record companies, and publishing as belonging to the same organization or guild. This is because products from all of these industries are displayed on the same floor at retailers, but the reality is that there is very little exchange between these four categories and I don't think the probability is high that this will change moving forward.

From another standpoint, the music business consists of three elements:

1. Tools and means for delivering performances (hardware)

2. Musical charts, digital files, and so forth that enable the above (software)

3. The artistry that is central to all music (artware)

Artware, a word I made up, is everything that supports the artist in his or her activities. There are some who dislike referring to music as a "business" as this work involves communicating to other people's sensibilities, but you cannot remain consistent with your intent on an ongoing basis without a business perspective. Many artists delegate the business aspect, including negotiations, to managers so that they can concentrate on their music, and I believe there is great wisdom in taking this route in terms of maximizing results. The areas of music publishing and recording revolve around the software aspect, and are run by a combination of artists and businesspeople who have professional expertise in business planning.

The musical instrument industry is founded on a fine balance of all three aspects. The value of an instrument is determined in large part by the degree to which it embodies artware. As for electronic musical instruments, because hardware and software inevitably tend to take center stage, misconceptions can arise without a demo for showcasing the musicality of the instrument, and this is truer the more novel the instrument. People like ourselves who are involved in design and manufacture must particularly keep this point in mind. Additionally, while electronic musical instruments benefit from technological innovation because they use a large number of light electric components—components that are used in the computer industry—we can just as well find ourselves caught in a trap of not taking artware into consideration. For the artist, the most important element for delivering a great performance is a musical instrument that he or she can use comfortably. The possibilities that derive from technological innovations also have a huge impact in this very crucial area.

In addition to seeking musical instruments that allow them to express their sensibilities, artists also seek to create sounds that have not existed before. Although it goes without saying that new sounds are created through new playing skills, many are also created through new "tricks." As makers of musical instruments, it is crucial that we consistently provide artists with tricks that are easy to use. My belief is that no matter how excellent a particular trick might appear to be, it must never require the player to adopt completely novel playing styles. While these things do often occur in the realm of electronic musical instruments, they are simply displays of designer arrogance. A wide range of new sounds have been discovered and come into use over the past fifty or so years, and these have all been the product of collaboration—and sometimes even battles—between artists and instrument manufacturers.

With the birth of electronic instruments, musical instruments gained the ability to interact with the external world for the first time in history. Business opportunities abound because the digital world has opened its doors to musical instruments, giving them access to networks, storage media, and CPUs. Opportunities exist in all three of these areas as well as in areas where they overlap.

People in the music world are self-sufficient and solitary in a good sense. This applies equally to performers as to designers and manufacturers. That said, even if people think that they are working all alone, in reality, they are being supported by a large number of people. For this very reason, it is absolutely necessary that they have a good advisor and the openness to listen to what others have to say. People who pursue music are the same as those who pursue venture businesses. Few musicians see themselves as running a venture business, but the joy they experience is the same as the joy that comes from starting up a new business. In Japan, we cannot afford to squander the current opportunity to start venture businesses in the music industry. The United States and the UK are the only countries where music hardware and software exports exceed imports in dollar amounts. In contrast to anime, which is enjoyed visually regardless of language, music is an area in which Japan lags far behind due to the language barrier. I believe, however, that instead of seeing this as a lag we should see it as a source of possibilities. The realm of music is a treasure trove for venture businesses.

Shortcut to Paradise

We typically do not feel tired when we are doing something we enjoy. It's interesting to note that we tend to grow bored quickly in endeavors where improvement comes easily. Pursuits with depth to them are interesting. The arts are such a field and more people should actively engage in creating art. Specifically, in the field of music, many people enjoy listening to music, but far too few play an instrument themselves. And people who compose music are rarer still, possibly due to the first hurdles being too high, which include learning to read music, theory, and various other elements of music. There are only a few people in my range of acquaintances who continue to write songs, if only as a hobby.

People who start learning music when they are young are very fortunate. Just as babies learn language from their parents through repetition, people who familiarize themselves with music at a young age, even if they do not keep up with their practice and move on to completely different fields, know how to enjoy music, and this, I believe, makes their lives that much richer. They have a higher-than-usual capacity to enjoy music without having to climb as many steps, and their scope of enjoyment is also expanded. If as adults they decide to take up another instrument, they will learn more quickly and will be less likely to quit.

While music education has had its ups and downs since it began in the Meiji era, it is something that we can be proud of. Of course, partly because of the way it is taught and partly because of the excessive expectations of parents, music education has also produced many dropouts, but that is a natural part of the process and may even be a healthy thing in the end. The sheer number of people forming clubs and bands in their schools and workplaces would have been unthinkable in the past, and all of this is founded in the basic music education provided in elementary schools.

The proliferation of PCs has opened the door to new possibilities in music. Music is a temporal art, and therefore it moves forward in real time. Bach was once asked how he could play so well. He is said to have replied to the effect that he merely hit the right keys at the right time, as denoted on the music sheet. Although others may find it difficult to hit the keys at the right time in "real time," we can create music in "non–real time" by treating the timing and pitch as digital data and inputting this data into a computer. That said, although a player might not need traditional performance skills, a different set of skills is required to create unique and interesting music on a computer. And writing good music requires the same sensibilities needed in traditional performance. Although there used to be only one narrow path to "music paradise" where people could enjoy making music, we now have a variety of wide paths thanks to music education in schools, the popularity of different kinds of music on TV and radio, and the opportunity to play in bands and create non-real-time music on computers.

While I had few opportunities to listen to music during my youth because of the disruptions of World War II, after the war I was able to access music by listening to the radio. When I reached my own version of "music paradise," I met a world of interesting people there, and I was very fortunate to have been able to join them. Along the way, I realized that while there is no such thing as a shortcut in any kind of work, if you are walking on a path toward a goal that you have set, the journey will be enjoyable and you will not feel tired. This, I believe, is because I live in "music paradise."

Piano Genes

The commercialization of electronic musical instruments began with organs. I also rode that wave from organs to synthesizers and then on to keyboard instruments. While the piano was an appealing target from an engineering standpoint, it required a large number of circuitry chips and the early LSIs were not up to the task of enabling a commercial product. While electronic circuitry for creating decaying sounds had existed since the time of vacuum tubes, there were a variety of technological hurdles in the way of creating the sounds of pianos, sounds that begin to decay and change the moment a key is struck.

In addition to circuitry, the feel of the key when it is hit was another critical element. Because pianos do not have the functionality of switching between different tones, the player must use varying strengths of key touch to express emotion. As such, key touch dictates not only the volume but all aspects of a piano performance. The action—the complex mechanism that transmits this touch to the hammer—is the most delicate part of the piano. The action that we find in modern acoustic pianos has basically not changed for over a century, and this speaks to the degree to which it has been perfected. The acoustic piano, just like the violin and acoustic guitar, has reached such a high degree of perfection that there is no more room for improvement.

That said, there is a huge difference between the pianos used in the time of Mozart and Beethoven and the modern piano, to the point that it would not be an overstatement to say that these are actually different instruments. One look at the pianos exhibited in the Hamamatsu Museum of Musical Instruments makes this clear. It's thrilling to think of how a composer, who had written a piano piece two centuries earlier, might feel if he could hear his piece being played on a modern piano. Rather than reject the modern piano, I think he would be inspired to compose for it. The first task of digital pianos is to prove that their expressivity is equal to or greater than that of acoustic pianos. If they are not able to do this, they will remain a substitute for acoustic pianos.

I believe that only digital pianos are able to achieve the "piano (soft)" that is indispensable in piano music. We are now seeing the beginnings of an era in which pianists and composers are seeking to create music that traditional pianos have not been able to express, and manufacturers are working to meet these needs. "Exploring the Future of Music," a concert that we held in 1987, provided a venue for these experimentations. We are very grateful for the ongoing support and cooperation of Toshiro Mayuzumi and Hiroyuki Iwaki, two people who advocated the potential of electronic musical instruments from early on.

While we have been developing electronic pianos since 1973, I proudly maintain that, from a technological standpoint, the inaugural year for digital pianos came in 1986 when we succeeded in developing a digital piano based on the Roland SA synthesis technology. I still remember feeling deeply moved at my sense that this technology had given us a vision into the future, and that it was the true heir to the piano. So we immediately organized the above-mentioned concert to announce the results of our development efforts. A review of the concert was carried in *Music Trade*, the equivalent of *The Music Trades* magazine in the United States. This review was a huge encouragement for us. We held the second concert in 1988 at Gotanda U-Port Tokyo Post Office Life Insurance Hall. The third concert, held at Suntory Hall in Tokyo in 1991, was an electronic musical instrument concert featuring a semi-grand piano model prototype and was titled "Concert for Exploring the Future of Music Featuring Electronic Musical Instruments and Orchestra."

The fourth of these concerts was again held at the Suntory Hall. It was very fortunate that we were able to have the presidents of all our overseas joint companies and the management of key Japanese suppliers at the concert. At this concert, we featured a digital grand piano that was not connected to external speakers. I believe this was the first piano concerto in which a standalone digital piano without external speakers played with a full-fledged orchestra. It was discovered during rehearsals that the piano's lows were interfering with the violin section and we were able to address this issue by setting up a shielding panel. This was something that we had not noticed when the piano was played alone.

▼ Toshiro Mayuzumi and Hiroyuki Iwaki at the "Exploring the Future of Music" concert.

The designs of modern acoustic pianos use two or three strings for different pitches to improve their sound, creating an exquisite level of balance. The differences in design between various manufacturers have to do with how they achieve this balance. Since the piano must be able to play along with an orchestra, significant changes cannot be made in the design that affect harmonies developed over many years of experience. Steps must be taken so that the instrument is able to play solo as well as in a concerto.

A replica of the piano invented by Cristofori, which introduced the prototype of the modern piano action, is on display at the Hamamatsu Museum of Musical Instruments. The instrument covers notes from G to C on fifty-four keys. Whereas rich lows were not available in Cristofori's day, modern pianos typically have eighty-eight keys. This is made possible by the availability of mechanisms that stabilize the strings. It would be extremely difficult to string a large number of the thick, long piano strings that produce lows on a wooden frame. First of all, they would not be able to tune. And the tension would be too much for a wooden frame to handle. For this reason alone, piano manufacturers must have been elated when iron frames became available and they were able to design pianos with expanded ranges of pitch. They also began to wind the piano strings with copper wire to increase their mass in order to produce a more powerful sound. However, by the time sounds produced on such strings reach the orchestra and the audience, they are different from what the pianist hears. In this area also, there are countless issues that need to be solved.

The fourth concert in the "Exploring the Future of Music" series was scheduled to open with Toshiro Myuzumi's *Rhapsody for the Twenty-First Century*, but due to a minor complication, the program had to be changed to *Romeo and Juliet* at the last minute. Had the program proceeded as planned by Hiroyuki Iwaki, the Myuzumi piece would have featured the original players who had performed nine years earlier. The change was unfortunate also because the concert would have flowed naturally into the second piece, Chopin's Piano Concerto no. 2 in F Minor. But setting all of that aside, I personally felt that the concert was amazing. The dynamic range in Respighi's *Pines of Rome*, the last piece played, was truly sublime. While I have heard this piece performed at concerts several times in the past, I have never felt so moved. This was a performance in which Rodgers organs, Roland harpsichords, and digital piano completely blended in with the orchestra. My hat is off to Mr. Iwaki, who was able to bring out the full power of the orchestra.

The second piece, the concerto, was to be performed with the digital piano not connected to an external speaker for the first time, and I felt an unspeakable nervousness until the music started. The wonderful concerto we were treated to owed much to the skills of pianist Akira Wakabayashi. In the questionnaires collected after the concert, many indicated that they had not been able to tell that the piano was digital. While there were a number of critical comments about the actual performance, it was great to know that the audience at least enjoyed the concert. I also felt that it would take some more time for perceptions of digital instruments to change.

The first "Exploring the Future of Music" concert was held in December of 1987, and the first concert in which we created a program centered around digital pianos was the one in 1988. A look at the review headlines of these concerts as they appeared in *Music Trade* gives an idea of the history of electronic musical instruments.

- 1987: "Daring Challenge: A Concerto on Electronic Piano! Roland's 'Exploring the Future of Music' Concert"

- 1988: "Electronics Takes on the Classics and the Beatles; Roland's 'Exploring the Future of Music' Concert 1988"

- 1991: "Roland's Ambitious Proposal: 'Exploring the Future of Music' Concert 1991 Is Held; Electronic Musical Instruments and Orchestra Play Together Seamlessly!"

- 2000: "Roland's 'Brand-New Classic Concert'; Powerful Showcase of the Evolution of Electronic Musical Instruments; Unending Applause. The Audience's Conclusion Was Unmistakable."

Thirty years ago, it was a "daring challenge" to use a digital piano in a classical concert. My feeling at the time was that they had given me some homework to do before our next concert.

And in 2011, we held a series of concerts featuring the digital V-Piano Grand in twenty-one countries around the world, titled "V-Piano Grand World Premiere." Wonderful performances were given in various countries by prominent pianists. In Japan, where the concert was called "The Yukio Yokoyama Digital Piano Recital," Mr. Yokoyama played Beethoven's *Moonlight Sonata*, Chopin's Ballade no. 1, and Liszt's Piano Sonata in B Minor, among other pieces. The technique with which he delivered these pieces was truly something to behold. In our US concert, David Benoit, a Grammy-nominated jazz fusion musician, made an appearance. The V-Piano was highly praised for its response to the excellent techniques of these amazing pianists from around the world.

I take pride in the fact that this series of concerts opened up a new era for digital piano in a wide range of genres including classical and jazz.

13

The Future of Electronic Musical Instruments

The Evolution and History of Electronic Musical Instruments

ELECTRONIC ORGANS DEVELOPED THROUGH THE COMPETITION AMONG various manufacturers who continued to incorporate technologies from the electronics industry. This process is evident when one studies the patent bulletins published in Japan and the United States.

In the 1900s, we begin to see a large number of electronic musical instrument prototypes that produce vibrations mechanically or with the use of rotating disks. Thomas Edison founded a light bulb company and a phonograph company in 1878. A well-known photo of him in his Menlo Park laboratory shows him sitting in front of a small pipe organ with his employees. While Edison was first involved in audio technology, with his wax-coated cylinder records, and expanded his work into the movie business, he was not involved with musical instruments at all. Since early movies were often accompanied by performances on theater organs, Edison probably had some connection to musical instruments, but there is no sign that he involved himself in that area.

▼ Thomas Edison (center) and his employees at his Menlo Park laboratory (1880).

With the invention of the vacuum tube came the invention of electronic musical instruments—instruments whose sound-generating components have no mechanical parts—although they could only play a single note at a time. Prominent examples include the ondes martenot, the trautonium, and the theremin, among others that I have mentioned in this book. The historical background as well as the anecdotes passed down to us about the era in which these musical instruments were invented are very intriguing, and books such as Fred Prieberg's *Music in the Technological Age* and Joel Chadabe's *Electric Sound* are recommended reading for musicians who aspire to create modern music. It is also interesting to note that all three instruments mentioned above were invented in Europe. One cannot fail to be amazed by the innovative nature of the ondes martenot, especially upon learning that a patent for this instrument was filed as early as 1928. Many musicians used this instrument to compose music. The Italian composer Ferruccio Busoni went so far as to say that the development of music was being obstructed by the limitations of musical instruments. Although as someone who was prototyping new instruments and struggling to simply make an instrument that would perform consistently, I was not as ambitious as I was only attempting to create commercially usable and very sellable electronic instruments.

The invention of electronic musical instruments exploded in the 1920s and '30s, and it is obvious from studying the circuit diagrams of all of these inventions that the vacuum tube—the latest technology at the time—provided the spark for this explosion. One must also not overlook the active involvement of composers and electronics developers. Active research continued after World War II. Germany

in particular was home to five electronic music studios, and Japanese composers made investigative visits to the Technical University of Berlin's music studio and the Studio for Electronic Music of the West German Radio in Cologne. I had the chance to speak with the composer Toshiro Mayuzumi, who wrote a piece for ondes martenot titled *Ectoplasm* in 1954, about what he saw at the studio in Cologne. He told me that this studio had been the inspiration for the electronic music studio at NHK.

The April 1956 issue of "Radio Technology" (I had contributed an article on a prototype I had made of a sweep generator, a measuring device for testing TV sets, to the November 1953 issue) featured an

▼ Clara Rockmore playing the theremin. Copied from a record jacket. Robert Moog is credited here as the recording engineer.

article by composer Makoto Moroi on his visit to the broadcasting station in Cologne titled, "Lullaby of the Twentieth Century? Special Feature: What Is Electronic Music?" This article also featured some thoughts from Toshiro Mayuzumi, and I remember being impressed by the extent and depth of these composers' research at a time when I was still just making TV sets and prototypes of electronic musical instruments.

At the time, music had to be recorded using tape recorder, an unimaginably time-consuming process compared to what we can do today with modern equipment. Before this, in the 1920s and '30s, live performances were the only mode of delivering musical pieces written for electronic musical instruments. This was before tape recorders were available, and when the ability simply to amplify sound was a major feat in itself.

Analog records had already been around for some time, so we do have recorded sound as well as film footage of theremin performances. The performances of Clara Rockmore, who was originally a violinist, created quite a sensation. I have a record of Rockmore playing the theremin, and while the instrument's tone is reminiscent of a music saw, its musical expressions are much more refined. The LP, which was recorded in July 1975, even has a circuit diagram printed on the jacket. Robert Moog is credited on this album as the recording engineer. I also prototyped a theremin, and though it was able to produce sound, I was not able to play it at all myself. The prototype was relatively easy to make, but the instrument was very difficult to play and I could make only sounds that resembled sound effects. This gave me a new appreciation of Rockmore's technique. The fact that not many theremin players have come on the scene also speaks to how difficult this instrument is to play.

An announcement was made in the August 1953 edition of "Soviet Culture" magazine that the Soviet Union's electronic musical instrument manufacturing division would be closing its doors. The reason given was that electronic musical instrument performances went against socialist realism. Apparently, it was against their principles to freely play music that could not be played on traditional instruments. In reality, however, it might have had more to do with the nonessential and non-urgent nature of electronic musical instrument projects, as this coincided with the period when the country was focusing on the development of its nuclear arsenal and rockets. In any case, it was unfortunate that the lineage of Soviet electronic musical instruments, which originated with the theremin, had to be derailed by shifting politics and ideology.

In October 1954, the Second International Congress of Catholic Church Music reached a resolution "opposing the use of electric organs that have no pipes." This should not be such a surprise as during medieval times, there had even been churches that opposed the pipe organ. In the Gothic era, the use of pipe organs was opposed for the reason that they were musically too elaborate for use in religious services.

The books and publications of the time make it clear that musicians in the early days of modern music were in search of something new. They were fed up with traditional instruments, and felt an aversion toward materials such as wood, horsehair, steel wires, and brass plates. According to the German-language publication *Music in the Technological Age*, the avant-garde musicians of the time were dissatisfied, complaining, "Old sound equipment has taken on a fixed character, and it cannot but prompt cultural-historical and sentimental associations," and, "Traditional instruments are burdened with something immeasurable, and are replete with feelings by which they are 'characterized.' The flute, horn, and oboe are of the past, and constitute the inheritance of tradition in both the literary and formative sense, an inheritance from which we cannot easily liberate ourselves."

These comments were made by composers and performers who were active at a time when possibilities for new sound-producing materials were beginning to take shape. I have become increasingly convinced that our mission as developers is to present new possibilities for audio-image expressions, including 3-D imaging, in ways that are easy to use.

In the United States—where people are known for proactively taking on whatever they set their minds to—research had been ongoing and in 1976, Herbert Deutsch published his book *Synthesis*. Deutsch had worked with Robert Moog in synthesizer development. This was just at the time when I was designing the System 700 modular synthesizer. I had the opportunity to get acquainted with the author so I obtained the Japanese translation rights to the book and in 1979 published the translation through a company called Pipers (presently Sugihara Shoten). I still remember the many eye-openers I gleaned from the book during the translation process of the first chapter, "Music after the Modern Era," and the second chapter, "A Short History of Electronic Music." It was clear that in the early years of electronic musical instruments, the composers and performers—who are more responsible for the soft than the hard aspects of music—were the ideological leaders in the field.

In 1950, Dusseldorf-based Jorgensen Electronic launched their clavioline. Based on one vacuum tube (dual triode valve vacuum tube), this was an affordable melody instrument that was easy to carry around. The Canary that I prototyped during my Ace Electronic Industries years and exhibited at the 1964 NAMM Show was a melody instrument inspired by this clavioline. Starting off as monophonic instruments, electronic musical instruments did reach a certain level of sophistication. But at the next level, that of keyboard instruments, musicians naturally sought instruments that could play harmonies. From a technological perspective, the ability to produce harmony became a point of challenge for engineers, and electronic organs became the specific target. With the advent of semiconductors, our design procedures as well as our thought processes were forced to undergo a drastic change.

The Timeline of Electronic Musical Instrument Technologies

A look at the developments in sound-generating technologies will shed some light on the history of electronic musical instruments. The development of electronic organs began as a search for ways to replace the functions of a pipe organ by electronic means.

1. *Turning the sound on and off, and adding tone series = the addition and subtraction of sound*

In pipe organs, when a key is pressed, a pipe with the corresponding pitch produces the sound. If another tone is needed, the airway can be switched to produce sound on another pipe with the same pitch but a different shape. In simple terms, an electronic organ is an instrument whose pipes have been replaced by electronic sound generators. And while it is different in that its sound emanates from a set of speakers, its basic principle as a musical instrument can be traced back to the pipe organ. The keys on an organ's keyboard were responsible for turning the sound on and off, but were not given the ability to add other musical expressions.

2. *The ability to choose harmonics = variable harmonics*

In 1935, Hammond Organ Company launched the first mass-produced electric organ, which had a mechanism whereby musicians could freely combine different harmonics using a set of sliding drawbars. This was the first instrument that came with a feature that allowed performers to choose harmonic combinations in real time. Since this alone did not create enough dynamics, it was later improved so that accents could be added.

3. *The ability to shape sound = variable envelope*

Sounds rise and decay differently in different instruments; whereas pianos produce decaying sounds, organs produce sustained sounds. Our next goal was to electronically reproduce the shapes of sound that were unique to each instrument. We had to consider many questions. What is the state of the sound when the key is first pressed? How does it decay once the key is released? To control the process, we used parameters such as attack (A), decay (D), sustain (S), and release (R). And we eventually gained the ability to change the settings on each of these parameters to create sounds that did not exist in nature. It was the analog synthesizer, first introduced around 1965, that opened the door to this new area. It would require more than another ten years for synthesizers to provide controls for the envelope, called the envelope curve, of the sounds of every key, a capability that was eventually made possible with the advent of LSIs.

4. *The ability to change the harmonic composition continuously = time-wise variability of harmonics*

By enabling the tone to change with time, we can add more richness to musical expressions. For example, the initial sound that comes from a piano hammer hitting a string contains many harmonics and has a complex waveform, and the sound eventually decays while the key is being held down. Its tone begins to resemble a very soft sine wave, and then completely decays naturally. This happens because the harmonic composition of the sound changes with time, and this was the effect that we had to achieve with electronic technology. To this end, the technologies that came out of the process of synthesizer development became very useful. Electronic organs, electronic pianos, guitar synthesizers, and other electronic musical instruments were all developed by fully incorporating this technology, and of course functions two and three on this list above.

5. *Storing waveforms = sampling technology*

If you needed a sound that closely resembled that of an existing musical instrument, an easy way to fulfill this need would be to directly record the sound of that instrument, store the sound on memory, and come up with a way to trigger it when you hit a key. This idea became a reality as the price of computers and memory came down. This technology is not without its shortcomings, however. Just as still photographs are realistic but static, sampled sounds are realistic but lack movement. This technology is particularly difficult to use with the human voice. Regardless of these limitations, however, this is a very convenient technology and has been widely used in production.

6. *Thinking in units of phrases = VariPhrase technology*

Digital technologies for synthesizing voices and waveforms have advanced, and there are a large number of products available on the market that combine several different types of technologies. While many musicians are interested in the possibilities this opens up, their frustration with the current options is somewhat vague, so it is not an easy task to reach a conclusion. Currently, electronic musical instrument manufacturers are focusing their research efforts on finding a way to combine technologies one through five above with waveform synthesis and a technology called *physical modeling*. To draw an analogy with computer technologies, I believe the technologies we have seen so far are akin to the program languages (machine language and assemblers, etc.) used in the early days of computers. This is not to say that these technologies are still undeveloped, but that, in terms of realizing the sounds that a musician may come up with in his or her mind, the methods provided by current technologies may not be a good fit with musicians who are better at doing things by feeling.

I believe that we will be able to open the door to a completely new area of music if we begin to look at music as being made up of units of phrases instead of units of notes. DJs are the ones who use phrases in the most direct way. This idea that the direct use of phrases has the potential to open up a new area of music is actually quite difficult to communicate to others.

While past experience is a crucial part of developing musical instruments, there are times when this can become a hindrance for moving forward with a new project. The advantage of a novice is that he or she is not burdened by what has previously been done and hence can dare to do things that others with more experience, who may be set in their ways, may not do. At the same time, novices cannot expect to grow unless they are humble enough to listen to what their predecessors have to say and maintain a flexibility of the mind. You cannot have true innovation by making something that is simply "different." Many people, after having been involved in a particular project for four or five years, begin to think that they know it all. While five years may seem like a long enough period of time to experience a variety of things, especially when you take into consideration the speed of change, it is still not enough time to gain a thorough understanding of music and all the elements that support it, as well as the ability to truly listen to feedback from musicians.

Concert reviews can be quite hard on new performers, but those who can learn and grow from these experiences are the ones who go on to have successful careers. I believe the same thing can be said for designing musical instruments. The real gauge of your success is the number of satisfied purchasing customers. If you have accumulated over a decade of experience, this experience can be rendered completely useless if market values make a pivotal shift. For example, the first LPs were sold in 1950, but at the time, few people could buy even two LPs with one month's pay. The LPs that you bought after taking great pains to choose them were precious items and you took exceptionally good care in handling them. People in our generation who seriously brooded over purchasing these LPs with our small disposable incomes would never think of touching the playing surface of these records with our bare hands. So the idea of DJing, where the DJ picks out phrases directly from the records, could only come from people who are nonchalant about these things.

Even some people involved in design are not able to understand concept six and tend to reject it out of hand. Musicians often grasp the idea intuitively. Typically, you have to literally see and hear the new design in action to have an intelligent discussion about its value. With this in mind, the only thing we can do is present a breathtaking demo.

New sounds have always come out of a need for new music and I believe this cycle will continue to repeat itself into the future. A variety of methods have been developed one after the other to create new sounds on electronic musical instruments—starting with analog synthesizers developed by Dr. Moog and continued with digital synthesizers—but the scope of manipulations and processing that could be applied to existing music and the human voice was limited.

At the 2000 NAMM Show, Roland was able to announce VariPhrase, a technology that gives users a completely new way of creating sounds. This technology takes finished pieces of music, disassembles them into their three elements—pitch, length, and tone—processes these elements, and then re-synthesizes them in real time. I believe this is a major success achieved by the Roland development team led by Tadao Kikumoto, chief of Roland's research laboratories. I look forward to vast amounts of music that will be created by future musicians using this new VariPhrase technology.

When I look back at the products we've sold commercially, the ones that we packed with as many functions as we could ended up being too expensive and did not sell well. However, these efforts made huge contributions in improving the level of our elemental technologies.

7.   *Next target: the sound space*

Electronic musical instruments are destined to deliver their sounds through a speaker. A musical instruments such as a pipe organ, where the architecture is an integral part of the instrument, produces amazing results if it is built in a good hall. But if the architecture or pipes are installed in the wrong locations, there is no way to correct the situation. Electronic musical instruments are different in this respect as they deliver their sounds through a speaker, which means that the instrument itself can be transported to wherever one wants and its volume can be adjusted to desired levels.

However, a constant drawback of electronic musical instruments has been that they lack the sound space created by a good architectural setting. Particularly in the area of organs, people have been comparing for decades two musical instruments in completely different price brackets: the very expensive pipe organ, and electronic organ, which costs only a tenth or possibly several tenths of the price of a pipe organ. That said, the ability to control the sound space is close to becoming a reality thanks to computer technology.

I believe the area of sound space has great potential for technological development. No one would have imagined thirty years ago that speakers, which were then considered to be a drawback, would be transformed into powerful tools. The volume of a sound is completely different from its richness. The sound of a pipe organ is rich even when it emanates from a small portable radio; one instantly notices the amazing nature of the sound. Conversely, music that one does not enjoy can sound noisy even if the volume is not particularly high.

Music sounds completely different depending on the venue in which it is performed. If an orchestra performs in a venue without any reverb, the different parts do not blend together, and the music is unsatisfying. In such situations, you cannot help but feel sorry for the orchestra. The right amount of reverb functions like a natural mixer so the choice of venue is a huge responsibility on the part of the organizer. In addition to this, even if everything sounds good during rehearsal, we are often surprised at the dramatic change in reverb once the seats are full. This difference can be more or less dramatic in different venues, but just in terms of reverberation time, there can be a difference of 0.3 to 0.6 seconds. A study of the seat arrangement at La Scala in Milan—where the box seats located on four floors are arranged as if to enclose the space and the 1,437 seats are all arranged in a slight curve facing the stage—clearly shows that its designers took into account the acoustics of the hall with its seats full.

While I have unfortunately not had the chance to listen to an opera at La Scala, I have visited the exhibit room adjacent to the hall. I was able to see the stage from a box seat on the third floor, and this gave me some idea of how the audience was able to enjoy an opera performance that used no microphones. Having set up RSS, Roland's 3-D sound-processing system, at home, I feel that we have finally gained the ability to create a good sound space for listening to music in one's own room, just as if one were sitting in one of the box seats. The sound quality of records has improved over the years, from SPs and LPs and then CDs, and we now have good-quality audio systems in our homes. While our equipment for reproducing music has dramatically improved in this process, the reproduction of sound spaces has just begun.

8. *You cannot divorce video from audio*

In Japan, we held the tenth "Organ Festival" tour in Tokyo, Hamamatsu, Nagoya, and Osaka in November 2000. When we held the "Organ Power" concert in the United States, the combination of stage performances and video went very well so we tried the same using only Roland equipment, which yielded good results.

The purpose of using video was to show the movements and techniques of the players to the audience. I believe the video shown at the front of the stage conveyed the passionate performance of the musicians to the audience. So we have come to a point where instrumentalists are able to incorporate video into their performance.

Since video-editing equipment is readily available for purchase, anyone can create and edit his or her own video with only a little effort. We at Roland envisioned that there would be business opportunities in the interplay between video and sound, so we entered this area and were able to exhibit our digital video editors at the SATIS Show in France in November 2000, as well as at COMDEX in the United States and Inter BEE at the Makuhari Messe in Tokyo. It will not be too far into the future that musical instrument retailers will begin carrying video equipment.

9. *Education is the most crucial of all software*

I will not repeat myself as I have already mentioned this in chapter twelve, but to briefly summarize, I believe that the area of music education, the function of which is to increase the number of people who understand the joy of music, will be the largest beneficiary of the information revolution moving forward. When approaching the use of new digital tools to disseminate educational content, it is best to do so with a blank slate. You do not need to pay admission to enter paradise. All you have to do is take your friends along.

Conventional music education has been plagued with the following issues.

(a) Typically, results would vary widely depending on the abilities of the teacher. And while this is thought to be what education is all about, it is no easy task to train a large number of able teachers.

(b) Though many textbooks have been published and various syllabi are available for different objectives, in reality there is no freedom in choice of learning material.

(c) Music education should preferably be given in private lessons, but this is not for everybody and this mode of teaching cannot accommodate large numbers of students. Group learning has its own benefits, and interactions with friends is something students will not find in private lessons. But when we focus only on efficiency in education, we almost always stray away from what is essential.

Roland has been offering the Intelligent System of Music (ISM) since 1987 to address the three predicaments described above. The choice of medium was difficult in some ways due to the speed of technological innovation, but thanks to the popularization of MIDI and the standard MIDI file (SMF) format, as well as to declining semiconductor costs, systems based on this concept are reaching a point where they are poised to play a central role in music learning centers.

The Door Has Been Opened

The guitar has a long history and I personally do not know enough to say which instrument was actually the prototype of the modern acoustic guitar. The guitar is among the instruments that have reached a level of near-perfection. The reason the guitar has been called a small orchestra is that the player can produce the melody, accompaniment, and rhythm all on a single instrument. With its pitch determined by frets embedded in its fingerboard, the guitar is one of the most popular instruments along with keyboard instruments. The sounds produced on its six strings have a richness as they resonate in the guitar's body.

However, the guitar can be found to be lacking in terms of sound volume compared to other instruments, so microphones are often used. Guitars with solid bodies—which have no sound chamber but are equipped with means to electrically amplify the sound—are generically called electric guitars. These guitars use steel strings whose vibrations are captured and converted into electrical signals by pickups. So the entirety of the electric guitar's sound comes from speakers. With this development, guitars were given enough volume and also the potential for creating a variety of tones with the use of electronic circuitry, pioneering entirely new fields of music.

The sizes of concerts also grew and guitarists increasingly took center stage. Although electric guitars replaced acoustic guitars as the mainstream for a time, folk and country music remained very popular. And as musical genres continued to diversify, acoustic guitars made a comeback with a consequent increase in the guitar-playing population. While the electric guitar made a huge contribution in terms of sound volume and the creation of new tones, its tonal characteristics were different from those of the acoustic guitar as it picked up the vibrations of the strings on a single pickup. If we were able to equip the guitar with six pickups, one for each string, each with its independent tone and volume control, we would at least be able to create guitar sounds with a stereophonic feel, and we might even be able to convert the tones of each string to different tones. By pursuing this idea, we would be able to provide musicians with a new playing field that transcends the boundaries of traditional stringed instruments. This idea was what led to the development of the guitar synthesizer—the electronic guitar.

Guitars have expanded their realm of possibilities from acoustic to electric and then on to electronic. I believe that each of these types of guitar has specific areas of music in which it is needed, and each is in a complementary relationship with the others.

Almost forty years have passed since Roland launched the world's first guitar synthesizer, GR-500, in May 1977. While this is a short period of time compared to the history of musical instruments in general, it is quite a long period of time in the history of electronic musical instruments. The launching ceremony for the GR-500, which we held at the Tokyo Grand Palace, was attended by a large number of press representatives and dealers. We had the good fortune of having the American guitarist Del Casher demo this new product for us. Accompaniment was provided by Godiego, a Japanese rock band that was beginning to gain popularity at the time. The guitar was featured in NHK's morning news and we were off to a good start, but our thunder was stolen when ARP launched a guitar synth of their own at the NAMM Show in June.

Although guitar synths drew a lot of competition with five or six manufacturers entering the market, it took a long time for them to become popular as they were still incomplete in some ways as musical instruments and there were certain limitations on how you could play them.

In 1995, soon after Roland launched the guitar synthesizer VG-8, existing guitar manufacturers began building guitars that were compatible with it, and this brought widespread acceptance to electronic guitars. In this process, we began to realize that elements such as "distortion," "muddiness," "twistedness," "convolution," and "noise"— elements normally considered to be obstructions to music— were all important to musical expression. The fuzz tone box, which added distortion to the electric guitar, was released in the 1960s and became an indispensable part of rock music, along with high-output amplifiers. It was a great advancement that these

GR-500 guitar synthesizer. ▶

▲ At the launch ceremony for GR-500, the world's first guitar synthesizer (1977).

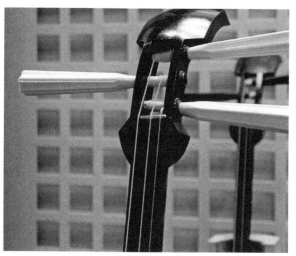

▲ The *tenjin*, or headstock, of the shamisen. The first string does not rest on the *kamigoma*.

noise components came to be actively used with the help of electronic technology.

Broadly speaking, there are five different types of distortion, and we can find an example of an instrument that used distortion being used in Japan long before electronic circuits were ever conceived of. This is the shamisen. While there are a variety of theories regarding the origins of three-stringed instruments, they appear to have originated in either China, Mongolia, or Central Asia and come to Japan by way of Okinawa. The shamisen, however, is clearly a Japanese creation that was improved on throughout the Edo period, resulting in what we have today. The fact that the large *bachi* (plectrum) used to play the instrument derived from the bachi used to play the *biwa* (Japanese lute) gives us a glimpse into its history of improvements. The second and third strings of the shamisen rest on a *kamigoma* (nut) at the top of the *sao* (neck), while the first string, the thickest of the three, does not rest on the kamigoma. Therefore, the first string creates a unique sound, which is clearly that of a "fuzz," or distortion, tone. This construction is called *sawari*. What this shows is that people had already been exploring distortion without the use of electronic circuits, so one might say that distortion was invented in Japan.

Even in the realm of acoustic instruments we have entered an era where we are making drastic transformations with digital versions of these instruments, all the while paying close attention to traditions that must be preserved. The following is a list of areas in which work has already begun:

- Digital pianos are exp anding the scope of piano music.

- Electronic organs are effectively replicating pipe organs more and more, even in subtle nuances of feel, expression, and more.

- Digital drums and percussion instruments are constantly creating modern beats on drumheads made of new materials.

- Roland's digital drum set, V-Drums, is bringing change to traditional drum sets.

- Guitars have transitioned from acoustic to electric and now on to digital.

- Recording equipment has transitioned to digital. Mixers will also change.

- Where there were once only DJs, we are now seeing the emergence of VJs, or video jockeys.

- Synthesizers can now be found on PCs, tablets, and smartphones.

- MIDI, used in conjunction with V-Link, will change live performances.

... and these transformations will continue.

In addition to expanding our product lineup from automatic rhythm to synthesizers, MicroComposers, echo machines, guitar synthesizers, digital pianos, organs, DJ equipment, and digital recorders, we at Roland have developed the following foundation technologies:

1. Musical Instrument Digital Interface (MIDI) interface

2. Structured Adaptive Synthesis (SA) System musical tone synthesis

3. Linear Arithmetic Synthesis (LA) System musical tone synthesis

▼ The first VariPhrase model, Roland VP-9000.

▲ TD-30KV, the latest model of the V-Drums, which became the second generation of digital drums.

▲ The V-Piano Grand. This digital piano has no strings above its soundboard.

4. Composite Object Sound Modeling (COSM) musical tone modeling

5. Roland Digital Audio Compression (RDAC) data compression

6. Roland Sound Space (RSS) 3-D sound-processing system

7. Feed Forward Processing (FFP) read-ahead audio processing

8. Variable Phrase Processing System (VariPhrase) variable phrasing

9. Visual Synthesizer CG-8, the world's first video synthesizer

The technologies used in electronic musical instruments are becoming increasingly specialized, and Roland is establishing separate companies to address this trend. Eighty years have gone by since the birth of the electronic musical instrument industry but I believe this is still a very young area with much more room to grow. "Turn your imagination into sound, into video, and into shapes . . . and combine them." These are the goals that Roland is pursuing. I believe that there are still many possibilities in the realms of both sound and video.

The Future of Electronic Musical Instruments

Two years ago, I made the decision to go on leave from Roland, a company that I have run for forty years since its founding, and launch a new company, ATV Corporation, where we are engaged in developing new systems that integrate electronic musical instruments with audio and video. Because of my age and the physical constraints that come with it, many may say that this is a foolhardy endeavor, and I think that it is only natural that one might think so. However, the work that needs to be done in the field of electronic musical instruments cannot be completed in a single generation. Rather, I believe my mission is to develop people who will be able to carry this work forward into the next generation. With that mindset, all difficulties have a way of transforming themselves into challenges, and it feels right to engage in this work on a day-to-day basis to fulfill this mission.

We have settled on a vision for ATV Corporation as a company that will engage in developing new concepts and ideas to match the new era. By moving forward with a positive outlook, we have seen a variety of different possibilities come to fruition and eventually reach the market. Reflecting on this new approach, I've come to realize how antiquated our previous way of doing things has been, and that we have missed many opportunities due to our attachment to preconceived ideas.

That said, it is also critical that we establish our foundations on the experience and technologies that we have accumulated over the years. Our goal is to combine these in a well-balanced way, and focus on new instruments, video equipment, and audio. One thing that I can say with certainty is that building on the central role and foundation of electronic musical instruments in their ability to produce sounds, adding video will be the primary focus of our development moving forward.

As I began to summarize the philosophy on which I founded ATV Corporation, I noticed that very little had changed in terms of vision from the time that I founded Roland. I was rather surprised myself to discover, after all this time, that a philosophy that led to the same conclusion had been present all along within me. And I am also very proud that to this day I have hardly wavered in my convictions as I engaged in the area of electronic instruments.

What I have to say is: "Music is live."

I believe the essence of music for the performing musician is in enjoying it on stage with a live audience. And the most important element of musical expression is to deliver it with conviction, again, live from a stage.

Moving forward, "We design the future" will continue to be the motto at both Roland and ATV Corporations.

My Journey with Performers: An Interview with the Author

Yuri Tachibana, Organist and Arranger

THE HISTORY OF MUSICAL INSTRUMENTS IS FOUNDED ON THE COL-laboration between quality instrument makers and excellent performers. This topic will be explored in this chapter. The following is from "What the Pioneers Have to Say," thirty-eighth installment, in the May 2009 issue of *RET's Press* newsletter for Roland Music School lecturers.

You have mentioned that you have met many performers in the process of developing organs. Who can you speak to us about today?

Ikutaro Kakehashi: Yes, the relationship between performers and manufacturers revolves around musical instruments. One of these musicians that I would like to speak about would be Yuri Tachibana. From what I know, Ms. Tachibana began her performing career as a professional organist playing the Hammond organ. Meanwhile, we had acquired, from the US-based Hammond Organ Company, the right to import and sell their products in Japan, and had been importing Hammond organs. So Ms. Tachibana and I have a very long history between us that has been mediated by this musical instrument.

So you were importing Hammond organs into Japan?

Kakehashi: Yes. Before we began importing them, the Omi Brotherhood Ltd., which was manufacturing and selling Mentholatum products, was importing Hammond organs as part of their corporate mission based on the Christian faith. Then I heard that they would be discontinuing their Hammond import business so I leaped at the opportunity and flew to the United States to state my case with Hammond directly: "Let us import your organs and I will sell more than you are selling now." And that's how Ace Electronic Industries, Roland's precursor, came to be the sole importing agent of Hammond organs to Japan. Soon after that, Hammond initiated a project to market a Hammond organ built-in with the FR-1 rhythm machine that we made. As an extension of that, Ace Electronic

Industries was put in charge of developing the industry's first organ with automated accompaniment, the Hammond Piper. The success of this project led to the founding in 1970 of our joint company, Hammond International Japan.

When I look back now, that was quite a daring feat as I hardly spoke any English. You could say that this was kind of like someone who had been tinkering with his or her homemade PC forming a joint company with IBM. Ignorance can be an advantage at times.

We began by making organs ourselves, and believed that the best way to go forward with the organ business was to sell products that would sell in the professional arena, so during our Ace Electronic years we began selling Hammond organs and also began making organs as an original equipment manufacturer (OEM) to Technics. These efforts eventually led to the Roland Music Atelier. Because we had been manufacturing OEM products for Technics, we knew a number of performers who were using Technitone and its dealers.

And then you personally met Ms. Tachibana after you developed the Music Atelier?

Kakehashi: I knew of Ms. Tachibana as an organist even before that, but our interactions became more in-depth after we launched the Music Atelier. As a maker of musical instruments, the development of the Music Atelier had been a mixed process for me, but Ms. Tachibana, as a performer, was able to draw from her experience with a variety of instruments in playing the Music Atelier. What I learned after meeting her was that we had a lot of common acquaintances centering around organs. It's interesting how people are connected with each other.

What do you find the most attractive about Ms. Tachibana as an organist?

Kakehashi: I think she has the wonderful ability to evaluate a variety of instruments and bring out the characteristics of each organ. For example, Music Atelier allows the player to create a variety of sounds before you begin to play. You can combine any of the tones, whether it be strings or brass, to create a variety of other tones that are better than the original. The tones in the early models were not sufficient to deliver orchestral or big band performances, and you couldn't play tones that had delicate nuances. But now, a variety of functions are available that allow one person to play the tones of a seventy- to eighty-piece orchestra. The Music Atelier is not an organ for simply playing existing repertoires but an instrument for expanding into new repertoires. The Music Atelier is a musical instrument that offers exceptional possibilities in terms of musical performance. In order to bring out the strengths of this organ, it is also crucial that the player have the ability to arrange, compose, and conduct music.

▲ Yuri Tachibana and the Roland Music Atelier AT-900.

Based on her extensive career, Ms. Tachibana is able to draw out the musical possibilities of Music Atelier beyond what developers such as ourselves are able to imagine. She is able to deliver wonderful performances that make full use of her ability to arrange, compose, and conduct music.

So you could say that Ms. Tachibana has been fulfilling the role of a pioneer for Music Atelier.

Kakehashi: Yes. I think a good example of how Ms. Tachibana's appealing performance was fully realized was at the concert held in São Paulo in November 2008, when Roland Brazil invited Ms. Tachibana to play. The year 2008 was the centennial of the first Japanese immigrants to Brazil and a variety of exchange events were held in both countries. This concert became a reality through the enthusiasm of Takao Shirahata, the president of Roland Brazil, a Japanese Brazilian himself, who knew of Ms. Tachibana's amazing playing. I think she was able to deliver the kind of music that the packed audience of eight hundred most wanted to hear. From what I hear, as half of the audience were of Japanese descent, many people in the audience were seen teary-eyed as they listened to songs such as "Sakura Sakura," "Kokyo," "Ringo Oiwake," "Yosaku," and "Shimauta." When she played the Brazilian tune "The Girl from Ipanema" the audience all joined in a huge chorus. While I was unfortunately not able to attend, this performance, which only a Japanese player could deliver, had a direct impact on the audience, making this an exceptionally wonderful overseas concert.

So this concert came five years into your organ development. We are excited to think of what the future might hold.

Kakehashi: What you could say about any endeavor, not only about musical instruments, is that you may not reach your goal in one fell swoop, but you will get results if you take one step at a time and make the right judgment calls along the way.

What is important is one's intent to get started with something whatever it takes, which in our case were the V-Drums, guitar synth, and V-Accordion. Once you get started, the ones who carry out the work are the engineers and other people in charge, so these people may have the most difficult task [laughter]. On top of that, we must not forget that the history of musical instruments is invariably founded on the cooperation of excellent performers. The most important thing is not to quit, once you've started, until you succeed. This goes without saying, but you won't succeed if you quit along the way. Roland will continue to develop new products moving forward based on this conviction.

Electronic musical instruments continue to evolve almost on a daily basis. Can you tell us about any recent concerts?

Kakehashi: One concert would be the "Isao Tomita Tale of Genji Art Festival," held at the Yokohama Minato Mirai Hall in November 2011. This was presented as a comprehensive form of art that featured an organ performance by Ms. Tachibana of Isao Tomita's 1989 piece *The Tale of Genji, Symphonic Fantasy*, a puppet dance performance by Hiroshi Hori, and video, which added color to the musical performance. Ms. Tachibana arranged this monumental piece—which Mr. Tomita wrote for orchestra—for organ, but this was not on the level of simply replacing the orchestral instruments with organ tones. Ms. Tachibana extracted the essence of Mr. Tomita's orchestral piece and arranged it into her own *Tale of Genji*, which she played solo on a single organ. I have been involved with organs for a long time, but this was the best performance I had ever heard; something that no one else has been able to mimic.

Even before this concert, I had edited a variety of videos to accompany performances by Ms. Tachibana and a large number of other musicians. Mostly I remember working on videos for Ms. Tachibana's performances, which were invariably infused with a rich musical landscape. Thanks to these experiences, I had the opportunity to edit video for *The Tale of Genji, Symphonic Fantasy*, and eventually produced two versions. The first one for the actual day of the concert was a video that gave color to the background to match the music as it was performed along with the puppet dance. I created another version that included the puppet dance for shows that would not be accompanied by a live puppet dance performance.

In December 2013, Ms. Tachibana held an organ concert at Kioi Hall in Tokyo, primarily playing pieces written by Isao Tomita. Included in the program was the theme from the 1974 NHK period drama series *Katsu Kaishu*, which drew much attention at the time as a new piece of music that redefined Mr. Tomita's image. Ms. Tachibana drew on her personal worldview to arrange all of these songs for organ. Mr. Tomita and film director Nobuhiko Obayashi were also present at the concert to discuss music and film, making this a wonderful concert to end the year 2013. I had the opportunity to edit the background video for the songs performed at this concert as well, so it was a very meaningful concert also for myself personally.

The combination of music and video has become commonplace in concerts these days.

Kakehashi: Yes. I began with the belief that this new approach of combining video with music to enhance the mood of performances would create new styles of performances. This was realized at the third Roland "Organ Power" concert, which we held at the same time as the 2001 NAMM Show in the United States. This was a revolutionary, world-first concert in that the system was configured so that the video would cut to a different shot when Ms. Tachibana switched a registration [tone-setting] button.

I was fortunate enough to be recognized for the development of the MIDI standard, and we have verified that it can be used in the field of video as well. I proudly claim that Roland's CG-8 and V-Link are the world's first video synthesizers. Video performances that people can simultaneously view, listen to, and become mesmerized by will be the norm for performances moving forward. I believe that this is another contribution I have been able to make in this age without samples.

My Journey with Performers: An Interview with the Author

Oscar Peterson, Pianist

THE FOLLOWING IS EXCERPTED FROM "WHAT THE PIONEERS HAVE TO Say," first installment, April 2006 issue of *RET's Press* newsletter for Roland Music School lecturers.

An Artist Who Believed in the Future of Digital Piano

Please tell us about your first encounter with Oscar Peterson, a world-renowned maestro of jazz piano.

Kakehashi: The first time I visited the NAMM Show in the United States was in 1964. While there, I noticed a newspaper ad for a concert that featured Duke Ellington, Oscar Peterson, and Ella Fitzgerald. There was no way I was going to miss a concert with such a great lineup of artists, so I went out to the Hollywood Bowl. I didn't know about car rentals at the time so I took the bus, transferring buses along the way, and purchased the cheapest ticket, which cost four dollars. Of course, my seat was all the way at the back, and it was quite a large venue so the players looked no larger than peas [laughter]. But the concert was really very good, although there certainly must have been a lag of about 0.2 to 0.3 seconds for the sound to reach my seat.

That really is an amazing lineup.

Kakehashi: When I mentioned this to Gene Trademan, who was VP at the precursor company to Roland Canada, he said that he would talk to Oscar Peterson and ask him if he would be interested in stopping by the Roland factory when he was on tour in Japan.

So that is where it all started.

Kakehashi: Yes. I think it was around 1977 or 1978 that I first met him, so that would be almost thirty years ago. He was kind enough to visit our Takaoka factory in Hamamatsu during his Japan tour. This was about five or six years after I had started up Roland. He tried out the latest electronic piano that we had at the time.

Honestly, I had a preconceived notion that Mr. Peterson might not be that interested in electronic musical instruments because he always played a Bösendorfer piano. My image of him was that he was an acoustic player. But this was actually unfounded, and he was knowledgeable not only about electronic pianos but about synthesizers as well. We were actually quite surprised at the extent of his knowledge.

When was the next time you met him?

Kakehashi: I visited a musical instrument show in Canada called the MIAC Show and I had the opportunity to visit him at his home then.

At his home?

Kakehashi: Yes. He had a studio in his basement. It was quite a large studio and there was quite a bit of gear there, including recording gear made in Japan. He also had a wide range of synthesizers from many manufacturers, and operated all of them himself. And he was using Roland's MicroComposer MC-8 to operate them.

▼ With Oscar Peterson.

MC-8?

Kakehashi: He was making music on his system synthesizer using an MC-8. Like I said before, he was a very famous artist and I had this image of him as an acoustic player, so I remember being surprised at how he was making music, operating all of this gear himself. Mr. Peterson was known for breezing through very fast passages and delivering amazing performances, so I used to imagine he must have a sequencer built into his body. When I asked him, "Why do you use the MC-8?" he replied, "The

MC-8 can play faster than I can," to which he added, "It can play really fast without making any mistakes" [laughter]. I know he must have been half joking, but still this meeting left a lasting impression on me.

How was he using the MC-8?

Kakehashi: He was recording his own playing. He gave me a tape with a recording of his playing and made me promise that I would not let anyone listen to it until he gave me the go-ahead. At the time, I was just surprised at the fact that he was an adept user of the MC-8, so I stored the tape away just as I had promised. In December 2007 when we received the sad news that he had passed away, I looked for the tape as I wanted to listen to it but was not able to find it. I was quite distraught, but a few years later I finally found the tape. From what was on the tape, you could tell how he was experimenting with many things in his basement studio. At the time, he purchased an MC-4 after the MC-8.

I see. So you and Mr. Peterson gradually became closer until he eventually appeared in a Roland electronic piano commercial in 1982.

Kakehashi: Yes. I think it was the second or third time we met that I asked him if he would appear in a commercial, and he replied, "Sure," without even pausing. At the time, Mr. Peterson was appearing in a commercial for a certain coffee product, but I had made my casual request without knowing anything about this [laughter].

So you negotiated with him directly?

Kakehashi: Yes, and that's how that commercial came to be. It was shot at a small studio in Osaka in the middle of the night, so all the nearby restaurants had closed and we had nowhere to go for a meal. If I remember correctly, I think we ate at some food stand [laughter], although I don't remember what we had.

Mr. Peterson was already very well known at the time, so why do you think he readily agreed to appear in your commercial?

Kakehashi: It all came from his generosity. Also, I think that he was very excited about the future of digital pianos. Electronic pianos at the time still had quite a ways to go, but I think he understood that the instrument had future potential. This was at a time when no right-minded person who played the piano would have anything to do with electronic pianos.

So Mr. Peterson already felt then that digital pianos had possibilities for the future.

Kakehashi: That's true. If he didn't, there would have been no way that he—world-famous person that he was—would agree to appear in our commercial.

So what kind of response did you get once this commercial aired on TV?

Kakehashi: It had a major impact. That said, I think many at Roland, particularly the younger people, didn't actually understand what it meant to have Mr. Peterson appear in a Roland commercial. Now they were all amazed, going "Wow!" [laughter].

Yes, it was quite a surprise.

Kakehashi: Don't you think so? You would be surprised, wouldn't you? People just didn't know very well at the time what Mr. Peterson meant to the world of music and what he had accomplished. So I think the impact would be greater now. There aren't that many commercials that can hold their own thirty years after they were made.

That's true. It was so simple and easy to understand.

Kakehashi: I'm very grateful for that. So our relationship continued after that and I visited him at the Osaka Festival Hall when he was touring Japan in 2005. I was also invited to a reception at the Canadian embassy as a representative of his Japanese friends. And when he was awarded the Praemium Imperiale in 1999, I was invited to the awards ceremony as one of his friends along with Sadao Watanabe, George Kawaguchi, and Toshiko Akiyoshi.

Did you meet him every time he was here in Japan?

Kakehashi: I contacted him every time he was here. Sometimes he would call me. There were also times when he wanted a piano to warm up with so we would haul a Roland piano to his hotel room.

I don't think many people know that Mr. Peterson was using a Roland electronic piano for warming up.

Kakehashi: That's probably true. After all, he would play a Bösendorfer piano on stage. But you couldn't bring an acoustic piano into your hotel room and make all that noise. So on these occasions, Roland would take the latest electronic piano to his hotel room.

This story speaks volumes about the trust and confidence the both of you had in each other.

Kakehashi: With Mr. Peterson, it was more of a personal relationship than simply a relationship between an artist and an instrument maker. Similar relationships between player and manufacturer can often be lacking in this personal aspect.

So perhaps Mr. Peterson understood your passion for music and for creating musical instruments.

Kakehashi: Perhaps. When we launched a new product, he would insist on purchasing it himself and not accept our offer to send it to him as a gift. He had purchased all the Roland products that he owned. Honestly though, although he was testing them after he had actually purchased them himself, we would have loved to have him take a look at our new products right off of the production line [laughter].

▲ Oscar Peterson in his home digital recording studio.

I see.

Kakehashi: In late January of 2006, he gave me a call and the first thing he said was, "Congratulations!" I asked "What for?" and he said, "I just bought an RD-700. It's very good and I was just calling to let you know that I'm happy to be able to play this piano." I was very happy to hear that.

Is there any remark by Mr. Peterson on Roland pianos that left an impression on you?

Kakehashi: For example, he wouldn't say things like such and such an aspect of the product was good or bad. He was constantly interested in new pianos, would purchase them one after the other, and use them and play them on an ongoing basis. The fact that he was using these instruments in this way was good enough for me. He was a customer who truly loved our products, and he would even call me up directly to let me know. I am very grateful for this. So he never commented on any particular aspect of the piano, but you would naturally get an idea of the "how" and "what" of making the product better just by listening to what he had to say.

When he purchased the CD-2 recorders, they weren't for himself but for donations he was making to schools. Mr. Peterson worked hard for the advancement of music education through these donations of musical instruments. The

Canadian people have a special place in their hearts for Oscar Peterson, as can be seen in the decision by the Canadian embassy in Tokyo to build the Oscar Peterson Theater on their premises in 1991.

Kakehashi: My relationship with Oscar Peterson goes back many years. I was invited to his home many times and we spoke at length about music and musical instruments. Mr. Peterson told me one or two years after the MC-8 was launched that he would like to try using it in his live performances. This must have been sometime after 1982, because the MIDI standard had already been developed.

As I mentioned earlier, I asked, "You are able to play any phrase that you want. Why would you want to use a sequencer?" and he replied, "Because the MC-8 will play it even faster!" I still remember the smile on his face as he said so.

As it turned out, I did not receive a go-ahead from him regarding the tape that I received from him, which I promised not to let anyone else listen to until he said it was okay to do so. I listened to the tape and there were three pieces on it. The first piece was apparently a recording of him practicing, since there were spots where he would stop playing midway through. Eventually, you could hear him say, "Take one," which was followed by a melodious piano tune that sounded like he had connected to a Rhodes piano or perhaps to a synth. There was also a piece that featured piano and synth tones, and had a magnificent cosmic feel to it. I think that of the three tunes, the second and third might be a single piece. I was very moved by this precious experience of having this opportunity to listen to this world-class maestro all to myself.

At the time, Mr. Peterson said, "I don't like to spend time reading manuals. I'd rather use that time concentrating on playing myself." For my part, I felt that I'd love to see him use MIDI extensively and expand his horizons even more, but I remember I didn't feel it was appropriate to counter his comment at the time. When I asked him, "By the way, what is the title of the piece on this tape?" he said, "Let's just call it 'Night Dancer,'" and laughed heartily. I assumed this was an unpublished piece so when I finally listened to it I took a photo of the tape case and sent it to Mrs. Peterson. In return, she sent me a tape with a recording of the piece he wrote for the 1988 Calgary Olympics, accompanied by the comment, "Please use this tape with the other one as you wish."

So I am currently thinking of the best way to make this tape public. My plan is to use this piece sometime in the future with one of my video edits. This is sure to become a very precious, one-of-a-kind work [laughter].

My Journey with Performers: A Dialogue

Isao Tomita, Synthesizer Artist and Composer, with Ikutaro Kakehashi

▲ With Isao Tomita at Mr. Tomita's home in Tokyo.

THE FOLLOWING INTERVIEW IS IN TWO PARTS. THE FIRST PORTION WAS conducted at the Tomita residence in Tokyo, November 30, 1999. The second was conducted at Roland's Hamamatsu Research Center on January 21, 2013.

My Encounter with Synthesizers

Kakehashi: Mr. Tomita, you made your debut with synthesizers, but you were doing a lot of work even before that, such as in TV programs. For example, when I listened to the music you wrote for the *Shin Nihon Kiko* album (released only in Japan), I realized what a broad range of areas you worked in. Can you tell us a little bit about your work in the field of broadcasting and recording prior to your synthesizer years?

Tomita: I started working in 1952 on a minor NHK program. We didn't have synths back then so we used orchestras and acoustic instruments. The Hammond organ was one of the only electric instruments we used; the other one we used was a vibraphone, which was equipped with a motor. So I began working when acoustic instruments were the norm. At the time, the program I focused on the most was *Rittai Ongakudo* (Stereophonic Music Hall), which aired stereophonically on two radio stations, with NHK Radio 1 and 2 airing the left and right channels, respectively.

Kakehashi: That was the program where the announcer would ask, "Do you hear this from the right? Do you hear this from the left?"

Tomita: Yes. There was always an announcement asking the audience to adjust the balance. It went on for three minutes before the actual programming started. At the time, I was in my twenties and just starting out, but I was given access to a large eighty-plus-piece orchestra so I became quite absorbed in this project. The pay at NHK at the time was an hourly rate, so the pay for arrangers and composers was the same whether you wrote for an eighty-plus-piece orchestra or a four- to five-person ensemble. To tell you the truth, this was probably one of the reasons veteran arrangers were reluctant to take these jobs, but we were young and it was a lot of fun. So I was one of these younger arranger-composers.

As you surely know, the norm for audio up until that time was that you had a speaker in the middle, like a Cyclops, but this program broadcasted through two speakers and truly reminded us of the joy of having two ears, so I was stoked. That's where I learned all the tricks of creating tone. For example, I learned that if the oboe and flute, two woodwinds, play in unison, the resulting tone will not be something in between the two, but a mixture of two independent tones. I also learned which of the two should come above the other to create a more effective duet, and ways of making the best use of strings. This was where I learned the basics of the things that I later did on synthesizers.

Kakehashi: That being so, I'm sure many people will recognize your name from the credits on the *theme for the "Shin Nihon Kiko* album, as the composer of the it's theme. What was the timeframe that you writing for that program?

Tomita: That was when steam locomotives were still around so . . . I can't really say, but it would have been sometime between the mid-fifties and mid-sixties. Steam locomotives were used on regional lines and there were still a lot of single-track lines. All those lines have now been upgraded to double-track, so it would have been quite a while ago.

Kakehashi: I see, that long ago.

Tomita: We didn't have synthesizers back then so we would have entire orchestras come in to record these theme songs. In terms of orchestration, my favorite
composers were Rimsky-Korsakov, known for his famous *Scheherazade*, the
French impressionists Ravel and Debussy, and Stravinsky and Respighi, who
were influenced by these composers. I was completely stoked. Compared to
these pieces, the orchestration of Mozart and Beethoven felt monochromatic. I
was intrigued by how different the music sounded even though the instruments
used were the same.

Kakehashi: This was at a time when Japanese cinema was still very popular.
Did you have anything to do with music for film?

Tomita: I was still just starting out during the heyday of Japanese cinema so I
never worked on any major films. I started working on films when they were well
into their declining years. So I ended up working more in the area of TV music,
which was up and coming at the time.

Kakehashi: The record *Switched-On Bach* by Walter Carlos (now Wendy Carlos)
made a huge impression on those of us who were developing synthesizers. And
just as we were all marveling over that record, you came out with the album
Snowflakes Are Dancing, and specifically the track "Clair de Lune." When I heard
your record, it was as if until then I had only seen paintings painted with straight
lines, and all of a sudden I was shown a painting that used all sorts of curves
and complex colors. As a developer of musical instruments, I knew that a lot of
work had to have gone into creating those sounds. It was a kind of music that
we wouldn't even have thought possible, let alone actually attempt to make. It
had a huge impact on me.

I assume this new music came out of your interest in Debussy and Stravinsky,
which you just mentioned, but wasn't it quite a challenge to begin using a
synthesizer?

Tomita: First of all, we didn't have any information in Japan at the time about
what a synthesizer was. So we had heard rumors about people having made
these things called synthesizers but we didn't know what we could use them
for. The defining moment that I became aware of synthesizers came in 1969, a
year before the Osaka Expo. I just happened to be at this store in Osaka that
sold imported records and purchased *Switched-On Bach* there. I realized that
this development would allow me to deliver an orchestral performance all by
myself, and thought that maybe I could do this too. That was the thought that
got me started.

I looked and asked everywhere but I couldn't find out where I could purchase
one. At the time, the Hong Kong market would get foreign-made products,

such as Gibson products, sooner than we got them here in Japan, so I asked around there but they didn't know either. Yamaha was also an agent for a lot of companies so I asked them and their reply was, "Never heard of such a thing." Eventually, I heard from a trading company that a manufacturer in Buffalo, New York, was making what they called a Moog synthesizer. I didn't know anything about the manufacturer so I was quite anxious, but I decided to import one through the trading company, as this was the only lead I had.

I met Dr. Moog at the time, and he told me about an exceptional Japanese musical instrument engineer named Kakehashi. So had you already met Dr. Moog by then?

Kakehashi: The first time I met him was in Frankfurt. I met him several times after that, including once when he invited me to his home.

Tomita: I didn't know you at the time so I remember wondering who he might be referring to. *Switched-On Bach* was amazing, but as you say, it was like a line drawing. I think the people who used synthesizers at the time didn't think too much about the tone and used the tones just as they came out of the instrument and combined them. I was aiming for something else. My focus in orchestration up to that point had been to create a sense of colors. I also realized that the synth would produce a variety of different tones when you tweaked its filters. So I decided that, in contrast to *Switched-On Bach*, which came across like a baroque line drawing, I would produce a piece based on Debussy's music, specifically a piano piece that had not been previously colored by orchestration, and doing so would allow me, a person of Asian ethnicity, to compete squarely. After all, the French impressionists were influenced in no small part by the Orient, such as by Japanese gagaku musicians who performed at the Paris Expo.

▲ Walter Carlos's *Switched-On Bach* (1968).

So that's how I got started but it was a lot of work. Importing the thing was just a nightmare. The customs official confronted me, "You've got to be kidding me. This is a musical instrument? Show us evidence." But that's what it was, a musical instrument. So all I could do was telex Dr. Moog to ask him to send me some supporting document but his reply didn't come as soon as I had hoped. All procedures would halt unless I could prove my case, so I was at a loss. I showed them the album jacket of *Switched-On Bach*, which showed the Moog synthesizer, but they wouldn't accept it as proof because he wasn't playing it in the picture. The eccentric way he was dressed didn't help either. I eventually showed them a photo of Keith Emerson playing the instrument in a concert and they were satisfied with that, but it was a lot of work. At the time, Haneda was the international airport for Tokyo, but since their storage space was limited, the synth was relocated to a warehouse in Baraki, Chiba. It took about a month for me to actually take possession, and I was even charged storage fees for that duration. I had been telling them all along that it was a musical instrument, but the official would say, "You are obligated to pay because you are at fault in that you were not able to prove that it was a musical instrument." I knew putting up a fight would further delay delivery so I ended up paying the fee. Things were hard enough up to that point, but there were many more challenges to follow.

Leading Up to the Release of the Masterpiece "Clair de Lune" on the album *Snowflakes Are Dancing*

Kakehashi: So after this whole ordeal, you presented the completed album, *Snowflakes Are Dancing*, to various record companies. What was their reaction?

Tomita: I presented it to many record companies. I visited them actually carrying cassette recordings with me. Young executives would say, "This is very interesting." Some would say that they couldn't picture it in their minds just from the sound of it and that they wanted to actually see the synth. They would naturally get excited once they realized that this music came out of this strange contraption. At this point, judging from their reactions, I was thinking that this was going to go well, but when they went back to their companies and talked to their salespeople, things started to get a little iffy. They'd ask questions like, "What section are we going to categorize this in, in the first place?" It wasn't popular music, nor was it classical or film music. So we went out to see what section *Switched-On Bach* was being categorized in and we found out that it had been placed right next to a sound effects record called *The Nostalgic Sounds of Steam Locomotives*. In the end, people in upper management would not accept it, saying that something like this was not going to sell, or it was too unconventional.

But I had already put in close to a year making this record, and I'd also purchased a lot of gear, including an AKG echo machine, CompuMix, and an Ampex sixteen-track recorder. A Japanese record company offered to release the album on a contract fee that was next to nothing, but that wasn't going to do it for me so I flew to America.

I heard that Peter Manves, the director responsible for *Switched-On Bach*, had transferred from CBS Columbia to RCA so I contacted him thinking that I might be able to get some kind of reaction from him. I was confident that my work had a completely different aspect to it in that it was created from the perspective of color and there was nothing like it around at the time. So I took the tape to him, thinking that he might be looking for another hit in a similar market, and sure enough, he responded. He asked me, "Why don't you release this in Japan?" When I told him that the companies couldn't figure out where to categorize it in record stores, he said, "Just go to any local record store over there. You'll find *Switched-On Bach* under classical, popular, electronic music, and of course in the sound effects section. It's in all of those sections, so go take a look. If I

▲ "Clair de Lune" by Isao Tomita (1974).

were you, I would go ahead and not worry about what shelf it ends up on." So we went ahead and it turned out to be a success. He even set up a press conference for the album.

Kakehashi: I see. We in the musical instrument industry can relate to getting different reactions from people in Japan and the US.

Tomita: And then a little while later, I started getting calls from many Japanese companies: "Looks like your album is selling well in New York. Would you be interested in releasing it here through our company?" Things like that.

Kakehashi: After that, you became interested in outer space and expanded the themes of your work. I brag about how I had the opportunity to create a data file with a coded message for your *Bermuda Triangle* album, which I also play on the album.

Tomita: Thank you very much for that. At the time, the rasping noise made by computer data was very unusual so I decided to ask you to produce that as one of the sounds in the piece. But the phase got inverted when JVC (Victor Company) inserted that sound. So almost no one was able to decipher the message that I had snuck in. So are computers not able to handle inverted phases?

Kakehashi: There are ways around it, but it would require quite a bit of ingenuity and you would need a Tarbell system. There weren't that many people with these capabilities around at the time, but you still got a response quite early on didn't you?

Tomita: Yes, it was a sushi chef and a student who figured it out. They were enthusiasts who had nothing to do with computers. No one figured it out in America.

Kakehashi: Well, Tarbell was much better known in the US.

Tomita: But the thing is, the material used to make records in the US was of lower quality so I think that might have had something to do with it, along with the fact that it was phase-inverted too.

Kakehashi: I see. This was going to be played back from a cassette tape so it wasn't going to work unless the data would reproduce the highs properly and had distinct square waves. Still, I didn't expect anyone to figure it out so soon, so I was surprised.

Tomita: Apparently they had no means of printing it out so they sent me photos of what appeared on their computer screens. It showed the text exactly as we had entered it.

Kakehashi: At the time, I was really surprised to see you persistently, carefully, and meticulously working on producing that rasping noise.

Tomita: I thought that that sound would be appropriate for that scene even if it didn't contain any of those symbols, just as a sound effect that depicted a signal that an ET visiting on a UFO might transmit.

Kakehashi: Still, simply recording any kind of rasping noise would have done, so it's amazing that you stuck to your intention, knowing that it would make a difference. After that, you became interested in sound images. What was it that piqued your interest in that area? Your *Bermuda Triangle* album contained the sound of a rocket launch. Can you tell me how you became more conscious of three-dimensional sound images?

Tomita: Around 1970, there was a huge boom in four-channel stereo in Japan, with different companies coming out with about four different formats, including JVC with their CD4 and Sony with their SQ formats. I was in the RCA camp so I used JVC's format, CD4. I became very interested in this as everything was discrete and you could hear sounds coming from every direction.

Typically in classical concerts, the players sit in a formation on the stage and the audience listens to the sounds that they make. The music is over there and reaches the audience three-dimensionally. I think this is what the familiar stereo system is based on. With synthesizers, however, I'm doing the multitrack recording all by myself so there are no fixed positions, and there are actually no players, so I can locate the sound wherever I like. I can make it go around and around or do anything I like with it. It would sound unnatural if you were to do that with non-synth instruments, but with sounds made on synths, there's no such thing as unnatural, no matter how you move them around. It's kind of like animation in that there is no original form that it's based on. For this reason, I thought that synthesizer records might as well be recorded in multi and that's why I delved into four-channel stereo. I produced a number of pieces in that format but unfortunately four-channel stereo did not continue long after that. Having said that, we can now control six channels in DVD audio and other media, so I'm working on a lot of things now to revive my dream.

When you think about it, this relationship between the stage and the audience is simply an extension of how music has historically been listened to. Your sound field can actually be anywhere that you happen to be. In our daily lives, when we're strolling through town or walking on the beach, we hear sounds from all around us. In a sense, we spend our lives immersed in this cosmos of sound. So what's wrong with having something like that in music? That's the thought that I had when I began working on three-dimensional sound fields. For me, that's the most satisfying way that I can deliver my music to the audience. But unfortunately, two-channel stereo is still the mainstream in CDs and records.

Kakehashi: Yes, that's true. The conditions and systems available in the listeners' homes are still limited.

Tomita: Yes, so I feel a bit disheartened because I feel like the listeners are still listening to a miniaturized version of my music. I'm hoping that I can create the sound field that I envision using DVD audio.

Kakehashi: Thank you for trying out the RSS [Roland Sound System] when you were working on *The Tale of Genji*. For us, it's relatively easy to make sound "move" or "run" but the technology to make the sound drift around or stop in a certain location is quite challenging. We had developed the RSS at just the right time, and Mr. Yamato [an engineer at Roland] was working hard on the project, so I think it was great timing that we had the opportunity to work with you then. Where did you come up with the idea of making a ghost drift about in your piece?

Tomita: I think we were able to create an amazing effect for that performance. I was in front of the stage conducting so I could not hear the effect with my own ears during the performance, but based on the audience's reaction, I think it came out just as we had intended. When you move sound on regular left-right speakers, it's essentially just the sound on one speaker getting smaller and the other getting louder. With RSS, you hear the vengeful spirit of Rokujo Miyasudokoro coming right up to you and then moving away from you. The spirit drifted in a way that almost made you feel her cold hand might touch you at any moment, so I think it was a great success. Western people seem to like ghosts even more than the Japanese [laughter], so this was very effective.

Kakehashi: We manufacture musical instruments so you and I have been connected through technology and different gear. The first one was the MC-8, which happened to be the first product that came out of my obsession with computers at the time, and in recent years we have connected through the RSS that we just mentioned. My belief is that the human voice is the most amazing musical instrument, which until now you couldn't "play." The human voice is a great musical instrument that has all the right pitches and can even convey meaning. With technology that we are currently developing, we are coming very close to being able to play voices and use them with MIDI. As we move forward with our research, we're hearing from people who are developing sound generators for computers that this area of technology, in which we use the human voice as the raw material, is an exciting one that they would very much like to work in. Our first focus was on manipulating the voice but we are now finding out that this is not the only possibility. We showed you this technology in the past while it was still under development. We have advanced our research since then and it's become much more usable than what we showed you earlier. So I think you would be able to make use of other new aspects of this technology.

Tomita: What about the problem with formant?

Kakehashi: We've solved that.

Tomita: I see. If you've solved that, we won't be getting any more Donald Duck voices.

Kakehashi: With sampler technology, when the player played a note that was an octave higher, the sound would decay quicker, which meant that you couldn't play harmony. But with the new technology, players can play harmony in real time.

Tomita: I see.

Kakehashi: The relationship between people on the hard side of things, the musical instrument makers, and those on the soft side, the artists, has not changed since the time of Beethoven. We have finally reached a point where we have more latitude in working with materials such as semiconductors and silicon. You and I have experienced the transition from vacuum tubes to transistors, then on to integrated circuits, and then to the present time where we have access to CPUs and memory without having to be too conscious of cost. In that context, what are your dreams for new fields of music moving forward?

Tomita: Many people like to differentiate between acoustic and non-acoustic instruments, but I started out with orchestras before I came across synthesizers, so I don't have his differentiating mindset. Electricity already existed in nature in the form of lighting and the ancients no doubt had heard the sounds associated with it. And our biology, all of us, humans and animals alike, we're governed by electrical effects. So just as flutes and pipe organs were made by ingeniously utilizing energies that already existed in nature, I see no difference in musical instruments that use electricity, which is also a natural energy. Pipe organs are amazing mechanical achievements. The pipe organ was invented in a time when people were playing their folk instruments, one instrument per person. And while the pipe organ did not use electricity, it enabled a single player to produce sounds that surpassed that of even orchestras. Through human ingenuity, a mechanism was made for manipulating the flow of air—something that occurs in nature—culminating in an amazing pipe organ. How long ago were pipe organs invented?

Kakehashi: The other day, I saw a report on NHK about an organ that was dug up in Greece. I would say over two thousand years ago. It already had pipes and a keyboard too.

Tomita: Was the keyboard black and white?

Kakehashi: No, they didn't have black keys yet then. And the scales were the opposite of what we use now. The pitches got lower as you moved to the right. It ran on a hydraulic pump.

Tomita: I think you could say that those were mechanical too. Whether you're using mechanics or electricity, you're using energy found in nature so there is no particular need to differentiate. What we need to focus on is the diversification of musical instruments. Thanks to that diversification, people who could only play guitar have gained the ability to operate synthesizers. The birth of electronic musical instruments has brought about an amazing expansion in the range of our expressions. By making use of this huge range of possibilities, musicians are now able to create expressions that would have been absolutely impossible to achieve in the past, even if the idea had been there. Also, people who could not express their talents because they only had traditional instruments to work with now can, with the arrival of synthesizers. I see a lot of people like this coming on the scene now. As for myself, although I liked orchestras, thanks to synthesizers I've been able to express things that I would not have been able to with orchestras. I think we will see more and more of these types of composers, moving forward. I believe a wonderful world awaits us, because as listeners, we have all these diverse options to choose from.

The Allure of Synthesizers

Kakehashi: I think it was around 1969 that I spoke with Dr. Moog at the Frankfurt Messe and we hit it off, saying, "Let's make synthesizers that are more affordable!" The next time I met him was on a ranch near a lake, which had kind of a desolate feel.

Tomita: Yes, I've visited that ranch too. It is kind of desolate.

Kakehashi: When I spoke to him there at the ranch, he told me that he couldn't go ahead with our earlier plan because of the venture capital that had come into his company. I remember feeling disappointed and saying, "Oh, that's too bad, since I'd made preparations for this meeting." This was at a time when we had just started up Roland and we were developing our first synthesizer. We met numerous times after that and I remember that when we spoke I would often lose track of time.

Synthesizer music that came out around 1968, including *Switched-On Bach*, all sounded like the musical equivalent of a straight-line drawing. Then in 1974, you released *Snowflakes Are Dancing*, an album that in a way shattered the limits of synthesizer technology of the time, and I still remember how amazed I was at the album's expressivity and musicality.

Tomita: At the time, *Switched-On Bach* was very popular, and I felt some sense of rivalry toward it. I'd gone through a lot of trouble importing this amazing device from the US, so there was no point in doing the same thing. Once you start fiddling around with the synth, you begin to realize that that is kind of what you will naturally get with the music of Bach and other baroque music if you use a sequencer to simply play the sounds produced on the synth's oscillator and record them. But that wasn't going to cut it for me.

One of the strengths of the synthesizer is that you have full freedom to create sounds that are completely different from the sounds of normal orchestral instruments such as the flute, oboe, bassoon, clarinet, trumpet, horn, and trombone. That's what makes it so much fun.

Kakehashi: From our point of view, we knew that making music on a synth was a lot of work, so listening to your records, we realized that you were doing things that we had not even thought of. We were amazed at that. This was your passion for music.

Tomita: I must have liked what I was doing. I'm quite the enthusiast, you know.

Kakehashi: You had the passion to create your own music regardless of how much work it entailed.

Tomita: I remember very well the time you visited me. Who was it that came with you that day?

Kakehashi: That was my second son, Ikuo. That was at your studio in Atami. Prior to that, I visited you alone and you told me that you would be building a studio in Atami.

Tomita: That area has beautiful beaches, and close to this Hamamatsu Research Center where we are now, there's beautiful Lake Hamanako. Having said that, I grew up during the war, so I tend to get better ideas in desolate surroundings. In Atami, everyone else was there to relax at the resort, and there I was, toiling on the System 700 and a multitrack recorder alone. I realized I couldn't concentrate so I eventually moved out. I guess the poor man's mentality is a part of me so I find myself getting better ideas in desolate surroundings. People ask me, "You can make good music in nice settings, can't you?" But no, it's the opposite for me. How about you?

▲ With Isao Tomita at Roland Research Center in Hammamatsu.

Kakehashi: I don't care too much about my surroundings, because when I'm working, I tend to over-concentrate to the point that I even forget to eat.

Tomita: I force myself into a situation where I won't be distracted and there is nothing else for me to do. But by doing that, I run the risk of going off in strange directions, so I make sure that I have conversations with people who come to visit and talk about what I'm working on, among other things.

Orchestral Pieces on Synthesizer

Kakehashi: You have created orchestral works done entirely on synthesizer. And I was intrigued to hear that you have also done pieces recently in which you have matter-of-factly included synthesizers in an orchestral arrangement, such as in *Symphony Ihatov*, inspired by the works of the author Kenji Miyazawa.

Tomita: The parts played on synth are the parts that were written for foot-operated and hand-cranked organs that come in where the children sing the "Taneyamagahara Pastoral Song" in the first part of the piece. In the "Night on the Galactic Railroad" I used synths to conjure images of a hand-cranked organ. As for ensembles with orchestra, I used synths in parts of the soundtrack for *The Tale of Genji* and throughout the entirety of the soundtrack for *Jungle Emperor Leo*.

Kakehashi: So you simply use what you feel you need in the music that you seek to create?

Tomita: Yes. If an orchestra worked for delivering the piece, I'd use that. If synths worked, I'd use them. This gives you a vastly broader range of expressivity. Actually, in terms of composing skills, solo piano pieces are my weakest area. Just as if I were painting, I think I can create better with a wider range of materials on my pallet for creating different colors. It's easy to narrow your range, but to expand your range, it's definitely better to have a lot of different sounds.

Kakehashi: You have been performing orchestral pieces on synthesizers, and I had been wondering what you were actually doing.

Tomita: We're now in a time where the definition of what constitutes composing is becoming blurred. I regularly find myself reaching for the computer in my composing process. When I was studying composing, we didn't have means for acquiring information such as we now have with the Internet, so we had to go to school and learn things like harmony theory, counterpoint theory, and musical form theory properly from a teacher. But now, you have access to all this information on the Internet. And there is information out there that is not even in the textbooks. The range of possibilities has expanded so I think this is a great time for young people.

Kakehashi: We now have animated characters come up on screen and sing. From the manufacturer's standpoint, we're very interested in the mechanism behind these things, for example how video and everything else is being controlled from the keyboard via MIDI.

Tomita: Recently, Hatsune Miku (a humanoid persona voiced by a singing synthesizer application) sang with a choir directed by an orchestra conductor. It wasn't like some programmed character just popped out and the orchestra played along to that. You could say that it was rather human in the sense that they could make the character recognize the musicality of the conductor and sing along to it. This was something that became possible due to advancements made in MIDI technology. I don't think it would have been possible without it.

Kakehashi: Personally, I was happy to hear that they used MIDI.

Tomita: At first, I thought MIDI was something you could only use to play music and combine the sounds of different instruments. However, looking at its switching, and different ideas of how you can use it, I see now that you can expand your range of applications, and I feel that this latest development has taken the technology to one of its extremes.

To Be Inspired by the Sound Field and Sound

Kakehashi: I would like to move on to our next theme. From listening to your works so far, I get the feeling that you are very conscious of the "sound field." Controlling the sound field is a challenging art, isn't it? In working with the sound field, there are many types of delivery media, such as TV, DVD, and Blu-ray. I have a feeling that you might have a vision for how certain attributes of these media might inspire your creative process even more. What are your thoughts on this?

Tomita: In terms of surround sound, there is a perception that you can't get a true surround effect unless you purchase equipment costing upward of ¥1 million, and many people therefore say that it is simply out of their reach. But if you just wanted to enjoy surround at home, there are surround systems available for ¥40,000, complete with amplifier and other equipment, and they all play SACDs, CDs, and any other media. Although this might sound like an advertisement, I do hope that more people recognize this fact and go out and purchase these systems. In fact, when you say that I'm conscious of the sound field, it goes back to a time before we had music. We had no music in my primary school years and I assume you must have had a similar experience. We had good military songs, nationalist songs, and Ministry of Education songs, but all Western music was outlawed so we had no way of listening to it.

Kakehashi: Yes, songs. They were more like song classes than music classes.

Tomita: During the war, enemy fighter planes would be flying around. If they were on the other side of the mountains, you couldn't see them but you could hear them. In these situations you had to figure out where the planes actually were. You might think that they were way out over that way, but actually they might already be very close by. So you had to listen to the sounds and anticipate lest you be taken by surprise. Because if they found you, they would come after you with their machine guns.

Kakehashi: We used to play guessing games based on the sounds of the engines. "That's a Grumman . . . No, it's a Lockheed."

Tomita: I think I was inspired more by the sounds I heard around me than by music per se. The sound reflections that you hear at the Echo Wall and Three Echo Stones in Beijing's Tiantan Park are other examples. Young kids today have so many fun things to play with, like video games and anime, and their curiosity doesn't seem to extend to how a certain sound sounds. When I was a kid, my parents were busy with their work and had no time for us. I think that it actually turned out to be a good thing.

Kakehashi: Hatsune Miku made her debut with the *Symphony Ihatov*. And further, Roland has launched the VP series, which plays vocals with lyrics and inflections simply by singing as you play the keyboard. Don Lewis played this in 2007 at Roland's Electronic Arts Hamamatsu Awards ceremony, where you were honored. Are you interested in trying this type of gear?

Tomita: Yes I am. I think Hatsune Miku shares similarities with the traditional *joruri* puppet theater of Japan where two or three *kuroko* puppeteers manipulate a single character doll. And these dolls exude a power of conviction that makes them even more compelling than live humans. The mechanical dolls of Hida Takayama are also manipulated from above by multiple puppeteers who separately manipulate the head, eyes, and hands. I went to see a Hatsune Miku concert in Tokyo Dome and I thought, "This is Kenji Miyazawa's world!" Hatsune Miku is a virtual idol, and precisely because she is a human-made figure she is able to express the essence of the human soul in a richer way. She is a character that you're not really sure which dimension she's from. In her Opera City concert, we had Naoto Otomo conducting the orchestra, a choir of 150 singers, and a child choir group. Hatsune Miku was the prima donna of the concert so she couldn't just sing but actually had to lead everyone else. I think she truly fulfilled this role. This was all thanks to the work that people were doing behind the scenes. She truly led the orchestra and choir.

Speaking of the world of Kenji Miyazawa, I see Matasaburo of the Wind and the character Campanella in "Night on the Galactic Railroad" not as flesh-and-blood humans but as characters who have come from another dimension that is slightly removed from our reality.

Kakehashi: Because they jump dimensions.

Tomita: I planned to have Hatsune Miku appear in "Matasaburo of the Wind" and with Campanella in "Night on the Galactic Railroad." We didn't think that the audience would get it if she abruptly came in, so we set her up as an entertainer in "The Restaurant of Many Orders." Hatsune Miku appears on the PC screen and sings, "In this transient body, I'm confined to the screen." The joruri puppet theater, mechanical puppets of Hida Takayama, and the actors who play female roles in kabuki are all human creations. They could simply cast real women but they intentionally cast men. So these virtual characters have an allure that you can't get from real people.

Kakehashi: You have made public how you create your work, but I don't think we are seeing a successor who is capable of creating the mood that you create. It appears that you are always one or two steps ahead.

Tomita: I don't think that I'm a step ahead at all. I just like to surprise people. Even at this age, I still haven't outgrown that childlike quality. I'm just like a kid. Just like a kid might be fascinated by the movements of a bug. I'm guessing you must be like that too, in a way. That's why I think you're able to involve yourself in development.

Kakehashi: I work in my studio where the scenery is not as good as it is here. I guess that must be my poor man's mentality right there.

Tomita: In a desolate place, like me ...

Kakehashi: It's not exactly desolate!

I Like to Surprise People

Kakehashi: You mentioned that you like to surprise people, and you really surprised us when you invited Hatsune Miku as the soloist for the concert. I thought that MIDI must be at work in the background as I was watching the concert. Can you tell us about some of the things you set out to accomplish as well as some of the challenges you might have faced?

Tomita: Preparing for experimental concerts such as this one, you tend to run out of time quickly, and the audience is already there before you know it and there are things you're not able to do anything about.

Kakehashi: In the end, it turned out very well. I got a sense that the tension of doing a live performance may paradoxically have had a relaxing effect.

Tomita: Mr. Otomo's conducting was great. The confidence he exuded was amazing. Most conductors frown at the prospect of incorporating electrical elements into an orchestra. Some won't even try to hide their consternation, thinking that nothing good can come from incorporating these elements into pieces that can be performed solely by the orchestra. If the conductor feels this way, the members of the orchestra won't play their best and the synth player will feel less confident. From this standpoint Mr. Otomo was great. He was very flexible in how he handled things.

Kakehashi: Normally, you would expect there to be a lot more tension.

Tomita: That's true. During the show, there was a part where Miku got the lyrics wrong. This was the first time Miku got her lyrics wrong. But you know, even Misora Hibari got her lyrics wrong occasionally. So there was nothing so bad about Miku getting it wrong. Actually, it was an operator error.

Kakehashi: There are things you can say after the fact, aren't there? But we didn't notice that and it sounded really amazing from the audience's perspective. Everyone joined together in a banzai, and I felt like joining in as well.

In your closing comments, you mentioned that this was something you had been conceptualizing for ten years, so I was quite surprised that what came out was Hatsune Miku, as I had not heard anything about her during that time. There was no Hatsune Miku ten years ago, was there?

Tomita: The concept I meant was that I wanted to create the world of Kenji Miyazawa. It was only February of last year that I encountered Hatsune Miku.

▼ With Isao Tomita and his wife, Akiko.

Kakehashi: So your concept was based on the world of Miyazawa. People like us, who work on the hardware, have a peculiar limitation in that we tend to think that intangibles and things we can't clearly see are things that cannot be utilized. We understand that there is more freedom in the world of content and music but at the same time it can feel more difficult to us.

Tomita: At first, I thought that the best Miku could do was roughly follow along to the orchestra's performance conducted by Naoto Otomo. So I spoke with Hiroyuki Ito, president of Crypton, the developer of Miku, and he suggested setting up sections with ritardando. For example, gradually slow the performance down on the fourth beat to the third beat, and do a fermata on the fourth beat, and then on the upbeat go straight back to in tempo. I thought that using a ritardando would make things interesting. But human ritardando will be different each time, even with Mr. Otomo's level of virtuosity, so I thought that it would be impossible to match Miku's performance with the orchestra.

Creating Original Sounds

Kakehashi: As long as she's the singer, you need to give Hatsune Miku's voice a unique character. Take a human singer—they might have overslept, might not be in the right emotional state, or their voice might not have the usual punch or luster. These things are difficult to express physically but they are real nonetheless. You can't adjust for these things with conventional tone controls. You once mentioned that there was a secret in the tone control of one of our amplifiers. Can you tell us what kind of tone control you were talking about?

Tomita: This was an Ace Tone guitar amp. What I wanted was the tone control section of the amp. I don't play the guitar but I wanted to create a different tone from the ones I made on my Moog synth. Would that have been resonance? Perhaps a two-tiered volume control?

Kakehashi: No. All that the circuit did was enhance the bass, mid, or treble.

Tomita: I was tweaking one of the knobs, which I would move by only about 0.3 millimeters, and it would create this interesting sound like a swishing sound.

Kakehashi: That wasn't designed into the circuit so I assume you found that sound in that particular area. There's nothing else there.

Tomita: In "Clair de Lune" you hear all these tones sweeping upward on top of the harpsichord. You can't create that sound on the Moog alone. I've heard that people tried hard to make that sound on their Moog but the truth of the matter is that you couldn't get that unless you were using an Ace Tone amp. That feature was a great help. I would move the knob only by about 0.3 millimeters and come back after dinner only to find out that the sound wasn't there anymore. Things would change with the temperature too.

Kakehashi: With the early Ace Tone guitar amps, we aggressively cut frequencies under 120 hertz based on the idea that guitars didn't need low end. I personally thought that, although this might have been the consensus then, there might be musicians who actually wanted more lows, so we extended the cutoff down to ninety hertz. This might have been an unusual frequency curve for guitar amps but we intentionally did things like that at the time. Current tone controls don't include the circuitry you're speaking of.

Tomita: In any case, it was a tone that you couldn't get on the Moog alone so everyone was mystified. I didn't tell anyone this secret, that I had been using an Ace Tone amp. You couldn't get that tone on a Gibson or Fender amp, but you could get it on an Ace Tone. I was wondering whether maybe you had built in some kind of special trick.

Kakehashi: No, we didn't. Sounds are so mysterious because sometimes you get sounds that you just can't explain.

Tomita: Synths are a treasure trove of hidden sounds. They can be hidden in the most unexpected places and you find them by chance. In "Clair de Lune" I wanted to create an effect that you might describe as a sharp cembalo tone sounding in a forest in the distance. There you are in front of a lake and the moon is reflecting on its surface. I was able to find a tone that was a perfect match for this scene.

Kakehashi: Mr. Tomita, thank you very much for sharing with us today your passion for music, many interesting stories including the challenges you faced during the production of *Symphony Ihatov*, and your discoveries with the tone control.

http://www.atvbooks.net/mv/017E

My Journey with Performers: A Dialogue

Hector Olivera, Organist, with Ikutaro Kakehashi

THE FOLLOWING IS FROM "WHAT THE PIONEERS HAVE TO SAY," TENTH and twenty-second installments, in the January 2007 and January 2008 issues of *RET's Press* newsletter for Roland Music School lecturers.

We Knew Each Other Before We Met

When was the first time that the two of you met?

Kakehashi: It feels like we've known each other for a very long time [laughter].

Olivera: It feels like we've known each other since our previous lives [laughter]. I feel like we've known each other long before we actually personally met and shook hands, because I'd been an enthusiastic user of Roland's first rhythm machine, TR-77.

Kakehashi: We'd been yearlong friends; a friendship mediated by our products. I've carried a strong passion for developing organs, and so I got my first opportunity to work with Mr. Olivera when we developed Roland's first organ, the Music Atelier. Technological revolutions had been ongoing at Roland prior to that, but back then, Roland organs were not able to keep up with Mr. Olivera's virtuosity.

Olivera: I think it was over ten years ago when we met at the entrance of the hotel across the street from the NAMM Show, and I said to you, "I'd like to work with you someday."

Kakehashi: Yes, I remember that. We had already started our organ project at that point, but we were not ready to mention anything in public yet [laughter].

Mr. Kakehashi, what drew you to Mr. Olivera in the first place?

Kakehashi: People who play classical organ usually play classical pieces exclusively, but Mr. Olivera has a wider repertoire. He could of course play classical organ pieces, but also had a very wide repertoire in jazz and popular music. And he didn't just play, he could deliver the music with feeling. There was no other player who could do that. The intent to go beyond the limitations of existing musical instruments, such as embodied by Mr. Olivera, is what gives meaning to playing a new instrument. Music Atelier was based on organs and its functions have been expanded from that starting point. To cultivate new fields with this new musical instrument, it was essential to enlist the assistance of creative performers like Mr. Olivera; someone who understood the possibilities of newer genres of music such as jazz and popular, as well as the classics.

Olivera: There are many performers who are much better than me in certain genres of music, but in terms of newer genres of music, I think that there are many who don't get the concept. When these types of people attempt something new, they tend to go to the extreme, such as playing Bach pieces or the *Concierto de Aranjuez* in fusion style. But you don't need to do that. With the *Concierto de Aranjuez* for example, if you could reproduce its beautiful guitar parts on Music Atelier, you would be recognized as a good performer. However, in order to reproduce the guitar part, you need to know how the guitar is played.

Kakehashi: Well, you can reproduce an entire seventy-piece orchestra, let alone guitars [laughter].

▼ Hector Olivera.

The Trick to Drawing Out the Advantages of Music Atelier

Your performance of Rhapsody in Blue *is a great example of this, isn't it?*

Olivera: I use sequencing depending on the music, but I play *Rhapsody in Blue* entirely in real time without any sequencing. To do that, you need to know about a variety of detailed elements including the inflections of clarinets, the breathing in muted trumpets, the bow strokes of string instruments, and piano pedal work. As such, *Rhapsody in Blue* is the best material to communicate the advantages of Music Atelier to pianists.

That's true, because the lower keyboard on Music Atelier has seventy-six keys, which is enough range to play a piano piece.

Olivera: Pianos in Beethoven's day had seventy-six keys so you can play all the sonatas from that period on Music Atelier.

One would think that in order to master Music Atelier, in addition to being able to play the upper and lower keyboards and the pedalboard, you would need to master the timing at which you operate its buttons and many of its mechanical features.

Olivera: That's correct. I was originally a classical pipe organist so I was used to operating the stops by calculating the time lag between the time I would switch the tone as I played and when the instrument would actually produce that sound. To play Music Atelier, it's important to master its button operations. We did over one hundred takes to record the *HMS Pinafore* prelude on my latest CD, *Heroes*. That was because I wanted to record a performance played in real time from top to bottom without overdubs or comping different parts together. The biggest challenge was the timing for switching the presets [tones and rhythm patterns]. I think the CD I did eight years ago was pretty good, but it was not perfect from the standpoint of switching between presets. I think this latest CD will give you a good idea of how much I have mastered Music Atelier.

Kakehashi: You have extensive knowledge of computers and machines, which you incorporate in your organ playing, but I think what is even more important for the modern organist is that, first of all, you have to be an excellent conductor and arranger. I've heard you play certain pieces on many different occasions but even if you were playing the same piece, they sound fresh and new each time. I think you must have these abilities as a conductor and arranger to make the best of the capabilities of the modern organ, not only Music Atelier.

Olivera: Yes, those are very important aspects. The conductor needs to know, for example, the different playing styles of oboes, or the range of trumpets. To produce a trumpet sound on the organ, you have to play it as if you're playing a trumpet, not an organ.

The Evolution of Players and Musical Instruments

Aside from playing Music Atelier, in what other areas has Mr. Olivera contributed to making instruments better?

Kakehashi: Mr. Olivera has given us a variety of ideas, not necessarily all of them verbally. Even an engineer like myself can point out weaknesses in the instrument by listening to Mr. Olivera play. We cannot make better instruments unless we also have ears for music. The important thing is to listen. When we ask an artist to play an instrument that we have made, without exception, we hear new sounds that we had not even thought of. The artist uses the registrations and his or her playing technique to produce sounds that were not on our minds in the design stage. I think similar things happen with classical instruments, although I think Music Atelier has the potential to create a wide range of new tones. This is why designing organs is so exciting.

Olivera: For example, the latest Music Atelier comes with more than forty differ- ent types of brass tones, whereas the early ones only had three or four. But I was combining those in different balances and made a wide range of brass tones, which quite surprised the engineers. Once you understand the characteristics of your tool, you can expand its envelope. To do that, it's important to take time to listen to the preset tones. Something I say often to students is, "You have wonderful technique, but there are two things that you need: your ability to listen and imagination."

Mr. Olivera, you will be giving private lessons in Osaka and Tokyo during this visit. What do you feel are some of the areas that aspiring organists can work on to improve their playing?

Olivera: I feel that many of my students in Japan tend to turn up the volume too high. Not the volume of the organ itself though. What I'm saying is that when they are creating sounds by mixing different instruments, they tend to turn up the volume of these individual instruments to full volume. If you turn up each instrument to full volume on the mixer, you won't have any elbow room for your sound. You don't have to set the twelve-step volume control to twelve all the time. Use six as your baseline and then if there are sounds that you want to emphasize, turn them up to nine, ten, or eleven. I would suggest that people keep this in mind when creating their tones.

▲ With the Roland digital harpsichord C-30. From left to right: Hector Olivera, Paulo Caius, and myself.

Kakehashi: You're not necessarily going to get a rich tone just by turning up the volume all the way.

Olivera: Yes, that's what I think.

Mr. Olivera, do you still make discoveries of new possibilities on Music Atelier?

Olivera: I've played Music Atelier for ten years now and I would say that I know everything there is to know about the instrument's functions and preset tones. Yet there still are times that I find new ways of using it that I've never even thought of before. The instrument itself is constantly evolving so I don't think a time will come when all of its possibilities are discovered.

The Possibilities for Music Atelier Continue to Expand through the Cooperation between Developers and Players

Roland has added three new models to its lineup of Music Atelier organs, and you have been playing Music Atelier AT-900 in your concerts in Japan. What did you think of it?

Olivera: The first thing I want to say is that it sounds great! Of course it has carried over the sounds of earlier models, but I think the new technology has added more depth to the sounds. The four "articulation voice" tones [violin, trombone, cello, and tenor saxophone] that are a product of the new SuperNATURAL technology allow players to express subtle changes in tone, vibrato intensities, and portamento and pizzicato tones realistically and in fine detail.

Kakehashi: The keys on electronic organs are basically switches that turn the sound on when they are pressed and off when they are released. It had been a longtime goal for developers to express the legato effects produced on violins and trombones on this instrument, and this has become possible with the incorporation of the latest technology.

Would you say that the addition of the D-Beam, a feature that is also used on instruments such as the HandSonic digital percussion, is another highlight of the new Music Atelier?

Kakehashi: D-Beam is a technology that allows you to change or add effects to the sound while you are playing. This was another function that became possible with advancements made in digital signal processing technologies used in the sound module. In addition to making changes to the sound, the gestures of the players using the D-Beam may have the effect of attracting the audience's attention. In the eighteenth Roland Organ Festival, held in November 2007, you played "My Romance," in which you used the D-Beam to add a slide pipe effect to your trombone tone. You did so with hand gestures that mimicked how a trombone player would hold the slide pipe, and that left a huge impression on me. Hats off to you for your creativity in communicating that particular feeling through those actions.

Whenever we add a new function, your reaction is always, "Oh, with this function, I can play such and such a song, or deliver such and such an expression," and you often present new ways of using these functions that the developers could not have even imagined. From a developer's standpoint, it's a great joy to receive such reactions from players.

The new Music Atelier comes with an extensive range of advanced functions. As a developer, what do you have in mind for the future of this instrument?

Kakehashi: There is no such thing as 100 percent for any instrument, and you don't know what will be in demand in the future as musical trends shift. That said, with modern organs, I think we are transitioning to a framework where we can leave the hardware pretty much untouched and evolve the instrument's performance through software additions.

Are you saying that it is an instrument that is capable of flexibly responding to changing times?

Kakehashi: One caveat is that, while electronic musical instruments have the advantage of being able to do anything thanks to their electronic nature, this can also be a double-edged sword. Where we have to draw a line is that we must never infringe on the territory of the player. With any instrument, developers must exercise self-control in terms of confining themselves to "providing possibilities of expression." I don't think it is right for instruments to evolve all by themselves and overtake the skills and sensibilities of the players. In this respect, Music Atelier is a musical instrument that we have developed by receiving input from and working with players such as Mr. Olivera.

The Joy of Making the Best Use of a Variety of Functions When Playing

When you say, "Never infringe on the territory of the player," this also manifests in how the functions of its sequencer are kept as simple as possible.

Kakehashi: Yes, that is true too. You could enter all the data in the organ and wow your audience maybe once, but that would not be a product of the player's expressivity. You cannot call it a good musical instrument unless the players themselves are able to feel the joy of playing it. Music Atelier has been around for over ten years, and this was the concept that we based its development on from the very beginning. I think we've been able to communicate the joy of playing this instrument to many people thanks to the help of players such as Mr. Olivera.

Olivera: We players need certain "functions" to play, but we don't need "gimmicks." None of the acoustic instruments, including clarinets, violins, and pipe organs, have gimmicks. So I think in the near future, Music Atelier, in that it does not have any gimmicks, will go on to establish an identity such as what acoustic instruments have established.

Kakehashi: Electronic musical instruments have historically been playing "catch up" with regular acoustic instruments. But there was a time in that history where attempts were made to go beyond acoustic instruments, with the help of gimmicks. The history of Music Atelier started at the point where we said, "This is not going to work," and stopped taking that approach. So we received a lot of input from Mr. Olivera and other artists in terms of what Music Atelier should provide as an organ.

▲ Hector Olivera with his mother.

Olivera: Speaking of this seesaw affair between the musical instruments' technological advancement and musicians, the articulation voice feature that comes with the new AT-900, AT-900C, and AT-800 was a function that I couldn't grasp at first. However, after going through the score, and studying it like, "Okay, so let's give this note a portamento like this," for example, I'm now able to use it without thinking about it. Of course, it's still not perfect, but I think I've just about caught up with this advancement of the instrument.

Also, *Danse Macabre* by Saint-Saëns features a part where the woodwind section plays short notes in triads, and I use harmony intelligence that lets you create harmony out of a one-part melody. You might think a function that allows you to play a chord with a single finger to be a gimmick for beginners, but if you use it effectively, such as in this piece for example, it becomes a function that enables musical expression. Some people might see the D-Beam that I used in "My Romance" to simply be a pitch bender, but the D-Beam allows you to control the pitch in much subtler ways so it is ideal for reproducing the feel of instruments that have unstable pitches such as trombones. Thanks to this feature, I was able to play the organ as if I were really playing a trombone and not simply playing a trombone tone on an organ. These new features have enabled me to play each orchestral instrument with real feeling and now I can play orchestral arrangements as if I've really become a conductor!

The audience might have wondered, "What is he doing?" as I looked this way and that each time I played the cello, contra bass, or French horn, but that was me getting into the mood of a real conductor facing an orchestra as I played [laughter].

Kakehashi: It would be safe to say that you are the first player to have perfectly compiled an orchestral score onto a three-stave chart for organs. That is the reason you have been able to fully use all of these functions on Music Atelier. What was amazing was your idea of compiling the orchestral score onto a three-stave chart.

Olivera: Another feature that I had been asking Mr. Kakehashi to add was the harmonic bar. In the past, you could have this show up on the display and operate it there, but these new models have physical harmonic bars so I can continuously change the tone as I'm playing.

Looking Forward to the Growth of Future Musicians

Olivera: When I come to Japan to play concerts every year, I also visit many parts of the country to give seminars, where I meet a wide range of aspiring organists. One young man told me that he had liked to play with jazz organ sounds until a few years ago and now he's interested in using orchestral tones. I think this was a result of listening to seminars and watching concerts held not only by me but also by other Music Atelier players such as Tony Fenelon and Yuri Tachibana.

Kakehashi: I think for up-and-coming organists, copying the performance of top players like yourself is an important aspect of their study. In that respect also, we need heroes like you.

Olivera: I recognize that it is very important to be an inspiration to people. I hold CD autographing events after my concerts, and for me what is more important than signing autographs is to see the expressions on their faces and see that they've been moved by the concert. Of course it is a lot of fun playing on stage, but my favorite activity during my visits to Japan are the seminars where I have a chance to directly speak with students. I've visited music schools and high schools with you, and I genuinely feel that I receive as much energy from seeing the excited expressions on their faces when they've learned something new. I very much look forward to seeing what kind of players they will grow into and what kind of music they will gift the world with.

▲ Mr. Olivera's mascot, "Harry."

Sources

Audsley, George Ashdown. *The Art of Organ Building*. New York: Dover, 1965.

Barnes, William H. *The Contemporary American Organ*. Toledo: Fischer & Bro., 1930.

Bowers, Q. David. *Encyclopedia of Automatic Musical Instruments*. New York: Vestal, 1973.

Briscoe, Desmond and Roy Curtis Bramwell. *The BBC Radiophonic Workshop*. London: BBC, 1983.

Carmi, Avner and Hannah Carmi. *The Immortal Piano*. Translated into Japanese by Sumi Gunji as *Ongaku no Tomo Sha*. Tokyo: Ongakunotomosha, 1984.

Chadabe, Joel. *Electric Sound: The Past and Promise of Electronic Music*. New York: Pearson, 1996.

Dan, Ikuma. *Personal History of Japanese Music*. Tokyo: NHK, 1999.

Deutsch, Herbert A. *Synthesis: An Introduction to the History, Theory, and Practice of Electronic Music*. New York: Alfred, 1976.

Dorf, Richard H. *Electronic Musical Instruments*. New York: Radiofile, 1960.

Douglas, Alan Lockhart Monteith. *The Electrical Production of Music*. London: Macdonald, 1957.

———. *The Electronic Musical Instrument Manual: A Guide to Theory and Design*. Blue Ridge Summit, Pennsylvania: GL Tab, 1976.

Electronic and Electric Musical Instruments. (Supplementary volume to *Musen to Jikken*). Tokyo: Seibundo Shinkosha, 1961.

Fujieda, Mamoru. *The Archaeology of Resonance*. Tokyo: Ongaku no Tomo Sha, 1998.

Furuta, Minoru et al. *Organs in Japan*. Tokyo: Japan Association of Organists, 1992.

Goode, Jack C. *Pipe Organ Registration*. Nashville: Abingdon, 1964.

Hammond, Laurens. Electrical musical instrument. US Patent 2230836 A, filed January 19, 1934, and issued February 4, 1941.

———. Reverberation apparatus. US Patent 2211205 A, filed October 7, 1939, and issued August 13, 1940.

———. Musical instrument. US Patent 2262179 A, filed July 30, 1940, and issued November 11, 1941.

Hammond Organ Company. *Fifty Years of Musical Excellence, 1934–1984*. Chicago: Hammond, 1984.

——. *When Electrons Sing: The Story of Hammond Organ Company*. Chicago: Hammond, 1966.

Hiyama, Rikuro. *Musical Instrument Industry*. Tokyo: Kyoikusha Shinsho, 1977.

——. *The Story of Piano*. Tokyo: Gendai-Geijutsusha, 1986.

Hubbard, Frank T. *Three Centuries of Harpsichord Making*. Cambridge: Harvard University, 1965.

Irwin, Stevens. *Dictionary of Electronic Organ Stops*. New York: G. Schirmer, 1968.

——. *Dictionary of Hammond Organ Stops*. New York: G. Schirmer, 1939.

Junchen, David L. *Encyclopedia of the American Theatre Organ*. Vol. I. Pasadena: Showcase, 1985.

Kindaichi, Haruhiko and Aiko Anzai. *Songs of Japan*. Vol. 1–3. Tokyo: Kodansha Bunko, 1977.

Kitamura, Tsuneji. *Piano Common Sense for Beginners*. Tokyo: Ongaku no Tomo Sha, 1982.

Klotz, H. *The Organ Handbook*. Translated by Gerhard Krapf. St. Louis: Concordia, 1969.

Koel, James A. *The Lowrey Story*.

Leslie, Don. *The Don Leslie Story*. Unpublished private writings.

Lewis, Walter and Thomas Lewis. *Modern Organ Building*, 3rd ed. London: Reeves, 1939.

Markowitz, Jerome. *Triumphs and Trials of an Organ Builder*. Macungie, Pennsylvania: Allen Organ Company, 1989.

Millard, Andre. *Edison and the Business of Innovation*. Baltimore: Johns Hopkins, 1990.

Minagawa, Tatsuo. *Baroque Music*. Tokyo: Kodansha Gendai Shinsho, 1972.

——. *The History of Musical Notation*. Tokyo: Ongaku no Tomo Sha, 1985.

Motegi, Kiyoko. *Musical Instruments of Japan: Their Materials and Sounds*. Tokyo: Ongaku no Tomo Sha, 1988.

Nagashima, Yoichi et al. *The World of Computers and Music*. Tokyo: Kyoritsu Shuppan, 1998.

Nagata, Kyoji and Kozo Chifuji. *The Folk Music of Japan: Western Japan Version and Eastern Japan Version*. Tokyo: Gendai Kyoyo Bunko, 1998.

Nakamura, Toyo. *The Century of Popular Music*. Tokyo: Iwanami Shinsho, 1999.

Nomura, Koichi, Kenzo Nakajima, and Kiyotatsu Miyoshi. *Unofficial History of Western Music in Japan*. Tokyo: Radio Gijutsu Sha, 1978.

Osaki, Shigemi. *Cultural History of Musical Notation*. Tokyo: Ongaku no Tomo Sha, 1993.

Prieberg, Fred K. *Music in the Technological Age*. Atlantis: Zurich, 1956.

Rosen, Charles. *Piano Notes: The World of the Pianist*. New York: Free Press, 2004.

Rubin, David M. *The Audible Macintosh*. Berkeley: Sybex, 1992.

Sakai, Hisao. *Auditory Perception and Acousticopsychology*. Tokyo: Corona Sha, 1978.

Sakata, Hiroo. *Do Re Mi So La*. Tokyo: Kawade Shobo Shinsha, 1995.

Sullivan, Anita T. *The Seventh Dragon: The Riddle of Equal Temperament*. Bloomington: Unlimited, 2005.

Tsuji, Hiroshi. *The Song of Winds: Pipe Organs and Myself*. Board of Publications, United Church of Christ in Japan, 1988.

Vail, Mark. *The Hammond Organ: Beauty in the B*. San Francisco: Backbeat, 1997.

———. *Vintage Synthesizers*. San Francisco: Miller Freeman, 1993.

Watanabe, Hiroshi. *Musical Machinery Theater*. Tokyo: Shinshokan, 1997.

Williams, Peter. *A New History of the Organ, from the Greeks to the Present Day*. Bloomington: Indiana University, 1980.

Yamato, Akira. *The Golden Age of Jazz and the Century of America*. Tokyo: Ongaku no Tomo Sha, 1997.

Postscript

I started writing this book to address the question of how we can approach the "age without samples." Since that time, I have made many new discoveries, resulting in a longer process than I had anticipated. Upon rereading the book, I realized that the past year had been a year of huge changes.

Advancements in PCs and IT equipment such as tablets and smartphones have changed the way we work. As a result, the chasm in areas such as information access, opinions, and even ethics has widened between people who are current and use these technologies in their work, and those who have been left behind by these advancements.

I feel that the "age without samples," once an abstract idea, is now right in front of us. In this new age, the way to proceed if you've found your purpose is to initiate action and not stop once you are on your way. You will always succeed if you keep at it until you succeed.

Having the needed resource in Japan has been a crucial element for this industry. By using standard technology, you greatly expand the possibilities for your business. And in terms of marketing, my belief is that businesses are born where there is a difference. That is, if you are able to create a difference, say in terms of performance or price, you will have a powerful product. This may sound like common sense but it is actually quite difficult and this is what makes it worth taking on as a challenge. Whether starting up a company or developing a product, you must have the conviction, "I am going to turn this into a business!" And then by discarding preconceived notions, you will be able to find new opportunities.

By using the QR codes provided, readers of this book can access a variety of visual materials. The QR code, like MIDI, is a common global standard, which is also shared free of charge. I am delighted that such technology has enabled us to read tomorrow's newspaper, so to speak.

I have known Mr. Larry Morton of Hal Leonard since we worked together in the early days of Roland, and we continue to be good friends to this day. I was very happy to be given the opportunity to work with him again on the publication of this book.

I am grateful for his gracious support and unwavering friendship.

▲ With Larry Morton.

List of QR Codes and URLs

If your device does not handle QR codes, please visit the sites at the URLs shown below to access visual material related to the content of the book. Please note that the visual content may be changed without notice.

Back Cover: http://www.atvbooks.net/mv/000E
Chapter One: http://www.atvbooks.net/mv/001E
Chapter Two: http://www.atvbooks.net/mv/002E
Chapter Three: http://www.atvbooks.net/mv/003E
Chapter Four: http://www.atvbooks.net/mv/004E
Chapter Five: http://www.atvbooks.net/mv/005E
Chapter Six: http://www.atvbooks.net/mv/006E
Chapter Seven: http://www.atvbooks.net/mv/007E
Chapter Eight: http://www.atvbooks.net/mv/008E
Chapter Nine: http://www.atvbooks.net/mv/009E
Chapter Ten: http://www.atvbooks.net/mv/010E
Chapter Eleven: http://www.atvbooks.net/mv/011E
Chapter Twelve: http://www.atvbooks.net/mv/012E
Chapter Thirteen: http://www.atvbooks.net/mv/013E
Yuri Tachibana: http://www.atvbooks.net/mv/014E
Oscar Peterson: http://www.atvbooks.net/mv/015E
Isao Tomita: http://www.atvbooks.net/mv/016E
Hector Olivera: http://www.atvbooks.net/mv/017E